364.1593

D0683189

Branse
Rah
To

Items should be r
not already requ
in writing or b
barcode lab
at your loca
Renew onli
Fines char
Damage to

PENGUIN BOOKS

The Doctor's Wife is Dead

...on-fiction work with the pulse of a courtroom Tierney's book is a moving account of Ellen Langley's ...nd last days, but it's also a study of Famine-era Irish ...Men dominate, be they grimly professional gents in tall ...rs and grey waistcoats or feckless scoundrels using women as chattel' *Irish Times*

...nishing book . . . a vivid chronicle of the unspeakable cruelty ...perpetrated by a husband on his spouse at a time when, in law, a wife was a man's chattel' *Irish Independent*

'Truly illuminating . . . brings great clarity to a tangled ...e . . . Tierney's exploration of the case's influence on Irish and ...glish lawmaking and literature is particularly intriguing, drawing comparisons with Kate Summerscale's similar work in *The Suspicions of Mr Whicher' Sunday Times*

...iveting . . . meticulously researched and deftly told' *Irish Examiner*

'Opens in gripping style and rarely falters . . . fascinating and well researched' *Irish Mail on Sunday* (5 stars)

A dark tale of spousal abuse, illicit sex and uncertain justice, set ...gainst a backdrop of poverty and privilege, marital inequality and deep religious divide between Catholics and Protestants. Tierney archaeologist, and his skill in unearthing the past is on display as ...digs deep into the historical record of a murder case so shocking and controversial that it was debated in parliament . . . Tierney writes with passion . . . and deftly weaves a plot that's filled with surprising twists and turns' *History Ireland*

ABOUT THE AUTHOR

Andrew Tierney, a native of Nenagh, Co. Tipperary, is a distant
descendant of Ellen Langley. Trained as an archaeologist, he is working
on the inaugural Pevsner Architectural Guide to the Irish midlands.
The Doctor's Wife is Dead is his first book.

The Doctor's Wife is Dead

The True Story of a Peculiar Marriage,
a Suspicious Death, and the Murder
Trial That Shocked Ireland

ANDREW TIERNEY

PENGUIN BOOKS

Leabharlanna Poibli Chathair Baile Átha Cliath
Dublin City Public Libraries

PENGUIN BOOKS

UK | USA | Canada | Ireland | Australia
India | New Zealand | South Africa

Penguin Books is part of the Penguin Random House group of companies
whose addresses can be found at global.penguinrandomhouse.com.

First published by Penguin Ireland 2017
Published in Penguin Books 2018

001

Copyright © Andrew Tierney, 2017

The moral right of the author has been asserted

Typeset in 12.02/14.25 pt Garamond MT Std by Jouve (UK), Milton Keynes
Printed in Great Britain by Clays Ltd, St Ives plc

A CIP catalogue record for this book is available from the British Library

ISBN: 978-0-241-97909-9

www.greenpenguin.co.uk

MIX
Paper from
responsible sources
FSC
www.fsc.org   FSC® C018179

Penguin Random House is committed to a
sustainable future for our business, our readers
and our planet. This book is made from Forest
Stewardship Council® certified paper.

In memory of my grandmother Maura Hanly
(née McCutcheon), 1916–2013

Contents

List of illustrations ix

Genealogical charts xi

Prologue: Nenagh, Co. Tipperary, 3 May 1849 1

PART ONE

1 'My poor unfortunate wife' 5

2 'Sworn to find a verdict' 9

3 'Things that ought to be buried in oblivion' 25

4 'A handsome mansion, pleasantly situated' 33

5 'A very subtle thing' 39

6 'Ellen Poe of the city of Dublin, Spinster' 51

7 'The quietest creature in the world' 56

8 'Private and pecuniary affairs' 60

9 'A very bad room' 69

10 'By the doctor's orders' 78

11 'As small as the black hole of Calcutta' 88

12 'Every kindness and good treatment' 96

13 'Thou shalt not escape calumny' 107

PART TWO

14 'My anxiety to vindicate my character' 113

15 'The new Bernard Cavanagh' 121

CONTENTS

16 'Allowing for the frailties of our nature'   131

17 'How say you, Charles Langley?'   136

18 'The book of fate'   150

19 'Sweet dear Solsboro'   164

20 'God grant I may never again dream such a
   dream as I dreamed last night'   175

21 'Mrs Langley's constitution'   179

22 'Who would not have done similarly?'   186

23 *Suppressio veri*   192

24 'Woman's frailty and sinful passion'   200

25 'The interposition of a kind Providence'   205

Acknowledgements   215

Note on sources   217

Notes   219

List of illustrations

p. 13 Barrack Street, Nenagh (now Kenyon Street) (Courtesy of the National Library of Ireland)

p. 21 James Jocelyn Poe (Courtesy of Charles Poë, Dorset)

p. 23 Rev. James Hill Poe (Courtesy of Charles Poë, Dorset)

p. 34 Map of Donnybrook estate, dated 1810 (Courtesy of Tipperary Studies, Tipperary County Council Library Service)

p. 74 Frances Poc (Courtesy of Charles Poë, Dorset)

p. 116 Nenagh Gaol (Courtesy of the National Library of Ireland)

p. 165 Solsboro (Courtesy of Limerick Museum and Archives)

p. 206 Possible portraits of Charles Langley & Anna Poe (Courtesy of Fedelma Tierney, Portroe)

GENEALOGICAL CHARTS

THE LANGLEYS OF LISNAMROCK

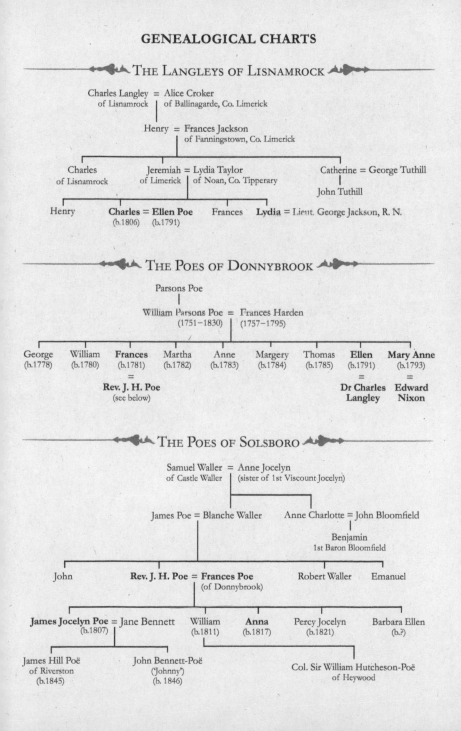

Charles Langley = Alice Croker
of Lisnamrock | of Ballinagarde, Co. Limerick

Henry = Frances Jackson
| of Fanningstown, Co. Limerick

Charles — Jeremiah = Lydia Taylor — Catherine = George Tuthill
of Lisnamrock — of Limerick | of Noan, Co. Tipperary

John Tuthill

Henry — **Charles = Ellen Poe** — Frances — **Lydia** = Lieut. George Jackson, R. N.
(b.1806) (b.1791)

THE POES OF DONNYBROOK

Parsons Poe

William Parsons Poe = Frances Harden
(1751–1830) | (1757–1795)

George	William	**Frances**	Martha	Anne	Margery	Thomas	**Ellen**	**Mary Anne**
(b.1778)	(b.1780)	(b.1781)	(b.1782)	(b.1783)	(b.1784)	(b.1785)	(b.1791)	(b.1793)
		=					=	=
		Rev. J. H. Poe					**Dr Charles**	**Edward**
		(see below)					**Langley**	**Nixon**

THE POES OF SOLSBORO

Samuel Waller = Anne Jocelyn
of Castle Waller | (sister of 1st Viscount Jocelyn)

James Poe = Blanche Waller — Anne Charlotte = John Bloomfield

Benjamin
1st Baron Bloomfield

John — **Rev. J. H. Poe = Frances Poe** — Robert Waller — Emanuel
(of Donnybrook)

James Jocelyn Poe = Jane Bennett — William — **Anna** — Percy Jocelyn — Barbara Ellen
(b.1807) — (b.1811) — (b.1817) — (b.1821) — (b.?)

James Hill Poë — John Bennett-Poë — Col. Sir William Hutcheson-Poë
of Riverston — ('Johnny') — of Heywood
(b.1845) — (b. 1846)

Prologue: Nenagh, Co. Tipperary, 3 May 1849

In the chilly pre-dawn air, a group of women gathered on Barrack Street, a busy commercial thoroughfare running south-east from the town centre. They faced a modest two-storey house, with a garret in the roof lit by two small skylights. Few who passed the house would have imagined that its sole surviving adult occupant was, according to one contemporary observer, 'connected with most respectable families of [the] county'.[1]

When, after several minutes, the door remained closed, the women began hissing and jeering. Then, one of them picked up a stone and hurled it at the house.

Others followed her example. Their missiles crashed through the windows, striking a grandfather clock in the hallway. Within minutes they had shattered every pane of glass in the facade. Then, surging forward, they pushed their collective weight against the front door, determined to break it down. As they heaved, there was the sound of a key struggling in the lock.

The battered door suddenly swung open.[2] Several men emerged from the interior of the house, carrying a pale timber coffin on their shoulders.

It was this the women had been waiting for.

The emergence of the coffin through the front door – a common sign of respect for the dead – had not been intended; in fact, the master of the house had expressly forbidden it. Instructing his housemaid, Mary Clancy, he had been emphatic on this point: the coffin should be taken out by the side gate. But the terrifying sound of crashing glass and the assault on the front door had frightened the servant into compliance with the mob outside.

As the small funeral cortège moved silently down the street, its modest character was clear for all to see. The coffin of thin boards, plainly cut and hammered together without trimmings or embellishment, was little better than that of a pauper – the sort of coffin that had become a common sight in a town suffering the effects of prolonged famine. The pall-bearers bore it upon unprotected shoulders, without the napkins or silk shoulder scarves ordinarily seen at respectable mid-nineteenth-century funerals.[3] Equally notable, the husband of the deceased was not present.

A further indignity was invisible to the mob: the lack of shrouding around the body. Even the Poor Law Guardians, who oversaw the town's overpopulated workhouse half a mile further down the road, considered clean white linen to be the only acceptable vestment for interment. In this case, though, the corpse had been left in an everyday chemise or undergarment.[4]

In provincial Ireland, public anger flared occasionally in protests against evictions, and, more recently, the inadequacy of famine relief. But those demonstrating so violently in Nenagh on this May morning in 1849 had come out to protest against a provocation of an unexpected kind: the suspicious death of a doctor's wife in her own home.

PART ONE

I

'My poor unfortunate wife'

The death of Ellen Langley was a death foretold.

On the morning she died, 1 May 1849, her husband, Dr Charles Langley, sent the following letter to his neighbour James Carroll, who was the town's coroner.

> *Dear Sir – My poor unfortunate wife having died, after an illness of ten or twelve days, in which she was attended by Drs Quin and Kittson, and having heard insinuations as to the cause of her death – although her death was not sudden – yet I am most anxious that a strict investigation should be held, as I consider it due to the public, and also for my own satisfaction. May I therefore request you will consider it a case to hold an inquest, as my sole wish is to have a fair, open, impartial and public investigation into her death. I know you will get a respectable and impartial jury on the occasion . . .*

It would soon be revealed that Dr Langley had written the letter three days before his wife had died.

In his anticipation of Ellen's death, and of the rumours attaching to it, Dr Langley was not alone. On the same day that he drafted his letter to the coroner, James Jocelyn Poe, his wife's nephew, had paid visits to the coroner and the police sub-inspector to request that an inquiry should immediately be held if his aunt should happen to die.[1]

Death came to Ellen Langley at 6 a.m. on 1 May.

As Dr Langley noted in his letter to the coroner, his wife's illness had been the subject of 'insinuations'. Determined to put a stop to the unpleasant rumours, he evidently felt confident that an inquest at the coroner's court would clear the air.

He was thoroughly familiar with the court's procedures. As chief medical officer of the local dispensary for eleven years, and an occasional private practitioner for seven more, he had often prepared reports for coroners' inquests. During the 1830s and '40s, Tipperary was arguably the most violent county in Ireland; reports of its agrarian violence were a constant feature of the London papers.[2] For a Tipperary doctor, attendance as an expert witness at inquests, quarter sessions and seasonal assizes was a common (if onerous) part of the job. As early as 1839, Langley and his medical colleagues in Nenagh had complained to the House of Commons of being forced, under threat of 'heavy penalties', to attend coroners' inquests, which involved 'serious liabilities and a considerable sacrifice of time and personal convenience'.[3]

Disputes between labourers and tenant farmers, caused by destitution or the threat of eviction, brought a stream of violent deaths through Nenagh's coroner's court before and during the Great Famine. In the spring of 1849 almost 3,500 paupers crowded Nenagh's four workhouses and a further 10,000 were on 'outdoor relief', assistance for those unable to gain admittance to an institution.[4] The week after Mrs Langley's death the *Nenagh Guardian*, the mouthpiece of the local landowning class, described the situation in stark terms. 'Destitution is every day becoming more appalling and wide-spread in this fertile but pauperised union,' it reported.

Groups of half-starved looking creatures patrol the streets daily, begging for food, and hundreds of men and women, who not many months ago were able-bodied and well-looking, might be seen covered with miserable rags, wending their way to the workhouse, either in slow straggling steps, or conveyed in donkey carts. There were 200 admitted into the Workhouses last week.[5]

Nenagh's population, just over 8,500 in 1841, actually increased by 22 per cent during the years of the famine as the starving and dispossessed fled from the surrounding rural areas into the town.[6]

Dr Langley and his colleagues in the town described the results of violence in cold and measured scientific language.

In one coroner's investigation in 1844, Langley had quickly summed up for the court the nature of the victim's wounds, describing 'an extensive effusion of blood on the surface of the brain under the dura mater caused by the rupture of the large blood vessels'. Prior to the victim's death, he surmised, the man 'was labouring under a severe concussion and compression of the brain'. From these injuries he inferred that death had been 'caused by a blow or blows of a stick, which violence, although dividing the integuments of the head to the extent of an inch and a half, yet did not fracture his skull; he was insensible and speechless, and continued so to the period of his death . . .'[7]

He was equally matter-of-fact in March 1846, when assisting the inquiry into the fatal assault on 35-year-old farmer James Cane, recording 'three wounds – one mortal . . . on the left side of the head, which fractured the skull, the broken bones driven into the substance of the brain, a flesh wound on left cheek, and a confused wound on left arm – which . . . were inflicted with a blunt weapon, and has caused death'.[8]

Police detection in Ireland was still in its infancy in the 1840s. In London and Dublin, small detective forces had been created within the Metropolitan Constabularies in 1842, but in rural areas of Ireland, doctors alone could offer a scientific view on an unlawful killing, and perhaps deduce the weapon from the nature of the wounds inflicted.[9] When Langley was called to examine the body of Jeremiah Halloran, a farmer who in 1845 unwisely intervened to stop a fight at a dance, he supported the witness who claimed to have seen the fatal blow. 'On opening the head,' reported the doctor, 'I found a rupture of one of the blood vessels, and also a wound as if inflicted with a stone.'[10]

Even lawyers and judges, practised in challenging every kind of evidence, might hesitate before undermining a medical analysis. When in 1838 his assessment of a victim's physical condition prior to an attack was called into question from the bench, the young Dr Langley had seen it as a 'direct imputation' against his character and applied to the Lord Lieutenant in Dublin to have the magistrate formally rebuked.[11] Quarrelsome and headstrong, he would not stand to have his medical competence publicly challenged.

At an inquest, it was the medical evidence that really counted. The circumstances of his wife's death would be judged by his own colleagues. That, at least, was what long experience had led him to expect.

2

'Sworn to find a verdict'

At 11.30 a.m. on 1 May 1849, just five and a half hours after the death of Ellen Langley, the coroner, James Carroll, the police sub-inspector, Charles O'Dell, and a group of townsmen, largely merchants and tradesmen, assembled at Dr Langley's residence on Barrack Street to commence the inquest. Dr Langley was present with his legal representative, John O'Brien, and a medical colleague, Dr Edward Kittson. A local solicitor, O'Brien Dillon, arrived with James Jocelyn Poe to represent Mrs Langley's family.

Mr Dillon proposed empanelling fifteen, three more than required, 'in case of any disagreement of the jury'. The coroner gave his consent and fifteen of the townsmen present were called to swear an oath on the Bible. Of these, only a single juror, Edward Davis, objected to being sworn. As a Quaker, he opted instead to make a solemn affirmation.

When James Acres was called to take the oath, Dr Langley objected. 'The ground is,' explained his solicitor, Mr O'Brien, 'that Mr James Acres was married to a cousin of Mrs Langley's.' Acres was dismissed, and the swearing-in continued without further contention.

At forty-three years of age, Langley was, according to a contemporary description, five feet ten inches tall, of slight build, with a dark complexion and black hair that was starting to grey, and 'a gentleman of substance and good social position'. A surviving photograph that likely depicts the doctor, taken a few years later, shows a good-looking man with an upright and dignified bearing. He wears a large necktie and crisply starched white shirt under a well-tailored waistcoat and jacket, and sports the elaborate sideburns fashionable in the mid-nineteenth century. [1]

The coroner read out the letter he had received that morning from Dr Langley concerning his wife's death, the rumours surrounding her illness, and his wish for an inquest. As he got near the end, Dr Langley stopped him.

'The remaining part of that letter,' he said, 'refers to a person whose name it may be as well not to mention, and whom I wished the coroner not to summon.'

'Very well, sir,' said the coroner, 'I will not read it.'

'What is the date of that letter?' asked Mr Dillon, solicitor to the Poe family.

'It is not dated at all,' said Dr Kittson.

'When was it received then?' said Mr Dillon.

'This morning,' said the coroner.

'Mr O'Dell, have you anything to say about this?' Mr Dillon asked the police sub-inspector.

'I was called on by Mr Poe,' he began.

'A letter,' Langley interjected, 'was written by me three days ago, which Dr Quin saw, but I thought it premature to give any notice till her death.'

'Mr Poe called on me also,' said the sub-inspector, 'to say that in the event of anything happening to this woman, I should consider myself under notice to hold an inquest.'

Left unresolved in this exchange was the question of why Dr Langley had drafted a letter referring to his wife's death three days before she died, or whether it was more than a coincidence that he had done so on the same day that his wife's nephew had gone to the police and the coroner to flag the need for an inquest.

The coroner instructed that the jury would begin the inquiry by viewing the body of the deceased in a room upstairs. The men filed up the dark, creaking narrow stairs at the rear of the house to Ellen Langley's small garret room at the top. Filling the doorway and outside passage, they squinted through glaring midday light at the gaunt body laid out on the bed. There was no external evidence of any violence, no open wounds or scars, but rather a haggard female frame, the features reduced almost to bone. A cholera epidemic had recently swept through the town, producing a great number of emaciated corpses; on the evidence of what the jurors could see, Mrs Langley's death was perhaps no different from a hundred others.

The coroner, thinking that the room in which they had been conducting their business in Dr Langley's house was very close, suggested they relocate to the more spacious schoolhouse a few doors up the street to hear further evidence. As the jurors stepped outside, the air was unusually warm, a sudden change from the severe chill that for several weeks had prevented farmers sowing their crop of potatoes and, only days earlier, had killed famine migrants on the mail packet to Liverpool. Even the swallows, normally swarming on to Irish shores by mid-April, had failed to appear.[2]

Both Dr Langley and his wife's nephew Mr Poe had provided the coroner with separate lists of people who might be interviewed to ascertain the exact cause of death, and an hour previously Mr Carroll had issued summonses via the police sub-inspector to request them to attend. When they had settled themselves in the schoolhouse, the coroner asked Mr Dillon (representing Mr Poe) to produce his first witness.

'In consequence of the very brief notice we got,' said Mr Dillon, 'it is impossible we could have secured the attendance of all our witnesses, some of whom reside out in the country. It would be totally impossible for us to have them here at this hour, if indeed we could have them this day at all. Besides this there will be a post-mortem examination which will occupy some time, and it would facilitate the administration of justice more by adjourning the further proceedings to tomorrow.'

Dr Langley, however, was anxious to proceed. 'All your witnesses are here but Thomas Pound,' he said.

'Well, he may be a very material witness,' said Dillon.

'The summonses were only issued at half past ten o'clock,' said Mr Poe.

'It is now only a quarter past twelve o'clock,' said Dillon.

'It is not my wish to hurry it on till you have all your witnesses present, I am sure,' said Dr Langley.

'Adjourn till three o'clock,' suggested Mr Dillon.

'If I adjourn at all, I will adjourn to tomorrow morning,' replied the coroner. 'This inquiry, gentlemen, stands adjourned to ten o'clock on the 2nd May.'

Each of the jurors was then bound in the sum of £10 to return at the stated hour, and the group dispersed.[3]

It was a peculiar sequence of events. The missing witness, Thomas Pound, was not a doctor who could speak to the circumstances of Mrs Langley's illness and death. He was a man who had briefly worked as a servant for the Langleys, and had left their employment by the time of Ellen's demise. Why, with a jury assembled and medical witnesses present, did Mr Poe's lawyer wish to delay proceedings over the absence of Thomas Pound? And why did the coroner agree to do so?

Ellen Langley's corpse remained in her deathbed in Barrack Street while the inquest proceeded in the schoolhouse. After the adjournment, a number of doctors came to the house and conducted a post-mortem examination.

Well after nightfall, a humble coffin was delivered to the house. Mary Clancy, the housemaid, followed her employer's instructions to dress the body in a simple chemise and night-cap, and with his help placed it in the timber casket, which she lined with straw. Normally, deceased family members were laid out in the parlour prior to their interment, but Dr Langley did not observe the customary formalities.[4] He and his servant carried the coffin outside to the yard at the rear of the dwelling, resting it between two chairs and screening it from the view of neighbourly eyes with a carriage cover.

Here, amidst the clutter of outdoor things, it would remain for two days and nights.

At ten the following morning, the inquest reconvened in the schoolhouse on Barrack Street, a stone-faced building four bays wide and two storeys high. It was often used for public gatherings of one kind or another – the occasional lecture, or meetings of charitable and religious societies at the weekends. On the morning of 2 May, the classroom grew clamorous as it filled with solicitors, witnesses, police constables and journalists. The fifteen jurors, all middle-aged, clad in dark coats and waistcoats and tall straight hats, sat on the chairs normally occupied by the small class of Protestant children. Called to adjudicate by virtue of their perceived respectability in the community, many of them worked from premises in or near Castle Street, Nenagh's main commercial thoroughfare, which ran perpendicular to Barrack Street.[5]

Two-thirds of them were members of the rising Catholic middle class that was beginning to challenge the political and economic hegemony of Ireland's Protestant elite and had begun to assume increasingly genteel manners and aspirations. Rody Spain, James O'Brien, Anthony Nolan and Edward Davis were rival linen and woollen drapers whose shops were on Castle Street. James Hanly, an ironmonger and hardware dealer, James Roche, a trader in wine and spirits, and Edward Jones, a coach maker, were their near neighbours. John Dwyer was a provision dealer, selling everything from saddlery to stationery, and, for a period, held the contract to supply milk to the workhouse; like several of his fellow jurors, he was also a town commissioner, responsible for the recently introduced gas lighting and street paving. Richard Cunningham was a saddler and harness

maker on Castle Street. William Gleeson and Bryan Consedine were in the boot trade. Besides the lone Quaker, Mr
Davis, there were three Protestants among the fifteen. Joshua
Cantrell, who was appointed foreman of the coroner's jury,
was a town commissioner and the only member of the group
who sat on the Grand Jury, an elite group of largely Protestant landowners who fulfilled some of the functions later
performed by county councils. Cantrell resided in the wealthy
Summer Hill area on the north side of the town. The other
members of the jury from the town's Protestant minority
were Benjamin Barrington, who imported steam-powered
machine-ground coffee from London, and Henry Harding,
a leather dealer with a premises in Silver Street.[6]

Dr Langley arrived with his sister, Mrs Lydia Jackson, and
her daughter Fanny. Nine years earlier, Lydia, who lived in
Limerick, had sent Fanny, then aged three, to Nenagh to live
with her brother and his wife, who were childless.[7]

James Carroll, an elderly man who had served as coroner
for at least twenty years, was formal and officious in his role.
He was an ironmonger and hardware dealer, and had no spe-
cialist legal or medical expertise. Like the majority of jurors
he had summoned, he was a Catholic. His position, unlike
others in the magistracy, was an elected one.[8]

'Gentlemen,' he began, 'the first thing for us is to hear the
evidence of the medical gentlemen, as a great deal depends
on their testimony.' He proposed starting with Dr O'Neill
Quin, who ran the medical dispensary at Silvermines, a small
village south of Nenagh.[9] Quin was distantly related to Ellen
Langley through his wife, Harriet.[10]

Dr Quin testified that, at Dr Langley's request, he had
visited Ellen Langley on 16 April, a fortnight before her
death. 'She consulted me,' he said, 'for a complaint under

which she thought she was labouring, but which I found not to exist.' Again at the request of Dr Langley, he visited Mrs Langley on 22 April, 'and found her suffering from severe diarrhoea, attended with excessive debility'. 'Her disease not abating,' Dr Quin continued, 'Dr Langley wished for a second medical gentleman, and Dr Kittson saw her with me on Tuesday, the 24th April; she complained of fullness of stomach, which was soon succeeded by vomiting of green bilious matter; the bowel complaint and irritability of stomach continued from that time to the period of death, assuming quite the character of English cholera.'[11]

A familiar ailment to any experienced jury, 'English cholera' was not cholera at all, but referred to a range of other diarrhoeal diseases, usually viral in origin, that would today be called gastroenteritis. English cholera often struck the urban poor in the summer months. It was understood to be distinct from what was known as 'Asiatic cholera' – cholera proper, caused by the bacterium *Vibrio cholerae* – which was rampant in various parts of Ireland, including north Tipperary, in the spring of 1849.[12] English cholera drained fluid from the system, producing 'thirst, cramps . . . collapse, suppression of urine, imperceptible pulse, and, in short, all the symptoms of [Asiatic] cholera'.[13] The doctors' decision to specify English rather than Asiatic cholera in the case of Ellen Langley was likely due to tissue damage not normally associated with the latter.[14]

Dr Quin noted that the conclusion he and Dr Kittson had drawn on 24 April was supported by the post-mortem examination he and four other doctors had made in Barrack Street the previous day. Two of these doctors, Dr Finucane and Dr Spain, he said, had been specially selected by James Jocelyn Poe, nephew of the deceased, to represent Mrs Langley's family.[15]

Conscious that the doctors' post-mortem report was likely to contain graphic language, Mr Carroll indicated that the ladies present, Dr Langley's sister and niece, may wish to leave.

After they had done so, Dr Quin proceeded to read out the report:

The external appearance of the body presented nothing unusual – on opening the chest we found both lungs extensively diseased, with large tubercles of long standing on each – the posterior portion of the right lung very highly congested. The heart of natural size, but soft, and containing some fatty deposit. On opening into the abdomen, we found the liver enlarged, particularly its left lobe, but presenting otherwise a healthy appearance. The stomach presented nothing unusual externally – the under surface appeared healthy, and contained about two ounces of thick viscid fluid. The spleen was enlarged and congested. The small intestines and peritoneal covering presented patches of recent inflammation, which we think sufficiently accounts for the diarrhoea under which she laboured, and ultimately caused her death.

O'Neill Quin, M.D.
Edward Kittson, Surgeon.
George Frith, Surgeon.
John Finucane, M.D.
Thos. Spain, Surgeon.

The evidence of tuberculosis would not have come as a great surprise to the doctors. The incidence of the disease was generally lower in Ireland than in the rest of the United Kingdom in the nineteenth century, but suddenly doubled during the period of the Great Famine.[16] It was not unusual for chronic sufferers to survive many years and ultimately die from an unrelated illness.[17]

When Dr Quin had finished reading the report, Dr Langley addressed his medical colleague directly – a freedom that was a distinctive feature of the coroner's court.[18]

'Will you tell the jury,' he asked Quin, 'whether you can swear, to your own knowledge, that she laboured under pulmonary disease for several years previous to her last illness?'

'You will allow Mr Dillon to examine first,' objected the coroner, referring to the Poe family's lawyer, 'and then you can offer whatever suggestions you please.'

'All that I can say is this,' said Mr Dillon, 'that from the various reports that were afloat both previous to and subsequent to Mrs Langley's death, her immediate relations thought proper to call for an inquest. Dr Langley also thought proper to call for an inquest. I think it was due to both of them that an investigation should take place, and on the part of Mrs Langley's family I have now to express our satisfaction at the post-mortem examination read by Dr Quin. It is the foundation of all, and on it I think the jury can find their verdict. They cannot go beyond it.'

Mr Dillon had evidently had a change of heart – or of instructions – since the first morning of the inquest, when he had argued for an adjournment on the grounds that the Langley's former servant Thomas Pound was not available. Following the post-mortem report, and the testimony of Dr Quin, there was no reference to Pound and the other witnesses; in the view of the Poe family's lawyer, the medical evidence was all the jury required.

'To avoid medical terms, and in order to be as simple as we can,' said Dr Quin, 'the verdict might be "died of bowel complaint".'

'Gentlemen,' said the coroner, addressing the jurymen gathered together on one side of the room, 'do you agree to

Dr Quin's evidence – is your verdict that she died of bowel complaint?'

There was a moment of murmuring between them. 'Dr Kittson ought to be examined,' suggested Mr Jones, the coach maker.

'Sure he corroborates me; his name is added to the other gentlemen,' responded Dr Quin.

'That is only on the post-mortem examination,' said Jones. 'We should like to hear his evidence.'

'No necessity,' said the coroner firmly.

Mr Dillon said he would call no other witnesses.

'The verdict may be that Mrs Eleanor Langley came by her death from bowel complaint,' said Dr Quin. (Though known as Ellen, she had been christened Eleanor.)

'It is *the jury* must find a verdict,' protested the juror William Gleeson; 'it is you who are finding one now.'[19]

Eight people, including two further doctors, household servants, a shopkeeper and a clergyman, were waiting outside to give evidence, and the jurors were surprised that these witnesses – whom many believed critical to establishing the veracity of the rumours circulating in the town – were not to be heard.[20] There was further agitated murmuring as the room was cleared to allow the jury to consider the matter for themselves. They were locked in and expected to remain there until they had agreed on a verdict – one based on nothing more than the evidence provided. But there were other things on their minds – above all, those rumours regarding the illness and death of Ellen Langley. One leading theory was that Mrs Langley had been poisoned by her husband. When news had got out of Mrs Langley's death, word spread that her husband had been arrested. Although this was not true, it probably reflected the state of public feeling concerning Dr Langley's relationship with his wife.[21] The jurors knew they must resolve the question of this death not just to their own satisfaction but to that of their wives, their neighbours and even their customers.

The jury sent out a request that they be allowed to scrutinize in greater depth the inquisition paper (the written statement they were expected to sign), the written evidence of Dr Quin, and the post-mortem report. The coroner ruled that such documents could not be allowed to leave his possession. Mr Jones, the juror who had been sent to enquire after them, retired to the conference chamber empty-handed.

After some minutes, the door opened and the various parties were allowed to return to the main schoolroom. Bryan Consedine, although not the head juror, was the first to voice the group's sense of disquiet. He was a strong-willed man who would, later that same year, publicly challenge decisions made by both the Poor Law Guardians and the Catholic Church hierarchy.[22]

'We will find no verdict,' he said to Mr Carroll. 'We adjourned from yesterday to today for the purpose of hearing evidence, and now you refuse to bring [the witnesses] forward.'

'I suppose you are not going to find your verdict upon public rumour,' said Dr Langley.

'Why not produce the witnesses?' asked Mr Harding.

'It is the business of the jury to find the cause of death,' said another juror. 'The jury are not satisfied with the information they have received.'

Further voices added their dissent, and, according to the reporter from the *Nenagh Guardian*, 'the greatest confusion prevailed'. The *Tipperary Vindicator* described the men 'conversing with the doctors and each other in several groups around the room', their voices conveying 'much earnestness', and 'a high tone'.

Mr Carroll struggled to make himself heard. 'Gentlemen,' he cried, 'are you likely to agree?'

Their response was emphatic. 'No! We'll give no verdict.'

James Jocelyn Poe, the 42-year-old nephew of the deceased, now moved to speak. The eldest of five children of Mrs Langley's older sister Frances and her husband, the town's Protestant rector, the Rev. James Hill Poe, James Jocelyn was a tall, slim, good-looking man, with lustrous dark hair. The

jurors would have known him as vice-chairman of the Nenagh Board of Poor Law Guardians and as land agent to the Earl of Orkney and his own cousin, Lord Bloomfield, as well as the heir to his uncle's estate of Solsboro outside the town. Given his stature in the locality and his position as the representative of the deceased, he may well have thought that his opinion would settle the issue. He decided to confront directly the theory that, he would have assumed, underlay the jurors' disquiet: that Ellen Langley had been poisoned.

'I have not said a word yet on the subject,' he began. 'Irritation of the stomach might produce the diarrhoea under which the deceased laboured. I got two medical gentlemen to assist at the post-mortem examination, Drs Spain and Finucane, to see if any symptom of poison could be found in the intestines. From the result of that examination I am perfectly satisfied no poison was found in the body. As next of kin to the deceased I do not press the matter any further after the testimony of the medical gentlemen.'

Perhaps fearing that he appeared confrontational, he made an addendum to this short address:

'I do not say anything of what may be the feeling of the jury.'[23]

Mr Poe's desire to conclude the inquest on the medical evidence alone must have puzzled the jurors. Next to him, but silent, was his 72-year-old father, the Rev. James Hill Poe. As the town's senior Protestant clergyman, he was a key figure in its public affairs. An active participant on the famine relief committee, which he occasionally chaired, he enjoyed good relations with his Catholic counterparts. But some tensions remained. Although he tolerated freedom of religious worship, he had firmly opposed Daniel O'Connell's campaign

for the political emancipation of Catholics when that question had arisen.[24] Now, he found himself sitting in the coroner's court, looking on as a body composed largely of Catholic merchants sought to hear evidence that might shed light upon his family's private affairs. While the evidence of doctors was seen as scientific and impartial, the testimony of other witnesses – servants, in particular – could prove embarrassing.

Mr O'Dell, the district sub-inspector of police, was less

circumspect. 'As this matter has occurred in my district,' he said, 'I beg to state I have used every exertion I possibly could to obtain the witnesses, and they are now in attendance if you wish to examine them.'

'Let us have them,' urged a voice from the jury.

'Any allegation that may be made,' Dr Langley announced defiantly to the jury, 'I am ready to meet it. I do not wish the matter to go any further, for if it is proceeded with, private circumstances will come before the public which will bring up evidence hurtful to the living as well as injurious to the memory of the dead. The jury are sworn to find a verdict according to the evidence brought before them, not on the reports they may have heard, or the stories of servants and gossips, and you have, I think, sufficient evidence to ground your verdict upon.'[25]

'It is a vicious taste for notoriety that would require it,' added Dr Quin.

3

'Things that ought to be buried in oblivion'

Bryan Consedine would have observed with interest Dr Quin's ready defence of his colleague. He and Quin had crossed swords earlier that year, when Consedine had pushed for an inquest into the death of a 56-year-old man in the town's auxiliary workhouse. The *Tipperary Vindicator* published an investigation which claimed the man had suffered 'starvation . . . bad treatment, inattention and want of care'. Quin, who had performed the post-mortem in that case, had insisted the man had died of natural infirmity and 'disease of the lungs'.[1] Now, as a juror at the inquest into Mrs Langley's death, Consedine once more found himself questioning Quin's diagnosis.

From Quin's testimony it became apparent that for several weeks Mrs Langley had been living apart from her husband in lodgings on Pound Street, a poor area in the western quarter of the town, before returning to Barrack Street just prior to her death. Consedine enquired as to the nature of the accommodation on Pound Street.

'There was a good boarded floor in the house,' said Quin, 'a large window, and she seemed to have enough of everything and not in want of any of the common necessaries of life. She –'

'Dr Quin,' interrupted Mr Poe, 'you must recollect you are here as a medical witness and not as an advocate.'

This sudden interjection suggested the reference to these lodgings on Pound Street was a sore point between the Poes and Dr Langley. For the jury, it was a chink in the armour that had been raised against them. Whatever Mr Poe's agreement with Dr Langley concerning the medical evidence, the subject of his aunt's lodging outside her husband's house was evidently a source of tension.

'Gentlemen, allow me,' said Dr Langley. 'If it is necessary I have the most respectable evidence to prove that for seventeen years we lived happily together. I have also evidence that for the last three or four months we lived unhappily, and that I did not treat her in the same affectionate manner as formerly, and I have documents, statements and evidence to warrant me in my change of treatment in her regard. There is no use entering on these matters.'

'But that conduct may have accelerated her death,' said Mr Gleeson, the bootmaker.

'It would be better to let the matter rest,' said Mr O'Brien, Dr Langley's solicitor.

But Consedine pressed: 'How was she fed?'

'She had sufficient to eat,' said Dr Quin.

'They have sufficient to eat in the poorhouse,' said Mr Jones, the coach maker.

'I do not know what she had to eat for it was money I gave her,' said Dr Langley. 'You must be aware, gentlemen, that as she was my wife, I was accountable for her debts. I cannot say what support she got, for it was money, not food, I gave her. I certainly tell you this: that I did not pamper her, nor treat her in the way I would have done had not matters come to my knowledge that induced me to change my manner towards her.'[2]

Evidently unable to bear public insinuations concerning

his aunt, James Jocelyn Poe stressed once again that as no poison was found in her body, his family did not wish to press the issue any further. Otherwise, he said, he would have had no hesitation in pressing for a fuller investigation.

Dr Langley was also tiring of the jury's persistence. 'It was intimated to me by Mr O'Dell,' he said, referring to the police sub-inspector, 'that there would not be any further proceedings in the matter, and consequently I am not now prepared with my witnesses.'

'I told you no such thing, sir,' protested the sub-inspector. 'I told you a conversation I had with Reverend Poe, and he said he would not press the matter after the evidence of the medical gentlemen.' He assured Langley that he had summoned Mr Abbott, the witness the doctor himself had requested, and who might speak on his behalf.

The jury too were getting impatient.

'Let there be no more cavilling – produce the witnesses,' demanded Bryan Consedine.

Consedine's distrust of the doctors' evidence was a deep-seated one. In addition to the earlier quarrel over the death of the pauper in the town's workhouse, he and seven other members of the jury were that same week arranging a public meeting to remove the town's Poor Law Guardians, who were in charge of the workhouse, for failing to secure the necessary medical attendance and accommodation for the poor following the recent outbreak of cholera.[3] Mr Poe and Mr Dillon were both members of this board. At the meeting, the following Sunday, the Poor Law Guardians' payments to four doctors to oversee the crisis would be held up as a classic case of double jobbing, given that they all held a variety of other medical posts and had little time for the extra work.[4] They included Drs Quin, Frith and Kittson, all of whom had participated in the post-mortem on Ellen Langley.

But there was little that Consedine and his fellow jurors could do to force the parties to the inquest to produce the non-medical witnesses.

'I will examine no witnesses,' said Mr Dillon, on behalf of the Poes. 'The case comes before the jury as a case would at the assizes, where, in default of witnesses, a verdict of "not guilty" is to be returned.'

This statement provoked further commotion among the jury – which in turn provoked the coroner: 'My God Almighty,' he exclaimed, 'if prosecutors wish not to produce witnesses are you to enforce them?'

'Perhaps I am not out of order in making this remark,' said James Jocelyn Poe, 'that having heard the evidence of five medical gentlemen, two of whom were selected by myself, namely, Dr Spain, and Dr Finucane, to act on the post-mortem examination, along with Drs Frith, Kittson and Quin – and they having found no trace of vegetable or mineral poison in the intestines – I am satisfied that the impression which had gone abroad, and which was also on the mind of the unfortunate woman herself, is quite contradicted by the evidence of these medical gentlemen, and I am quite satisfied on that point.'[5]

It was here that Mr Poe mentioned openly for the first time the real basis for the suspicions that had led to the inquiry – the fact that his aunt herself had believed prior to her death that she was being poisoned by her husband. The medical evidence, he was suggesting now, showed she was merely paranoid.

'Is it your wish to produce other evidence?' asked the coroner.

'The family are quite satisfied,' said Mr Poe.

'I tell the jury that I will produce no witnesses,' added Mr Dillon.

'And I'll give none,' added Dr Langley, 'for it would be dragging out things that ought to be buried in oblivion.'

He held up a parcel of folded documents for the assembled crowd to see. 'I have evidence in these papers ... I have respectable persons to prove that she said, almost with her last words, that herself alone was to blame in the transaction, and the fault was not mine.' The doctor's vague reference to 'the transaction' was left unexplained, but its purpose was clearly to insinuate some fault in his wife's character.

'If there had been little differences between the woman and her husband,' said Dr Quin, 'what need to create fresh uneasiness by bringing them to light afresh?'

'The most charitable way to end the matter,' added Mr Dillon, 'would be simply to return a verdict of "died of English cholera".'

There was uproar, and the cacophony again put a stop to the proceedings. The coroner ordered the room to be cleared of the public – leaving the jury once more alone to consider the matter among themselves. The *Nenagh Guardian* reported them 'pacing up and down the room' as they argued the various points of the case.

Several minutes passed, and the crowd of spectators waited impatiently outside the doors of the schoolhouse for readmittance, no doubt bringing inquisitive passers-by up to date on what was happening. The following day hundreds of people would stream into Barrack Street for the weekly market, centred in the market house opposite the schoolhouse, but such a commotion was unusual on a Wednesday.[6] There would be plenty of talk of this at the Royal Oak and the Victoria, and the five other pubs on the street, when people arrived from out of town.

At length the coroner, solicitors, interested parties and public were allowed to return inside. The morning was dragging on and the full intensity of the midday sun shone through the south-facing windows, raising the temperature in the room. Tempers were frayed and the resolve of the jurors was hardening.

'I would propose an adjournment of the jury,' said Mr Consedine, addressing the assembled parties, 'being firmly convinced that very important evidence has been suppressed.' There were cries of 'yes', and 'hear, hear' from his fellow jurors.

'I propose,' he continued firmly, 'that you adjourn this inquest to Saturday, when evidence may be forthcoming. You have no right to make a burlesque of this court. We were brought here yesterday from our business, and brought here today, yet no witnesses will be produced. I consider that nothing less than a burlesque.'[7]

'There are several ways for a woman to come by death besides poison,' said Mr Consedine.

'Hear, hear,' added several other jurors.

'By brutality, for instance, or ill-treatment.'

'You want to hear gossip,' said Dr Langley.

'No such thing!' replied Consedine.

Mr Dillon suggested drawing up a qualified verdict that would accommodate the scruples of the jury, stating that they had heard no evidence to contradict the findings of the post-mortem. The men rejected the proposal outright.

'We have suppressed no evidence,' protested Mr Poe. 'We have brought Dr Spain and Dr Finucane before you.'

'The jury are of [the] opinion, unanimously I believe,' said Mr Davis, 'that [the] deceased met with foul treatment.'

'The best way,' said Dr Langley, 'is to ask Mr Poe does he intend to bring any charge of foul treatment against me.'

'We have nothing to do with what Mr Poe thinks or intends,' said Rody Spain, a juror.

'We are bound by our oaths, and must respect them,' added Mr Cantrell, the foreman of the jury.

'Mr O'Dell, on the part of the Crown or the public, has to bring forward whatever evidence is to be produced now,' said Mr Poe.

'Mr O'Dell has done his duty,' said Mr Cantrell, 'he has his witnesses in attendance.'

'If witnesses are produced,' said Mr Poe weakly, 'they must be on the part of the Crown.'

In the face of this impasse, the coroner adopted Bryan Consedine's suggestion. 'The court of inquiry,' he announced, 'stands adjourned to Saturday next at ten o'clock in this room.'

Although Mr O'Dell had summoned the witnesses on behalf of both Mr Poe and Dr Langley, both parties had washed their hands of the case following the post-mortem results. Were there really grounds for a police sub-inspector to pursue the case in light of such a strong medical consensus? The role of the Crown was to investigate a case of unlawful death where there was some clear evidence of wrongdoing. Regardless of Dr Langley's dispute with his wife, the doctors had found no evidence of poison.

However, this was not a decision Mr O'Dell would have to make. During the two-day recess in the coroner's inquest, certain members of the Poe family, more emotionally involved and anxious for justice, would step into the breach.

*

The following morning, after the attack on the doctor's house in Barrack Street, Ellen Langley was buried. The cemetery, just 200 yards from the house, lay under the shadow of the church where for seventeen years Ellen had attended the weekly sermons of her brother-in-law, the Rev. James Hill Poe. Despite Mrs Langley's respectable station in life, her husband and family would raise no memorial there to mark her resting place.[8]

4

'A handsome mansion, pleasantly situated'

The small estate of Donnybrook in the parish of Bally-mackey, seven miles east of Nenagh, was a patchwork of neat fields, divided by straight hedgerows. It had been owned by the Poe family since Thomas Poe, a lieutenant in Cromwell's Parliamentary army, received grants of land in north Tipperary under the Act of Settlement in the reign of Charles II.[1] A handsome map, commissioned in 1810 by Ellen Poe's father, William Poe, shows the extent of the family lands, a faintly drawn escutcheon in one corner, bearing three crescents azure, derived from the arms registered by his earlier kinsman Dr Leonard Poe of Derbyshire, a physician to Charles I.[2] When William Poe married Ellen's mother, Frances Harden, in 1777 it was said he secured himself a 'handsome fortune',[3] which extended the estate to 600 acres.[4] The house at Donnybrook, built by her grandfather, or possibly her father following his marriage, was described in Lewis's *Topographical Dictionary* of 1837 as 'a handsome mansion, pleasantly situated'. It had a fine sweep of stone steps leading to a fanlit and pedimented door. Tall sash windows flanked the centre, lighting spacious reception rooms on the main floor.[5] A grander pediment crowned the parapet above, punctuated by a handsome thermal window in the attic where Ellen and her siblings, confined to a nursery, would have slept and played during their childhood years.[6]

Despite the widespread poverty in County Tipperary in

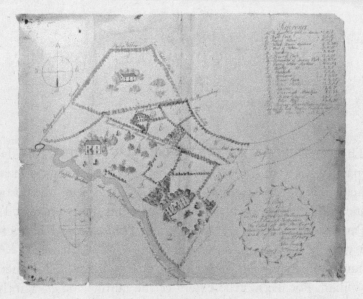

the early 1800s, Donnybrook, like most gentlemen's demesnes, had a carefully cultivated air of tranquillity. A view of the house, painted in the mid-nineteenth century, shows a rural idyll, the ivy-clad walls glimpsed through trees across a small park, with grass sweeping down to a racing brook. A line of white geese hover on the bank, while cattle graze serenely under the trees; a young girl, perhaps one of Ellen's nieces, plays with a small dog in the foreground, and in the distance the prospect fades into the golden haze of a summer's evening.[7]

To the rear of the house, servants tended an extensive walled garden, richly ornamented with formal parterres, providing fruit and vegetables to the kitchen and a pleasant retreat for quiet walks and solitary retirement.[8] Further west was a path through an orchard that ran as far as the Ollatrim River; and in the distance, on the other side of the water, the old ruined castle of Cappa – a remnant of the once wealthy native family of O'Meara, the last of whom still lived during Ellen's childhood years and was described as 'a gambler addicted to all sorts of gallantry, brave, hospitable, improvident, noble-mannered and wicked'.[9] From the high windows of their bedrooms, Ellen and her siblings would have seen substantial farms – Wilton, Elm Hill and Riverlawn – each with its own stone house of two or three storeys, leased out by Ellen's father to respectable Protestant tenants.[10]

On the walls of Donnybrook were portraits of ancestors, whose wealth had derived from the seventeenth-century wars of religion that had devastated Ireland's Catholic establishment. Several were given the name 'Parsons' in one form or another, from their ancestor Sir William Parsons, a seventeenth-century Chief Justice of Ireland. He had seen the arrival of the new English in Ireland in missionary terms: 'We must change [the Irish] course of government, apparel, manner of holding land, language and habit of life,' he wrote. 'It will otherwise be impossible to set up in them obedience to the laws and to the English Empire.'[11] As magistrates in the local town of Nenagh, his descendants enforced the English law that their ancestor had so strongly advocated, ruling as part of a small and privileged cohort of colonial families.[12]

Ellen was the second youngest of three boys and six girls. George, the first-born boy, had died young, perhaps as a baby, though the exact date of his death is unknown. Ellen's mother, Frances Harden, died in 1795 at the age of thirty-eight, when Ellen was just four years old. Her older sister Anne died at the age of thirteen.[13] The younger children were raised by their widower father.

Social life among Tipperary gentlemen often centred on

the hunt. A later memoirist recalled one of the Poes' neighbours at Castle Willington as 'full of anecdote and fun, as all such characters of that day were', enjoying a rough, hard-living lifestyle. 'In the hunting season,' he wrote, 'the hunting gentlemen dine together at the Hunting Club in Nenagh, or elsewhere; and, as may be well supposed, their violent and constant exercise by day occasioned them to take a booze at night, separating seldom till the dawn of day appeared, when the hounds and horses were all in readiness once more . . . The fox was always to be found both soon and near.'[14]

For young ladies living in rural Ireland, social life demanded constant travel. This was not without hazards: the eldest girl, Frances, broke her leg when her jaunting car overturned in 1805, killing her friend Miss Archer.[15] Smartly dressed in the high-waisted empire dresses of the period, the Poe girls would have looked to the 'fine barrack for two troops of horse' in Nenagh, where young officers of the regularly changing militia regiments were stationed.[16] Games were got up and wagers made at high stakes, such as for the ball game played on stilts in Nenagh in the summer of 1806, or the theatrical farce *High Life Below Stairs*, performed during July 1812 by the 6th Garrison Battalion.[17]

All around the town of Nenagh were 'houses with their doors wide and ever open to the weary traveller, anxious, all alike, to provide amusement to induce a lengthened visit'.[18] The novelist Sydney Owenson, who was a governess to the Poes' neighbours, the Crawfords of Fortwilliam, in 1801, described dinner parties of 'upwards of forty people' with 'singing, playing, and dancing away as merry as crickets'. 'Nothing can be pleasanter than our life at present,' she wrote in one letter, 'tomorrow we are to have . . . all the world to dinner, and music in the evening. We got a delightful piano and tambourine, and I do nothing but sing and play . . .'[19]

Frances married a distant cousin, the Rev. James Hill Poe, a Trinity-educated curate stationed in the nearby village of Toomevara, in 1806. It was a good match for the daughter of a minor landowner, and a coming together of the two north Tipperary branches of the family: James Hill Poe's older brother, John, was the owner of a fine estate at Solsboro on the opposite side of Nenagh, and sheriff of the county.

In 1815, the year of Wellington's victory at Waterloo, Ellen waved Frances and her husband goodbye when they moved to County Carlow so that he might take up a better-paid ecclesiastical post. It was a year of goodbyes. The younger of Ellen's two surviving brothers, Thomas, married in June of that year and established himself in Dublin, and Margery, the next eldest, became engaged to the son of a neighbouring Tipperary landowner.[20]

Although now twenty-four years old, Ellen remained unattached – whether by disinclination to marry or lack of suitors is unknown. Her younger sister, Mary Anne, married in 1819, and another, Martha – her last remaining sister at home – died soon after of an unspecified illness.[21]

Ellen stayed on at Donnybrook with her ageing father and her eldest brother, William. As heir to the estate, William would likely have occupied the house with his wife, four sons and three daughters, and would become responsible for his unmarried sister after his father's death. As the years passed Ellen remained at home, alongside her brother's growing family. His second-youngest child, born in 1818, was named in her honour.[22]

By the time her father died in 1830, Ellen was thirty-nine years of age and the probability of matrimony had faded considerably. Already in 1829, one of William's daughters, aged seventeen, had married and given birth to her first child.[23] Ellen had become not just the spinster aunt, but the spinster grand-aunt.

5

'A very subtle thing'

'Mr Coroner,' began Mr Dillon, 'before you go any further, may I request of you to order the presence of Dr Langley at the inquest.'

It was Saturday morning. The inquest had reconvened after a two-day adjournment, but Dr Langley was not present.

'He is at his own house,' said his solicitor, Mr Bolton.

'How can I order his presence?' enquired the coroner.

Mr Dillon said, 'I am informed he is not in Nenagh.'

'I saw Dr Langley last night,' Mr Bolton assured the court. 'I told him not to make his appearance in this room today, in consequence of the angry feeling exhibited towards him by the public, lest he might receive any bodily injury. I believe he is now at his own house.'

'Did you see him today?' enquired the coroner.

'I did not, sir.'

'I saw his phaeton coming into town by the Spout road this morning,' said Mr Cunningham, a member of the jury, 'and there was no person in it but the driver.'

The Spout road was the route that left Nenagh in the direction of Dublin – or, for those travelling to the capital by train, the route to the station at Templemore.

At the urging of the jury, a policeman was despatched by the coroner to the house in Barrack Street – and failed to locate the husband of the deceased. Dr Langley, it appeared, had left town.

*

The disappearance of Dr Langley was the first remarkable event on the third day of the inquest. The next was O'Brien Dillon's statement to the jury. Having represented Mr James Jocelyn Poe, nephew of the deceased, on the first two days of the inquest, he now had new clients. Whereas James Jocelyn Poe had expressed some tolerance towards Dr Langley, Dillon said, 'those more immediately connected with the deceased lady, Mrs Langley, have by no means been satisfied with this kindness and leniency towards him'. These members of the Poe family – 'nearer relatives to the deceased', according to the *Tipperary Vindicator* – had decided to retain Mr Dillon's services, with a brief to pursue the inquiry into Mrs Langley's death beyond the testimony of the doctors.[1]

Dillon never stated exactly who those 'nearer relatives' were, but they can only have been her siblings: Frances, Mary Anne and Tom. Their determination to retain O'Brien Dillon, despite his attempts to bring a close to the case on the Wednesday, suggests a faith in his abilities. The son of an apothecary from Pound Street, a poor area on the west side of Nenagh, Dillon was among the second generation of Catholics to benefit from the repeal of the prohibition against their practising law. Described in suspicious terms by the *Nenagh Guardian* years earlier as '"Gentleman Attorney" and ex-radical agitator', he had made his reputation in the emancipation campaign of his friend Daniel O'Connell which had granted Catholics the right to sit in Parliament in 1829.[2] During the Waterford by-election of 1826 he had fought a duel in defence of the rights of tenants to vote against their landlords' wishes.[3] Whatever the paper's reservations about his politics, Dillon commanded admiration, even among Nenagh's Protestant establishment. When he died in New York many years later, the editor of the *Nenagh Guardian*, departing from the paper's earlier assessment, commented that 'to know Mr Dillon was to respect him for he was one of the most perfect gentlemen ever known in his profession'.[4]

Also present that day in the coroner's court was Mr George Bolton of Bolton & Bolton Solicitors, who had been brought in to represent Dr Langley. Aged thirty-one, Bolton had an extensive legal practice with offices in both Nenagh and Dublin.[5] He occupied a large house close to the Rev. James Hill Poe's rectory on the affluent Summer Hill, on the northern side of the town, and acted as the Poe family solicitor, and as the receiver for the estate of the reverend's indebted elder brother, John Poe of Solsboro.[6]

Bolton's ties to the family of Dr Langley's late wife were not purely professional. During the preceding months he had been making social calls to Solsboro, where Anna Poe, at thirty-two the reverend's last unmarried daughter, was living with her brother's family. A photograph of her, taken a few years later, shows an attractive woman with soft features, sallow skin, large dark eyes and fine hair. When she was twenty, a Dublin weekly paper, praising the young ladies of Nenagh, described a Miss Poe as 'she who shines the fairest where thousands are fair'.[7] Although the estate was currently indebted, she and her siblings had good prospects. 'It may be satisfactory to you to know what my intentions are in the event of my surviving my brother, and his estate coming to me,' the reverend had written to his middle son, William, a few years earlier. 'I would charge the estate with five thousand pounds for the younger members of my family of which sum you should have one third.'[8] Anna might expect the same.

Bolton may have seemed a good prospect for Anna Poe. He was keen to get ahead in life, hard-headed and ambitious. The son of a lawyer, his politics were conservative and he would later rise to become Crown Solicitor for County Tipperary, advancing his career by prosecuting several high-profile cases against the rising tide of Irish nationalism. Many decades later, Home Rule MP William O'Brien would describe him as a man of 'craft and daring' – and as one of the three figures most responsible for the maladministration of Ireland.[9] It was to him, in his role of Crown Solicitor, that O'Brien would attribute 'the entire campaign of bloody reprisals' which followed the assassination of the Chief Secretary at the height of the Land War of the 1880s. His appearance later in life, according to one historian, was sinister and forbidding, 'tall, skinny, austere looking with . . . cold black eyes'.[10]

The extended Poe family, still in mourning for the deceased, were in attendance. The most prominent figure among them was the Rev. Mr Poe, the town's Church of Ireland rector and the brother-in-law of Mrs Langley. A portrait of him in late middle age shows a handsome man with bright, earnest eyes and a firm mouth.[11] His grand-uncle, Robert Jocelyn, had been Lord Chancellor of Ireland, and raised to the peerage as 1st Viscount Jocelyn; more recently, his first cousin, Benjamin Bloomfield, had been private secretary to George IV and created 1st Baron Bloomfield. The latter had been instrumental in elevating Nenagh to an assize town in 1838 and the construction of its magisterial new courthouse.[12]

Neither his wife nor his unmarried daughter, Anna, attended the inquest. The rector might have thought a coroner's court – especially one in which unpleasant testimony was to be expected – was not a fit place for gentlewomen. There might also have been an instinct to minimize the women's proximity to scandal – a subject he knew something about.

His own rise within the Church had been on the coat-tails

of his cousin Percy Jocelyn, the Bishop of Clogher, whose sudden fall from grace in 1822, as the result of a homosexual affair, had been the greatest British scandal of its time, and hugely damaging to the Church of Ireland. The Rev. Mr Poe had done all he could to help mitigate the disaster and was involved in settling the bishop's affairs in Ireland after his flight to Paris and later settlement in Scotland under an assumed name.[13] But the bishop's fall from grace caused considerable embarrassment to the Poes, who had traded heavily on their family connections with the Jocelyns. When another cousin died young two years after the scandal, a press pamphlet speculated that she had 'drooped and died from grief, induced by her uncle's infamy'.[14]

James Jocelyn Poe, who had represented the family on the previous day of the hearing, was there along with one of his two younger brothers, Percy Jocelyn Poe, then aged twenty-eight. Percy had been named in honour of his father's patron and born only a year before his public fall from grace. He had recently stood for election as a Poor Law Guardian to represent a portion of his family's estate, but, unlike his older brother, had failed to attract a single vote.[15]

A distant relative – William Poe of Donnybrook, also a nephew of Mrs Langley – and other members of the broader Poe family, filed into the room to observe the proceedings.[16] Dr Langley's sister, Mrs Jackson, and her daughter, Miss Jackson, constituted a rare female presence in the coroner's court, and were the only family he had in attendance. The doctor himself, having been so commanding a figure at the previous hearing, was conspicuously absent.

As the son of an apothecary, O'Brien Dillon was familiar with the world of chemicals, ointments and poisons. He knew that prussic acid (or hydrogen cyanide, as it is now more commonly known), with its contemporary application as a treatment for tuberculosis, deadly effects in overdose, and elusiveness to detection, was an ideal murder weapon for a doctor well versed in its chemical properties.

Dillon was not long into his interrogation of Dr Quin before he invoked the deadly poison.

'Now, Dr Quin,' he said, 'on the post-mortem examination you stated that her lungs were very much diseased. "Very extensively diseased" was the word. You know what prussic acid is?'

'Yes.'

'Would you not say from the state of her lungs that she must be a long time suffering under consumption?'

Quin confirmed that Ellen had been 'suffering from tubercles', and also that hydrocyanic or prussic acid 'is in many instances prescribed for the lungs'.

'Dr Langley never told you he prescribed for Mrs Langley, or gave her any medicine for her lungs?'

'He might have done so without my knowledge.'

'Of course, Dr Langley being a surgeon he knew the use of his medicines, and the effect they would have upon the patient?'

'He must know it,' replied Quin.

'Now, have you been able to ascertain, from the state of her bowels, having made a post-mortem examination, whether she had ever or at any time got hydrocyanic or prussic acid?'

'I [have] not. I have her stomach preserved this moment, in a sealed bottle, which is in my possession.'

'I believe it is difficult for medical gentlemen to trace the slightest particle of this poison. Does it not generally deceive them?'

'Oh, yes, it is a very subtle thing.'

'Would you not say if it was given gradually it would have the effect of diseasing the lungs?'

'I never used it to that extent.'

'Or if given gradually for the purpose of curing the lungs would it not, in some cases, have the effect of hastening or ultimately causing death?'

'I do not know.'

'But you knew it to be deadly poison?'

'Yes.'

'Hydrocyanic or prussic acid is a new medicine, I believe?'

'Yes, but lately brought into use.'

'Have you read the works of Professor Brera and Dr Majendie in reference to it?'[17]

'Not lately.'

'Why they were the first who discovered, in Paris, in the year 1809, that it was a medicine ... Then you must be an incompetent judge as to the exact effect it would have on a constitution, from its novelty as a medicine? You have not been able to trace it in the bowels?'

'No, but if there is a necessity for doing so I have it prepared to be sent up to Dublin for chemical analysation.'

'But the whole effect of it would evaporate in a short time – three days at farthest – so there is no use in sending it to Dublin.'

'I have known an analysis to take place three months after death.'

'Yes, for metallic poisons, but this is a fluid.'[18]

Dillon also interrogated Dr John Finucane, who had attended the post-mortem on behalf of the Poe family, on the subject of prussic acid. Dr Finucane said he believed Mrs Langley had died of a bowel infection but acknowledged the difficulty of tracing poison, had it been present: 'if a stomach was healthy prussic acid would have a tendency to evaporate the sorrow from it.'

'I have prescribed [prussic acid] myself in large quantities for consumption,' he said. 'It depends upon the nature of the disease and the strength of a person's constitution what quantity [of prussic acid] would deprive [them] of life . . . a teaspoonful or half a teaspoonful would immediately do so.' It produces 'convulsions, makes him insensible; it does not create irritation of the stomach, because it has not time . . . it creates a congestion of the lungs . . . [which] means that the lungs, or a part of them, are completely gorged or saturated with blood.'

He didn't know whether Dr Langley had given prussic acid to his wife, he said, but didn't think her case warranted it.

Crucially, he argued that there was no way of proving its use in the current case. 'The traces of it would disappear immediately,' said Dr Finucane. 'Mrs Langley's body was not examined until eight hours after her death.'[19]

A general panic about poison had spread across Britain and Ireland in the 1840s, and fears over the ease with which it could be acquired and administered were frequently the subject of sensational newspaper reports.[20] Less than a month earlier, a young Belfast servant woman had been charged with attempting to poison her employer's family by putting arsenic in their porridge, and only four days after the Langley inquest, the *Nenagh Guardian* reported the sentencing of a man in Aberdeen for poisoning his wife of twenty-seven years with the same toxin.[21]

For the jury, the doctors' medical evidence on this point

could be read in several ways. A commentator in the *London Medical Gazette* four years earlier had argued that lack of poison in the stomach was no solid defence against murder: '. . . knowing that there are easily understood means by which poisons may be lost – not to mention that the fatal dose may have been originally small – no difficulty has hitherto been experienced . . . in determining that poison was really the cause of death.'[22]

Proving the use of poison, however, was another matter. An acquittal in an earlier English trial had, in the opinion of a Fellow of the Royal College of Surgeons, produced 'a most baneful impression as to the facility with which such a crime might be securely perpetrated'. The question, he argued, demanded 'the most serious consideration of the profession and of the medical jurist in particular'.[23]

These fears had clearly been on Dr Langley's mind as his wife's health deteriorated, and the coroner's court heard of the steps he had taken to counteract them. 'She said she would like some wine,' said Quin in response to Mr Dillon's questioning, 'and she told me to ask Dr Langley for it; I did so, when he said – "I will give her everything in my house, down to port wine, but I will not give it to her with my own hands, for fear the people would conceive I poisoned her."' Instead, he got Drs Kittson and Quin to mix a decanter of wine for her every night while attending her.

'Ah, suspicion always haunts a guilty mind,' said Mr Dillon, on hearing of the doctor's caution.

There were other signs of the doctor's fears concerning how his wife's death might be perceived. The court heard that on 1 May, Dr Langley had seemed anxious while his medical colleagues inspected the body. 'Dr Langley wanted to go into the room when we were making the post-mortem examination,' Quin told the court, 'and I turned him out three or four times. "Now Langley," said I, "you shall not be in the room while your wife is undergoing an examination." When drawing up the result in his parlour, he wished to be present, and was turned out by me repeatedly.'[24]

The state of his wife's stomach, Langley would have known, was open to interpretation. Dr George Frith, the current dispensary doctor, who had attended to Mrs Langley for two months, admitted there could be poison in the stomach without his knowledge, but proffered another possible factor in her death.

'I saw the description of food she was in the habit of using,' he said; 'she did not observe to me she was limited in her quantity of food; but she said she was as regards quality; she stated to me that she got nothing but coarse brown bread, which she could not eat . . . she wished for white bread [and] she complained of the tea being bad.'

Several other witnesses would confirm that Mrs Langley frequently complained of hunger on account of the food she was given. Dr Kittson, who was cross-examined next, remarked that while 'brown bread would not irritate the bowels of a healthy person, if a person was suffering from chronic disease of the bowels the eating of brown bread would accelerate [their] inflammation'. He would not have prescribed it, he said.[25]

All the doctors were familiar with the impact a change of diet could have on an ailing constitution. Dysentery and diarrhoea had spread widely across Ireland since the commencement of famine in 1845 and, after typhus and relapsing fever, had been the biggest causes of death for several years. The Indian meal (maize) imported into government food depots from America during the late 1840s was notorious for causing digestive problems among a population used only to potatoes.[26]

Dr Frith also suggested that Mrs Langley's sudden change in lodgings in the period before her death could have impacted negatively on her health: 'A person accustomed to reside in a superior dwelling, if she was changed to bad and inferior lodgings, it might create irritation of the bowels, and a disorganization of the entire system.'[27] However, he warned that there was no firm evidence that it was indeed this that had caused the 'English cholera' from which he believed she had died.

Mrs Langley's change of lodgings would soon become a central question. Dr Spain said that although he had attended the deceased personally, and had known her for many years to be 'a delicate woman', her illness may have been 'super-induced from harsh treatment'.[28]

In cross-examining the medical witnesses, Mr Bolton drew a picture of a woman whose long-term ill health made her death an inevitability that needed no assistance from poison or bad treatment.

'What age was Mrs Langley?' he asked Dr Quin.

'About fifty-eight or sixty years.' This made her some fifteen years her husband's senior.

'Was she a strong or delicate woman?'

'I would say, decidedly delicate.'

'Had you a long time ago attended her for any disease?'

'I attended her for spitting of blood and heavy expectoration, during the last seven or eight years.'

'As a medical man, had you any idea she would live upon some of those occasions?'

'Upon my word, I was at her bedside from time to time, and I often thought frequently she would have died within twenty-four hours.'

'Was she in point of fact accustomed to attacks of diarrhoea?'

'She was.'

'What would be the effect of frequent attacks of diarrhoea on a constitution so delicate as that of Mrs Langley?'

'To greatly debilitate it, of course.'

'You would say then, the more frequent those attacks the less probable, in the course of time, would be the chance of recovery?'

'Yes.'[29]

6

'Ellen Poe of the city of Dublin, Spinster'

Unmarried women inspired contradictory opinions, according to a female correspondent in the *Dublin Inquisitor* in 1821: 'Having witnessed the decline of their youth and beauty without changing their condition [they] must be content to pass the remainder of their days in that quiet state of "single blessedness" which is often admired, sometimes pitied, and not unfrequently despised.'[1]

It was a situation that Ellen Poe may well have recognized prior to her marriage to Charles Langley. With no means of making her own living, she depended on the kindness of her relations. But they were not always in a position to support her. After her father's death in 1830, Donnybrook was left to her eldest brother, William, who had already experienced serious financial difficulties and been declared an insolvent debtor.[2]

William had quickly vacated the family home to paying tenants.[3] His financial difficulties were compounded by the £1,000 his father had charged to the estate for his younger daughters on their marriages, a sum equal to two years' rental income from the land.[4] Ellen would get £500 in the event of her marriage – by no means a great fortune, but a substantial sum for her insolvent brother to find.[5]

At some point in the midst of these unsettling changes at home, Ellen left Tipperary. By 1831 she was well established in the capital, describing herself as 'of the city of

Dublin' in a document that year, though her exact address is unknown.[6] Her younger sister, Mary Anne, was living on Denzille Street and, in the same year, her first husband having died, had married Edward Nixon, a Dublin wine merchant.[7] Ellen's niece, her brother William's eldest daughter, lived around the corner on Merrion Square with her husband and one-year-old baby.[8]

This part of Dublin had 'an aristocratic aspect', according to the *Metropolitan Magazine* a few years before, 'abound[ing] with magnificent mansions . . . a place of palaces'.[9] For Ellen, it offered the prospect of new social encounters. The winter social season began in October and continued until May.[10] Though shorn of some of its glamour since the Act of Union and the demise of Dublin's parliament, Merrion Square, in particular, remained a crossroads for high society. Its residents included Daniel O'Connell, who was about to take his seat at Westminster as the first Roman Catholic MP since the seventeenth century, and several other high-profile members of the legal profession.[11]

Ellen's brother Thomas lived with his wife in the pretty spa village of Lucan, on the River Liffey seven miles west of Dublin, which was regarded then as 'a place of fashionable resort and of pleasant occasional residence'.[12] In the summer people flocked here to take the waters in the handsome spa house, where they received treatment for their 'scorbutic, bilious, and rheumatic affections'. It also had an assembly room for concerts and balls. Thomas's home at Lucan Lodge was set within its own neat park beside the great walled garden of Lucan House, the seat of Mrs Vesey, his landlord, in a neighbourhood filled with wealthy gentlemen's residences.[13] Travelling between her siblings' homes in the vicinity of Dublin, Ellen may well have hoped to meet someone who would take an interest in her and provide her with a life and home independent of her immediate family. A single woman of this class had few other options in a world where genteel families looked down on paid employment and where access to family money often depended on marriage – in which case it passed to her husband.

Around the same time, Charles Langley, a Limerick man of twenty-five, had also found his way to Dublin.

He was connected, on his father's side of the family, to a wealthy Protestant family seated at Lisnamrock in County Tipperary. His mother, Lydia Taylor, was also from an Anglo-Irish landed family in Tipperary.[14] In 1798 she married Jeremiah Langley and they settled in the city of Limerick, then a growing mercantile centre. If his mother's reported age at her death is to be believed, she was forty-seven years old when she gave birth to Charles in 1806.[15]

Cadet branches of the gentry, unable to inherit property, had to survive independently of their families by making their way in the professions. Jeremiah Langley, as the second son of a Tipperary landlord, had chosen the law and established a legal practice in Limerick. His eldest son, in his turn, would become a naval officer, and would be killed 'in action with a Malay pirate on the Burmese coast' in 1827.

Soon after the birth of Charles, Jeremiah Langley took a house in Limerick's Richmond Place, a highly fashionable, crescent-shaped residential terrace then only recently completed. He 'fitted [it] up in the best manner, and laid out a large sum of money in additional improvements', including a greenhouse in the spacious garden to the rear. But there is some suggestion that he encountered financial difficulties early on in his legal career: in the winter of 1811, when Charles was five years old, he sought to lease out the house, offering 'immediate possession' to anyone who would agree to take it. It would accommodate 'a large family', according to his advertisement, and it must have weighed heavily upon him that it could not be his own. [16]

In August 1830, Charles Langley received his licence to practise medicine from the Royal College of Surgeons, Dublin, having gone through a public examination over two days.[17] During this period the college was criticized as 'a borough closed against talent unless gifted with wealth', 'a monopoly' and an institution 'hankering after exclusion'.[18] The students were, according to one contemporary account, a 'blue-frocked, black-stockinged, Wellington-booted assemblage of medical dandies', sporting gold rings and quizzing glasses, 'in short, the whole paraphernalia of puppyism . . . in the greatest possible profusion'.[19]

Early insecurity may explain Charles's preoccupation with money later in life. The death of his father in 1819, when he was just thirteen, and of his older brother in 1827, left him the solitary male in the family and the sole object of his mother and sister's attentions.[20] His uncle and namesake, Charles Langley of Lisnamrock, owner of the Coalbrook colliery near Thurles, was the only senior male figure on his father's side of the family to whom he might look for guidance, though he did have an aunt, Catherine Tuthill, who lived in Kilmore House, near Croom, County Limerick.[21]

In 1831 his primary concern was to find a means to begin his medical career. There were almost 500 dispensaries throughout the country: medical surgeries funded by a combination of local charitable subscriptions and Grand Jury taxation, and offering their services free of charge to the poor.[22] Appointments were controlled by local grandees who sat on the dispensary boards. According to one hostile contemporary observer, Daniel Madden, 'it was a common practice amongst them to set up dispensaries merely to provide for some needy relations who pocketed some seventy or eighty pounds *per annum* of the public money.'[23]

Dr Langley was elected to the Nenagh Dispensary post on 4 April 1831 following a general meeting of the subscribers in the town's courthouse.[24] Was he the beneficiary of the sort of patronage described by Madden? He was not, strictly speaking, the 'needy relation' of any of the people who had influence in the appointment. His uncle Charles's sphere of influence was the neighbouring town of Thurles rather than Nenagh, though he may have had connections there. Whatever his intentions towards his nephew, Charles's suicide only days after the appointment suggests a man tragically preoccupied with his own concerns.[25] But another significant local office had changed hands that year: Ellen's brother-in-law, the Rev. James Hill Poe, having spent sixteen years in Hacketstown, County Carlow, returned to Nenagh in 1831, when he became the town's Protestant rector. In such a role he wielded significant local influence.[26]

There is no record of any contact or understanding between Charles Langley and James Hill Poe before the dispensary appointment was made. What we do know is that, eight months after securing the Nenagh position, Dr Langley would marry the rector's sister-in-law, some fifteen years his senior.

7

'The quietest creature in the world'

Monday, 12 December 1831 was the opening night of a production of Sheridan's *The School for Scandal* at the Theatre Royal. The play was described by the *Freeman's Journal* as 'the mirror of the vices that disgrace high life, the facsimile of tea-table scandal, whispering gossip, sentimental hypocrisy, and speculative virtue'. In every character, wrote the paper's reviewer, 'we recognise an old acquaintance – sometimes perhaps ourselves.'[1]

Earlier that day, a short distance from the Theatre Royal, the Venerable Edward Barton, DD, Archdeacon of Ferns, officiated at the wedding of Dr Charles Langley and Ellen Poe at St Peter's Church on Aungier Street in Dublin, west of St Stephen's Green, where Ellen's brother, niece and several other family members had already been married.[2]

A solicitor on Charlemont Street had drawn up the marriage settlement, outlining the financial terms of the union. Charles was to receive almost £1,000 from his grandfather's estate at Lisnamrock in Tipperary. His mother had a life interest in this money, but it would come to him on her death. Ellen would bring £500 to the marriage, charged to the Donnybrook estate, plus a further £300 from an old debt due to her father by the Rev. Mr Poe's older brother. These modest sums would provide them with small annual annuities but would need supplementing from the young doctor's salary at the dispensary.[3]

*

The jury was intensely interested to learn about the state of the Langleys' marriage, and on the third day of the inquest this became a major theme for Mr Dillon. Among the various current and former servants called to give evidence was John Quigley, a groom employed by the Bennetts of Riverston in May 1849; he had worked for Dr Langley in the early 1830s.

Taking his place in the witness chair, Quigley recalled the very earliest period of the marriage. Dr Langley's 'tantrums', he said, had begun about nine months after the wedding.[4]

'Can you give us any striking proofs?' enquired Mr Dillon.

'I saw him on one occasion drag her off her pony, take a scissors and cut off her riding habit and then lock her up in her room where she was screaming all day,' he said. Frequently, he recalled, she would be abandoned there for extended periods, relieved only by the covert charity of the servants. 'Sometimes he would not give her a bit [of food] for two days, till I would bring it to her from the kitchen,' said Quigley.

There was, the *Tipperary Vindicator* reported, an audible reaction from the crowd as Quigley delivered this piece of evidence. 'He would often take a whim to treat her badly,' the former servant continued, 'for which she gave him no cause whatever; in fact, she petted him too much.' In contrast to her husband, he said, Mrs Langley was 'a kind-hearted, affectionate lady' and 'the quietest creature in the world'.[5]

He remembered that her distress was a continual cause of concern to the servants. 'My wife and I stopped in his house and we were obliged to keep a quilt before the windows to prevent her from throwing herself out,' he told the court. On one occasion, while she was imprisoned in her room, Quigley recounted how he took the decision to break the door down to liberate her; but he was caught in the act by his employer. 'The doctor struck me a blow of a large iron key,' he said. 'He knocked me down and blackened my eyes. When I got up I attacked him and gave him a good beating in return. I beat him well. I then left him; he turned me away.'[6]

Dillon moved on to the question of marital infidelity.

'Did you know Dr Langley to have any intercourse with other women besides his wife?' he asked Quigley.

'Yes, I knew him to send [Mrs Langley] to Solsboro on a visit for a week, and to be lying with his maid all that time; I went into his room one morning for the keys, and saw them both together; I let Mrs Langley know that.'[7]

'Do you think it a laudable thing to be interfering between man and wife?' protested Mr Bolton.

'I thought it my duty.'

Mr Bolton accused Mr Dillon of producing this witness merely for the entertainment of the press. 'I cannot possibly see,' he said, 'what those unhappy differences which occurred ten or twelve years ago have to do with the present inquiry; and I do not see the slightest good that can result from tracing the habits, the mode of life, and the angry bickering of Dr Langley and his lady. I think it extremely wrong to do so.'

'We want to know whether they lived happily together for seventeen years,' said Mr Dillon.

'There is proof,' offered Mr Cunningham from the jury, 'that they did not.'

Dillon also probed Dr Quin on the state of the Langleys' marriage.

'Recollect yourself now, Doctor: did Dr Langley and his wife live happily together?'

'I would not say they were happy together,' replied Quin.

'Do you ever recollect put[ting] her on a car to go out to Mr Tuthill's of Riverstown [*sic*] after having been beaten by her husband?'

'I recollect a great many unpleasant scenes,' said Quin.

River View, incorrectly named in the press as 'Riverstown', was a small country house in the parish of Knigh, four miles from Nenagh. It was leased by John Tuthill, a first cousin of Dr Langley, whose own estate was largely in County Limerick. Whether Tuthill and his wife were sympathetic to Ellen or merely accommodated her at the request of her husband is uncertain.[8]

Mr Bolton, listening to this evidence against his client, remained unmoved. 'I have heard of resurrection and of past events having been related, but I do not see what those questions have to do with the cause of death of the deceased – occurrences which took place eight years ago.' His client's indiscretion with his former servant maid might easily be overlooked as a commonplace misdemeanour among gentlemen, hardly counting as adultery. The mistress of Langley's grandfather, Kitty Doran, was so well known that she had even made it into popular song, according to the memoirs of Margaret Leeson, Dublin's most notorious eighteenth-century brothel keeper.[9] Similarly, although an act of 1828 had made it easier for women to prosecute their husbands for assault, the first law to address marital violence specifically would not be passed at Westminster until 1853 – and would not be extended to Ireland.[10]

The jury would need to hear more before deciding to what extent such ill-treatment may have contributed to Mrs Langley's death.

8

'Private and pecuniary affairs'

While Quigley's testimony shocked many listening in the schoolhouse that day, Dr Langley nevertheless had a long-standing reputation for being a difficult and combative character. He had fallen out with several people in the locality and, on more than one occasion, provoked physical attack.

Politically, he had pitted himself rather publicly against the local Catholic population. When Daniel O'Connell visited Nenagh in October 1837, his carriage pulled up outside Brundley's Hotel in the centre of the town amidst admiring supporters. Langley ventured forward and 'poked his nose' into the carriage where O'Connell was conversing privately with two colleagues. The doctor was roughly pulled away by someone in the crowd – and later mockingly accused of attempting 'to hear what instructions Mr O'Connell would give the Radicals of Nenagh'. Indignant at the manhandling he had received, he pursued a case against a Mr Gleeson of Liverpool for assault. Gleeson, he claimed, had incited the crowd against him. When cross-examined on his political views during the case, Langley proclaimed 'in a loud and distinct voice': 'I would oppose REVOLUTION in every shape!' – which reportedly drew 'immense laughter' from all those in the courtroom. Gleeson had been forced at great expense to return from Liverpool for the trial and was quickly acquitted when Langley admitted he had been 'more insulted than hurt' and all the witnesses testified against him.[1]

Dr Langley was then already well known in Nenagh through his medical practice at the dispensary, which had brought him into contact with a wide spectrum of the community. In the early years, the job was demanding and poorly paid. He had to keep the dispensary open for three hours each day, and he was required to visit patients in their homes. During 1839, for example, he made 1,145 house calls in the town, and reported 627 country visits, complaining in December of that year that his horse was 'rendered perfectly useless in the discharge of his duty' as a result of overwork. The board of the dispensary, clearly sympathetic, granted him the considerable sum of £10 to buy a new mount.[2] He specified that he wanted 'a good strong general horse . . . perfectly sound, and gentle in harness, in or about five years old, and capable of going eight or nine miles an hour'.[3]

His salary of £100 per annum would have been considerably lower than the income of the surrounding Protestant gentry with whom he socialized. Even a small estate such as Donnybrook yielded five times that. The largest estates near Nenagh were owned by families earning well over £5,000 per annum – most notably the Otways and Pritties.[4] As a result, Langley relied on other ways to make money, developing a local reputation for being hard-nosed in his financial dealings.[5] In the spring of 1840 he had a major falling-out with a colleague, Dr Dempster, who accused him of abusing his position as dispensary doctor for monetary gain. According to contemporary press reports, an unidentified couple had approached Langley in the hope of acquiring medicine to induce an illegal abortion. The doctor agreed to this, but asked for a fee that was double what they offered him. When they returned with the sum, he reportedly had them arrested. The couple then raised the much greater sum of £10 from among their friends to convince him to spare them from prosecution. News of the payment soon became public knowledge, and when the government decided to pursue a case against the couple, Langley said he would give the £10 he had received from them to charity. But Dr Dempster, a Scotsman practising in the town, insinuated that Langley had 'attempted to compromise a felony'. Enraged, Langley responded in a letter in the *Nenagh Guardian* under the motto 'Nic niger est, hunc tu Romane Caveto': 'He is a dangerous man, you, oh Roman, beware of him.' Without naming Dempster, no doubt fearing libel, he complained of a 'certain professional gentleman' who was 'well known for his political tergiversation and TREACH-ERY, towards his professional brethren'. This 'chameleon character', he said, had been 'wantonly misrepresenting the matter, in order to prejudice the public against [him]'.[6]

Dempster in his turn tried to sue Langley for £1,000 in damages. It was a massive sum in 1840, but his adversary had wisely avoided naming him in print and as a result the judge awarded only £20.

Some members of the dispensary board which employed Dr Langley had reservations about him on other grounds – also money-related – and the same year advertised for a doctor to replace him, emphasizing that the candidate's 'whole time' should be given to the job.[7] At the annual meeting of the Nenagh Dispensary, the secretary read out the minutes of the committee for the previous year, 'on which were recorded many complaints against Dr Langley, the Medical Officer of the Institution'.[8] Prior to the meeting, Langley had been forced to defend his position publicly. He wrote at the time:

> Whatever alleged errors may have been attributed to me
> during [the last nine years] they have arisen from causes

which all persons conversant with the daily routine of Dispensary duties can well appreciate, and which it is impossible for any Medical person entirely to avoid, when it is considered that the duties of his situation are confined to the poorer classes of society, who are not always the most tractable patients, or the best judges of the treatment they should receive.

The doctor complained that the dispute in this instance did not relate directly to his medical role but rather to his 'private and pecuniary affairs', in which he said the board had no right to meddle and which were 'totally unconnected with dispensary duties'.[9]

The main charge against him was that he was spending much of his time pursuing a moneylending business rather than attending to his medical practice. One member of the committee then moved a resolution that 'we are of the opinion it would be incompatible with the interests of the Institution to suffer Surgeon Langley to be put in nomination.' Another member moved that 'no Medical Attendant for the Nenagh Dispensary shall in future be allowed to interfere, directly or indirectly, with any Loan Fund, or any money-lending office whatever, under the pain of instant dismissal.'[10]

Langley's involvement with moneylending was somewhat complex. Firstly, he helped manage the Nenagh Loan Fund, a charitable institution with a board comprising wealthy and respectable gentry and merchant families such as the Bennetts and the Burrs. The treasurer of the fund boasted in 1840 that they had not a single bad debt on their books and that the fund 'has been of lasting benefit to many of our poor neighbours . . . Some of them declare they would not have a house to shelter them if they had not received its assistance.'[11] Those on the books included the whole range of the town's tradesmen, from carpenters, brogue makers, coopers and tailors to gardeners, washerwomen, butchers and weavers. Most numerous were the simple labourers, the poorest class of Irish, who subsisted on their patch of potatoes and, in some cases, the value of a pig they could sell for cash.[12] Langley owned the office on William Street from which the loan fund was run and derived a healthy rental income from it.[13]

But he had another angle on the moneylending business too. An official from the Loan Fund Board of Ireland, reviewing the status of these institutions, had viewed Langley's involvement with suspicion. In his report he remarked:

> It may be right to add, that from private inquiries I instituted, I learned that Mr Langley . . . has a private Loan Fund of his own, worked for his own benefit, at which he issues a considerable sum, processing defaulters at Quarter Sessions. It appears to me, such a proceeding unfits him to act as Manager of this [Nenagh] Loan Fund, inasmuch as there is a possibility of his granting Loans here to enable persons to pay up Loans from his private fund: and I think a communication should be made by this Board to the Trustee on the subject.[14]

Private moneylenders were the subject of intense local concern in the early 1840s. In May 1842 the *Nenagh Guardian* attacked the practice whereby certain banks 'have leagued with the small Money Lenders' in an underhand manner:

> By hints, nods, and false reports, the latter damage the credit of those they themselves give credit to; intimate to

the Managers that further security is necessary; so that the man seeking accommodation from the Bank is thrown back into the hands of the Village Shylock . . . We are creditably informed that a rate of Interest from 12 to 70 per cent is charged for the loan of money to the struggling population of the Town of Nenagh and the surrounding country. This is truly lamentable![15]

The practice had emerged when the usury laws were experimentally suspended in 1837 as part of the government's policy of encouraging free trade, a decision viewed by many as disastrous to Ireland's local economies. In 1843, when the Irish MP William Smith O'Brien failed in his attempt to persuade the government to reintroduce restrictions on usurious lending, the *Nenagh Guardian* commented wearily: 'For another year extortion may raise its burnished crest, and – serpent-like – plunge its envenomed fangs into the vitals of the needy. Rejoice, you usurers, with a great joy, for your wives and daughters may for another year robe themselves with the fruits of your abomination.'[16]

When challenged at a dispensary board meeting about his involvement with both a charitable and a private loan fund, Langley agreed that in future he would have nothing further to do with the former. Instead, he intended to keep his own moneylending business going. As the minutes of the meeting recorded, 'He would not be coerced as to the manner in which he thought proper to dispose of his money to advantage.'[17]

It was a situation many board members were uncomfortable with. A substantial contingent of the forty-four dispensary governors, led by O'Brien Dillon, proposed getting rid of Langley. But the doctor wasn't entirely without supporters, and other members of the committee agreed that he should be free to run his private business as he pleased. Supported by his wife's influential relations, he was voted back into his post at the dispensary by a majority of ten.[18]

Langley's moneylending activity continued into the darker days of the famine, and he was assiduous in chasing up repayments.[19] In June 1847, one of the most hopeless years, he had Jeremiah Howard, 'a pauper', thrown in prison until he got the seven shillings he was owed from him.[20]

During the late 1840s, desperation increasingly forced people into the hands of loan sharks and pawnbrokers, to such a degree that, having sold or pawned all their furniture to buy food, many were finally forced to part with even the clothes off their backs. In October 1847, one journalist reported the appearance of cartloads of paupers outside the Nenagh workhouse, whose bodies were barely covered with rags, which 'were no protection from either the wind or rain; their legs and arms were in many instances completely naked'.[21]

Many had been evicted from their farms in the land clearances that swept across Ireland in the later years of the famine, often ending up in poor accommodation in the towns. Here they were not immune to eviction either. Dr Langley, who had established himself as a landlord on a small scale in Nenagh, was as harsh in dealing with those who could not pay their rent as with those who could not repay their loans. In May 1847 he evicted John and Mary Kennedy from their lodgings on Pound Street. When they resisted, he had them arrested for assault. They were subsequently charged and bound by the judge to keep the peace for three years by paying a surety of £2 10s each. How they paid such a sum, probably a multiple of the rent they owed, is unknown.[22]

Local relief committees, attempting to buy and sell Indian

meal at an affordable price, urged landowners to contribute generously to their funds, and the more outspoken of them named and shamed those who didn't. Dr Langley was asked to contribute £3 to the fund in April 1846, and did so, but he was decidedly uncomfortable with the pressure put on landowners to contribute. At a poor relief meeting that summer, he defended an absentee landlord whose refusal to pay any sum towards the poor had been condemned as 'scandalous': 'Persons should be left to their own option as to whether they would contribute or not,' argued Langley. 'You cannot frighten men out of their money, if they are not inclined to give it.'[23]

The doctor's moneylending activities reflect something of his dissatisfaction with his career during the early 1840s. After ten years in the post of dispensary doctor, he was evidently tired of the hard work and modest remuneration. When an opportunity arose to resign, he was not slow in taking it. In January 1842, a year after his re-election as dispensary doctor, he was able to give up the position, referring to 'circumstances having lately occurred in my family which render it no longer necessary for me to retain the situation of Medical Superintendent to your institution'.[24]

He wrote that letter two weeks after the death of his 82-year-old widowed mother, who had lived in Eccles Street, Dublin; it is likely that an inheritance was the circumstance referred to.[25] The conflicts of the past were glossed over as the dispensary governors formally thanked him 'for the zeal and ability with which he ... conducted the duties of this institution for the last eleven years'.[26]

From now on money would be less of a problem and he could look forward to spending his time in more enjoyable ways. In the period leading up to his wife's death seven years later, he practised his profession at a remove from the daily needs of the poor, acting as a medical assessor for a company selling pensions and life insurance and sitting on the management committee of the fever hospital, overseeing the work of other doctors.[27] He would also occasionally appear as an expert witness in murder trials. Most importantly, he attended his private loan office twice a week to oversee the work of his clerk, Mr Prior.[28]

9

'A very bad room'

The woman who was born Ellen Poe came to the notice of the general public only in death. Over a century and a half on, much of what we know, or can infer, about her life and her character comes from the testimony of others, mostly men, on the subject of her final illness and her suffering. It adds up to a radically incomplete portrait but gives some insight into her state of mind during the last weeks of her life.

O'Brien Dillon, seeking to convince the coroner's jury of Dr Langley's continued ill feeling against his wife, called upon two people who bore intimate witness to the late stages of the Langleys' marriage: Thomas Pound and Eliza Rohan, who had worked as domestic servants in Barrack Street.

Eliza, a 'pretty looking girl' according to the press, had been hired as a housemaid in July 1848.[1]

'I lived in Dr Langley's service,' she said, when called upon by Mr Dillon. 'I was a servant maid in his house, living nine months with him [and] left him a few days before Mrs Langley left the house; that was about a fortnight before her death.'

Dillon enquired as to the doctor's treatment of his wife during this period.

'During the time I lived in the house he treated her very badly,' she said, 'he confined her to her room and put her on a low diet; he first confined her to her own room, the best room in the house; he afterwards confined her to the top room, what we called the garret.'

Dillon enquired as to the length of time Mrs Langley was kept there.

'She was confined in the garret two months before I left.'

And what kind of room was it? he asked.

'It was a very bad room with only one window in it,' she said. 'There were no window-shutters, the window was opposite the bed, there was a skylight besides the window.'

The bed was a good one, she said in response to a question from Mr Bolton, and there were sufficient coverings on it. But to Eliza, the doctor's intentions were clear. She heard him say, she told the court, that his wife 'would have a dreadful life, and die a bad death'.

Thomas Pound, the only male servant employed in the house, gave similar evidence. He had come to work in Barrack Street in July 1848. 'Dr and Mrs Langley lived pretty well together for the first two or three months after I came to them,' he said, but thereafter, 'no person could be treated worse than Mrs Langley was by her husband; he treated her in every disrespectful form.'[2]

Eliza recalled that Mrs Langley's incarceration began in October 1848. Initially her husband confined her to the house and garden, determined that she would see no one, and did not allow her to eat with him, making her take all her meals alone in her room. According to Thomas Pound, this isolation at meals began in January, four months before her death. 'The servant girl always took her up her breakfast; it was the doctor who prepared and gave it to her, because no one else could give it; the breakfast was sent from the doctor's table; with the exception of not getting eggs she got the same description of food that he used himself.' Eliza recounted, 'For the last six weeks she did not take breakfast or dinner with him; she used to take [them] in the garret room,' and, she later added, 'I often knew him to turn her out of the parlour at breakfast time.'[3] In response to these restrictions, Eliza would surreptitiously take her mistress breakfast in the kitchen if the doctor was out of the house.

From their testimonies, a complex picture of the doctor's treatment of his wife began to emerge. When Ellen fell ill in January 1849, Langley had been careful to see that she was attended by Dr Frith, and told the servants to get her whatever Frith ordered for her – beef tea, wine, white bread. When she recovered, after a fortnight, she was returned to her former diet – mainly brown bread, which was seen as unsuited to someone suffering from a bowel complaint. 'I never saw her get but strong coarse homemade bread,' said Thomas Pound. 'There was no white bread in the house.'

He testified that 'what she used to get for breakfast and dinner in the kitchen and garret was not sufficient for a child three years of age . . . she used to bring in white bread from the street; she bought some of it and she got more from Mrs Burr and other ladies.'

'Then, in point of fact, she was obliged to often beg her breakfast?' asked Mr Dillon.

'Yes, on account of not getting enough to eat at home.'[4]

There were murmurings of shock at this evidence from those in attendance.

Eliza testified that Mrs Langley's attempts to buy food were sometimes frustrated. She recalled that on one occasion her mistress gave her two shillings to keep for her: 'I had it in my box,' she said, '[but] the servant man told Miss Jackson I had it [and] I was obliged to give it to her; the doctor demanded it.'[5] (This was a reference to Fanny Jackson, Dr Langley's twelve-year-old niece, who shared the house with her uncle and aunt.)

It was at this point, Eliza said, that she began supplementing her mistress's diet by buying eggs and white bread out of her own money and bringing them up to her when her master was out.

Dr Kittson, too, testified that Mrs Langley had visited him for the purpose of getting food: 'She often came to my house while we were at dinner, and dined with the family; she told me, as well as I can recollect, that she often wanted a dinner; when she said so Dr Langley was sometimes at home and other times he was not.'[6]

The servants' testimony revealed further facts about the condition of Mrs Langley during her final months in her husband's house. In addition to hunger, they reported that she felt cold and in the later winter months was left in the garret without the warmth of a fire. According to contemporary thinking, she would have been especially sensitive to cold temperatures due to her tuberculosis.[7] Dr Langley had confiscated all her good clothes – 'her satin and silk dresses, her rings and watch', in Eliza Rohan's words – leaving her only six shifts to wear.[8] Eliza remembered that her mistress had no coat and just one shawl, and described her own attempts to relieve the effects of the cold by bringing her hot jars for her bed – a kindness that was repeatedly and deliberately frustrated by her employer: 'The doctor took away the jar when he found I used to be putting it to her,' she said.

Defiantly, she brought up another when the doctor was out. But he had ears and eyes in his niece, Fanny. According to Eliza, the girl was 'not very kind' to her aunt. She discovered and confiscated the second jar, and passed it to Dr Langley.

It is not unreasonable to guess that Fanny – a foster child in an unhappy home under the care of a domineering uncle – may have been subject to emotional manipulation, and unable to take an independent view of her aunt's situation.

Eliza described surreptitiously bringing her mistress down to the kitchen to warm herself, after which Dr Langley threatened to nail the door into the kitchen from the stairs.

The Rev. Benjamin Bewley, a Protestant curate who spoke with Ellen Langley in the days before her death, testified that she had 'complained to [him] that she was left very much alone'. The doctor kept her isolated: away from company, forbidden the parlour and, later on, the small garden at the rear of the house. Eliza was told not to visit her mistress during the day, being allowed up to the garret only to bring her breakfast and dinner. His wife's only companion in the garret was her small lapdog, named Silver, of which, according to Eliza, her husband did not approve. 'It was poisoned,' she told the inquest. 'I heard the doctor say he poisoned it with prussic acid.'[9]

In the early to mid-Victorian period it was the fashion for women to curl their hair in ringlets, or frouts, that hung down either side of the face, covering the ears.[10] Although there is no record of Ellen's appearance, a surviving portrait of Frances Poe, her sister, dating to the middle years of the century, shows exactly this arrangement. Eliza testified that her mistress 'wore false frouts or curls', and that Dr Langley 'used to half burn them, so as that they could be of no use to her, and then he would hang them on the door of her garret room, that she could see them'.

There was audible shock from around the room at this evidence.

Thomas Pound also attested to psychological abuse: 'I never saw him beat her, but heard him abuse her by the tongue; the parlour was convenient to the kitchen; we could

hear what they said.' The strain eventually became too much. 'About six weeks ago,' Eliza testified, 'Mrs Langley attempted to throw herself out of the window of her own house,' as a result of her husband's confiscation of her clothes. Twice Eliza had to intervene to save her.[11]

There was also concern regarding the presence of laudanum in the house, a commonly available opiate in the mid-nineteenth century which could be deadly in overdose and was commonly implicated in murder and suicide.[12] Although Dr Quin said he believed Mrs Langley was 'not in the habit' of taking it, Eliza told the court that Dr Langley had two bottles of laudanum in his room, 'each holding about a pint', and that he used to take it himself. Due to its potency it was normally administered in drops. 'I heard him say [Mrs Langley] could not do a better thing than take a glass of laudanum,' she said, provoking cries of dismay from those listening. 'That was about a month ago.'[13]

Thomas Pound testified that Langley had encouraged his wife to kill herself: 'I heard him tell her to go out to [their neighbour] Mr Burr's highest window, and throw herself down if she wanted to put an end to her life; but if she threw herself out of her own house she would get a lingering death, because her bones would be only broken.'[14]

It was a chilling piece of evidence. Those listening may have recalled the tragic death five years earlier of Mrs Tuthill, to whose home Dr Langley had on several occasions sent his wife after a quarrel. Mrs Tuthill had reportedly fallen from a window on the top storey of their house, 'a height of about 60 feet', dying instantly. She had been discovered by her husband 'bruised, her hair dishevelled, and the back part of her head broken in by the shock it sustained with the ground'. No one had witnessed the accident and no one had been able to conjecture how it had occurred.[15]

Just as Langley had prepared a defence against accusations of poisoning by employing other doctors to treat his wife, so he sought to allay any suspicion that might be directed at him should his wife throw herself to her death. Eliza recounted: 'I knew the doctor to lock himself in his room about a month ago; it was Miss Fanny Jackson and myself that used to lock him up, at his own request, and kept the key of the door in our room until morning; I don't know why he did this, but he said once it was lest the mistress would do anything to herself and that it might be laid to his charge; he was afraid she would kill herself; he had but one key for the door of that room; I used to open the door at eight o'clock in the morning.'[16]

He would have only one enquiry when he got out, she said: '"Did the mistress rest well last night?"'

Dillon asked her whether there was any reason why Mrs Langley should want to kill herself.

'I know no reason she should do anything bad to herself,' replied Eliza, 'unless it was that she got such bad treatment.'

That her husband's behaviour had a negative effect on Mrs Langley's spirits, the servants were in no doubt – but Mrs Langley herself suspected that there was something more sinister behind her own despair. Eliza explained: 'I always brought Mrs Langley her breakfast and she'd make me taste the tea before she'd drink it. Why? Because she was afraid the doctor was putting something in it to make her unhappy.'

This was a point of particular interest to Mr Dillon. It had emerged on the previous day of the inquest that Dr Langley made a great show of getting his colleagues to mix his wife's medicines and prepare her wine. Now it appeared that every morning he alone made his wife's tea.

'It was he made the tea, poured it out, and sweetened it,' said Eliza. 'Generally worse than he and Miss Fanny used.'

'Would you take upon yourself to swear there was anything put in her tea at any time?' Mr Dillon enquired of Eliza.

Mr Bolton objected: 'It is unfair to be asking suspicious questions, and it is improper to be giving illegal evidence to the jury.'

Dillon persisted: 'Could the doctor put something into her tea without your knowledge?'

'He could,' Eliza replied.

'Were you in the habit of bringing her an egg?' asked the juror Bryan Consedine.

'No,' said Eliza.

'Would he allow it?' he asked.

'No,' she said.

Mr Bolton asked whether Mrs Langley's dinner was the same as the doctor's and Miss Fanny's, and Eliza reported that it was. He queried her once more on the presence of Fanny during the preparation of Mrs Langley's tea.

'Miss Jackson was always present,' she said, 'when the doctor prepared the tea.'[17]

Whether Ellen's fears regarding the tea were founded or not, the testimony revealed a comfortless daily regime, deepening suspicion, petty reprisals and malign intent.

'By the doctor's orders'

Of all the evidence heard on the epic third day of the inquest, nothing was quite as grim and shocking – or as puzzling – as the thread of testimony that began with the evidence of Dr Francis Cahalan.

Something of an outsider, Cahalan was the only doctor in Nenagh to protest against the Poor Law Guardians' performance in dealing with the recent cholera epidemic. (Later, working at the front line of Ireland's famine crisis, in October 1849 he would contract 'a severe attack of typhus fever' from attending prisoners in the town's gaol.)[1] He was not among the cohort of professionals who had treated Mrs Langley during her illness and may well have been surprised to receive a summons to Dr Langley's house.

He recounted to the court: 'I did not attend Mrs Langley in her last illness; some time previous to that I was requested by Dr Langley to see her for the purpose of giving him a certificate of her having a certain disease – the venereal disease . . .'

At this there were utterances of surprise from those listening.

'The garret in which I saw her was most miserable,' he said; 'it was anything but comfortable and quite unfit for Mrs Langley, from the position which she held in society; there were no curtains on her bed; her room was opposite the servant's; there was a door to it, and the reason why I know there was, is that Dr Langley said to me, closing the door from the inside, "You see there is a running bolt to Mrs Langley's room, so that if Mrs Langley wishes to bolt herself in she may"; he assigned no reason to me for making this remark; he told me that he was desired by Mr Bolton to get the certificate.'[2]

Mr Bolton, the court now learned, had been active in his client's affairs even before the death of his wife. He had been advising his client to find legal proof that Mrs Langley had committed adultery with Thomas Pound, the servant man who occupied the room immediately next to hers in the garret on Barrack Street. Such proof – a medical diagnosis of venereal disease, contracted from Pound – would provide legal grounds for a divorce. (By the double standard of the law, Ellen Langley could not divorce her husband on the grounds of *his* well-attested infidelities.)[3]

In Ireland in 1849, there were usually three main stages to the process of divorce. Firstly, a decree of *divorce a mensa et thoro* ('divorce from bed and board') had to be obtained from the ecclesiastical court within the Church of Ireland. Then – where a third party was involved – a civil action was taken against them for 'criminal conversation'. If this proved successful, it allowed the plaintiff to introduce a private bill for divorce in the Westminster parliament, a lengthy and expensive process usually affordable only by the well-off.[4]

Mr Bolton, questioning Dr Cahalan, suggested that Mrs Langley had confessed her adultery to her husband. Dr Cahalan responded that, in his presence, 'Neither did Mrs Langley deny or admit that she had any criminal intercourse with her servant man . . . [Dr Langley] accused her of having criminal intercourse with the servant; she did not admit it, but cried and appeared much fretted, and very unwilling to undergo the examination.'[5] He observed, too, that 'She was in possession of all her faculties; she was not insane, but from her condition of mind she was actually bordering on insanity; she was in a most distressed and excited state, in consequence of which I would not be astonished at her having admitted anything.'

In the face of her husband's insistence, Cahalan said, Mrs Langley eventually consented to the medical examination, though 'with the natural repugnance a modest female would have'. Cahalan was distinctly uncomfortable. 'I told him I thought he was prejudiced against her.' Dr Langley remained in the room while Cahalan proceeded to carry out the examination. 'I examined her,' said Cahalan, 'and told him that she had not the disease he said, [but] he insisted she had, and requested of me to give him a certificate to that effect . . . I did not, nor would not, give him the certificate, for I was satisfied she had not the disease. I told him to call in any number of medical men he liked, to whom I would state my reasons and opinions for saying so.'[6]

Mr Bolton asked whether he had seen Thomas Pound before.

'I saw this man of Dr Langley's; prescribed for him a short time before; he called on me and told me to prescribe for him, but I did not examine him to see if he was diseased; he came in a few days after to say he was well.'

'Did he say he was sent by Dr Langley?' asked Dillon.

'No,' said Cahalan.

Though distressed by what had occurred, Ellen did not blame Cahalan. Before he left the room, he remembered, she thanked him for his kindness to her.

Thomas Pound was from Toomevara, a poor village six miles east of Nenagh, and may have been from a rather notorious family of that name associated with faction fighting and crimes of assault.[7] In 1845 the *Nenagh Guardian* had referred to an impending battle between 'the vile factions of the Pounds and Leamys' at Moneygall, a small village east of Toomevara.[8] A twenty-year-old man by the name of Thomas Pound had been imprisoned in Nenagh Gaol for twelve months for 'malicious assault' between March 1847 and March 1848.[9] If it was the same man, then Dr Langley had hired him not more than four months after his release from gaol. He was illiterate, and, according to Pound's own testimony, something of a ladies' man: ' . . . the women are fond of me,' he would later boast.[10] It may have been in light of this reputation that Dr Langley came to believe his servant man had acquired a venereal disease – one which might be usefully transmitted to his own wife.

Venereal disease was widespread in Ireland's garrison towns. The *Tipperary Vindicator*'s front page of 9 May 1849, which recounted the third day of the inquest into Mrs Langley's death, also carried a large advertisement promoting *The Silent Friend*, a book promising illustrated colour engravings of male and female anatomy and analysis of the causes and effects of human sexual behaviour. The book was promoted repeatedly in both of the town's newspapers throughout the years of the Irish famine. Several columns were devoted to detailing its contents. According to its publishers, the book would contain a frank discussion of the consequences of 'self-abuse', which they warned could lead to the destruction of the 'special and vital powers' of reproduction. Closely linked to disorders of the mind were 'disorders of the generative organs', which by 'undue and unnatural excitement' sapped the body, destroying 'the social happiness of existence'. Those more inclined to promiscuity would succumb to the dangers of venereal disease, which could suddenly 'break out and overwhelm the sufferer with wretchedness and horror at his fearful state'.[11]

Before he had begun his cross-examination of Thomas Pound that day, Dillon requested that the females – Mrs Jackson and her daughter, Fanny – should retire, 'having regard to public decency'. When they had left, Pound explained the background to his unusual accommodation in close proximity to the mistress of the house.[12]

'I slept in the top garret since I came to Dr Langley,' he said. 'There were three rooms in the top of the house; before I came Miss Jackson and the servant maid slept in the room opposite me; they were removed from that room about two months.'

'By whose orders were they removed?' enquired the coroner.

'By the doctor's orders.'

'When they left the room who occupied it?' asked Mr Dillon.

'The mistress, sir. It was the doctor's wish to have her there.'

Dillon probed further. 'After Mrs Langley went to that room, recollect yourself now, you are on your oath before God, had Dr Langley any conversation with you?'

'In about a month after Mrs Langley went into that room, Dr Langley and myself had a conversation, while going to Mrs Parker's of Castlelough; I was driving him in a phaeton; he told me he was much annoyed, and that Mrs Langley and himself had some angry words; he said to me he did not care if the devil took her.'

Pound explained that as Eliza was forbidden from attending Mrs Langley during the day, he himself took the opportunity to call on her when he could.

'I often went into Mrs Langley's room to take her eggs, without the knowledge of Dr Langley; he would not give her an egg, neither would he leave me boil one for her if he knew it; whenever I had an opportunity I attended her in her garret room . . . I used to steal her up a sup of milk for her tea; it was some of my own milk I gave her.'[13]

Despite this covert assistance, the doctor was aware of the servant man's familiarity with his wife and had encouraged it. Pound reported that his employer allowed his wife and the servant a single candle between them when retiring to bed in the garret and that he did not care whether Pound entered his wife's room or not.[14] Pound also testified that his employer had flaunted his own contempt for his wife by 'bring[ing] into the house, in the presence of Mrs Langley, at three o'clock in the day, women of ill-fame'.[15]

During this lengthy cross-examination it was Mr Bolton who first asked Thomas Pound about the alleged sexual encounter between himself and Ellen Langley.

'You say you were in her room; were you ever in her bed?' he asked.

The servant, who was by now accustomed to providing sensational evidence to the crowd, proved himself equally direct in his response.

'I was, sir.'

There were, according to the *Nenagh Guardian*, 'murmurs of indignation' around the court.

'When was that?'

'I cannot say, about the month of March; Dr Langley heard of it afterwards – he heard of it before he sent Mrs Langley to lodgings; when he heard of it she was turned out of the house.'[16]

Pound described the circumstances of the encounter. 'She used to have a jar of hot water to the soles of her feet, and the doctor searched the bed and took it away from her,' he said. 'When I was in the room she asked me to handrub her feet because they were cold, and then told me to come into the bed to keep her feet warm.'[17]

This intimate encounter occurred a single time only, Pound told the coroner's court, and was never repeated. But what exactly occurred between Mrs Langley and Pound in the small garret room would remain unspecified. Dr Langley evidently believed that there had been a sexual encounter between them, and the *Nenagh Guardian*'s report would boldly use the word 'intercourse' – but this was not a term used by Thomas Pound.

Pound gave an interesting explanation for his conduct. 'I would not dare to be guilty of what I was,' he said, 'if Dr Langley had a proper respect for his wife, or if she took breakfast and dinner at the same table with him, or if he had treated her with that respect which she deserved. I thought the doctor would not be annoyed with me for doing so.'

Pound had judged correctly. 'The morning after,' he explained, 'when Dr Langley found me in the parlour, he was laughing and making a humbug of me, asking me if I used to be going into her room, and saying he did not care whether I went [there] or not.'

This was a remarkable piece of testimony. In the absence of any obvious motive for inventing such an unsavoury story, it was, perhaps, natural to assume that Pound was telling the truth – and to focus on Dr Langley's response to the news that his wife had been intimate with his servant. It is important, though, to bear in mind that neither of the people who might have corroborated or contradicted Pound's evidence was available to testify. Dr Langley was absent from the coroner's court, having apparently left Nenagh for parts unknown. And Ellen Langley was in a coffin.

The story Pound told – of an intimate encounter between himself and an ailing, depressed, suicidal woman in her late fifties, initiated by her without the knowledge of Dr Langley – might have been wholly true. Equally, it might have been partly or wholly false. The encounter might not have been initiated by Ellen Langley. It might not have been consensual. The encounter might have been encouraged, before the fact, by Dr Langley. It might even have involved the connivance of husband and wife: could Ellen, believing she was being poisoned, have been so desperate for a divorce that she was willing to play along with the unsavoury scheme? Equally, the encounter might not have happened at all, or might not have involved anything more than a foot-rub: possibilities that may have crossed Dr Langley's mind after the medical examination showed no evidence of an infection.

Pound testified that, at his employer's behest, he had been examined by Dr Cahalan for venereal disease two or three days prior to the alleged adultery, and also by Dr Langley himself, who was convinced that he had an infection. Pound did not claim that Langley had ordered him to make advances on his wife, for the purpose of infecting her, but there had been an audible gasp from the onlookers in the court when Pound had mentioned the doctor's habit of supplying them with only a single candle to light their way to bed.[18]

Instead of trying to argue that there had been no sexual encounter between Ellen Langley and Thomas Pound – or, at least, that there was no proof that such a thing had happened – Mr Dillon focused on suggesting that Dr Langley had, in fact, been a direct party to it.

He asked Dr Finucane, 'Is there any medicine which could be given to excite the human passions – cantharides, for instance?'

'Yes, cantharides may be administered in a powdered or tinctured state, and will have the effect of exciting the animal passions,' said Finucane.

'And while in that state,' queried Dillon, 'the person to whom it is administered would permit any liberties to be taken with them?'

'Yes, [I have] heard of it given to common people to make the person fall in love.'

'And may be given to virtuous, honest people to produce these diabolical effects?'

'Yes,' replied Finucane. 'If continued to be administered for any length of time it would leave a trace on the bowels, but if only given once or twice it would not; it produces a disease called furora.'[19]

Cantharides, or 'Spanish fly', was used for a variety of ailments during the nineteenth century, particularly urinary and bladder problems. Despite the name, it was in fact derived from a form of beetle that had, according to one contemporary source, a body 'from six to ten lines long, the antennae or feelers black'. The odour of cantharides was strong: 'penetrating, unpleasant and peculiar, and their taste extremely acrid'. A well-known aphrodisiac, the substance was normally used as a cure for impotence in men and women because it caused an irritation or stimulation of the urogenital tract. It was highly toxic and could attack several parts of the body, often proving fatal in large doses.[20]

Establishing whether Dr Langley actually used such a

potion to affect his wife's behaviour was, however, extremely difficult if not impossible, and Dillon was evidently content simply to raise the possibility.

The jury might have been more influenced by Thomas Pound's account of Dr Langley's conduct after the alleged encounter in Ellen's garret room.

'The doctor kept me in his employment a week or so after the occurrence in question,' he said. 'He told me he was not displeased with me for doing what I did . . . He did not say he would give me any remuneration [but] he did give me a present of a suit of clothes, and said he parted with me in better friends[hip] than he thought he would . . . He said he would keep me in his employment only that he was afraid some remarks would be passed.'

Pound also testified that, immediately after terminating his employment, Dr Langley took him to Mr Abbott, a Commissioner for Taking Affidavits, to make a 'declaration' about his liaison with Mrs Langley.

'It was Dr Langley wrote the declaration,' he said.[21]

I I

'As small as the black hole of Calcutta'

In March and April 1849, Asiatic cholera spread across Ireland, thriving in poor and insanitary dwellings, of which there was no shortage in the famine-stricken country. The weakened condition of those suffering from hunger made them particularly vulnerable. The first indication that the disease was approaching Nenagh was its appearance in the neighbouring city of Limerick and some small outlying villages. In the same month that Thomas Pound made his advances on Mrs Langley, the disease was beginning to enter the town. A recent study, quoting an excerpt from the *Tipperary Vindicator* of 20 March, describes the state of Nenagh at the time:

> Hordes of the most wretched creatures infest the public streets from morning till night, many of them keeping up an endless cry and lamentation and terrifying people with their death-like appearance.[1]

Once the pandemic took hold, the death rate would be higher in Nenagh than in any of the major cities.[2] Most vulnerable were the already crowded hospitals and workhouses where paupers were crammed into miserable and unsanitary accommodation.[3] Next were the poorer parts of the town in their vicinity, where families lived in overcrowded proximity to each other and food and water were easily contaminated. In early April the Catholic clergy in Nenagh devoted a whole week to hearing the last confessions of those convinced they would die, assiduously preparing frightened souls for the next world.[4] Paupers were fleeing the workhouse in panic as the disease spread within its walls and families in the town abandoned their diseased relatives.[5] 'Alone of famine diseases,' writes the historian Ciarán Ó Murchadha, 'cholera could cause parents or siblings to shrink in revulsion from stricken family members.' It was the source of 'unique dread and terror'.[6]

Dr Langley was acutely aware of the approaching crisis. His first months as a dispensary doctor had been spent dealing with the great cholera pandemic of 1832–3 and he well knew the devastating effects of the disease in crowded environments. Already in March 1849 he was showing other doctors 'cholera medicines', which he had prepared in advance,[7] and his friend Dr Frith was the first to treat a case on the outskirts of Nenagh on the fourteenth of that month.[8]

The disease penetrated the town's interior streets quickly, spreading hysteria in its wake. Exactly a month later the *Nenagh Guardian* reported that 'the disease is extending to every corner of the union'.

> There have been five cases today in the Workhouses, in which there were 80 deaths since Sunday evening!! That, for five days, and during the previous week there were 100! who died of fever, dysentery, diarrhoea, and cholera. In fact, the mortality throughout the country is frightfully numerous, and should it continue for a lengthened period, very few of the population will be in existence!'[9]

For the poor, the risk of contagion was high. Even before the Great Famine, in the early 1840s agricultural labourers and their families, turned out of small farms, had been flooding into the town, living collectively and squalidly in single-room hovels 'in a most wretched and shocking state', as one contemporary observed.[10]

On 18 April the *Nenagh Guardian* described the town commissioners as apathetic, bemoaned the spread of cholera beyond the workhouses, and deplored the 'filthy, dirty, and disgraceful state of William-street and Silver-street, where the disease first made its appearance, and where it now prevails'. The newspaper also noted its spread to Glebe Lane, Ballally Lane and elsewhere, 'which even in healthy times, emit from their bosom foetid stenches and disgusting miasmas'. 'If the Board of Health are desirous to preserve the lives of the inhabitants,' complained the paper, 'let them take steps forthwith (as all other Boards of Health have invariably done) to have those lanes cleansed, and the interior and exterior of the habitations therein whitewashed.'[11]

Only days before the death of Ellen Langley, Dr Quin complained to the *Nenagh Guardian* that he and other doctors did not receive enough remuneration for the hazards they encountered in deprived parts of the town: 'We must go into every filthy lane and alley – into every dark and dirty room – into every miserable hut and disgusting cabin. We risk our lives . . .'[12] A local solicitor, Mr Kilkelly, commented around the same time on the unhealthy state of the town, where all the lanes had 'cess pools and dung heaps opposite the doors'.[13]

Amidst the filth were hundreds of beggars, most of whom were sent to gaol, which in some cases saved their lives. The only alternative was the workhouse, but as Dr Quin remarked, 'I never saw anything to equal the dislike people have of coming into the poor house – they would sooner die of starvation than come into the workhouse.'[14]

It was in the midst of this cholera epidemic that, on

4 April, Dr Langley decided to expel his wife from his house, a public declaration of her disgrace.

Mr Gabriel Prior, the clerk employed by Dr Langley to over-see his private loan fund, would later describe his own unwitting role in the explusion of Mrs Langley to her new lodgings in Pound Street: '[Dr Langley] told me to take a room for a single female as cheap as I could get it . . . for a shilling or thirteen pence a week; I took the lodgings, for which I agreed at 1s 6d [but] did not know at the time for whom I was taking it; but I did the same evening. I told Dr Langley if I knew the lodgings were for Mrs Langley I would not take them in such a place. In reply to me, he said he thought they were good enough for his wife.'[15]

Eliza Rohan accompanied Ellen to her new abode – and then quit her employment in Barrack Street.[16]

Several doctors visited Ellen's lodgings at her request, and her sister's family would have passed her lodgings every day on their way in and out of the town. 'The fact is this,' Dr Quin admitted at the inquest, 'if it must come out, I was very reluctant to go near her at all, and that was the feeling of all the medical men.' He said he feared being called to Dublin to give evidence in the event of a divorce.[17]

The doctor knew society's view of fallen women. A con-temporary pamphlet highlighted their plight in a culture which placed so great a premium on female virtue: '. . . there are no sinners who, by the usages of the world, are so absolutely lost, so cast out of sight, so abandoned to the bit-terness of their own tormented soul. A fallen woman the world counts it righteous to forsake and scorn. Even her own kindred turn their backs, and shut the door of home upon her.'[18]

Mrs Langley's expulsion from her home quickly became public knowledge. Mary Cleary, the occupant of a house two doors up on Pound Street, would later describe seeing her arrive that first day, in 'the small dark room with the broken window'. Helping her new neighbour settle in, she pushed the hood from Mrs Langley's bonnet into the broken pane, and several times invited her into her own cabin to warm her up. The cold was intense and, days later, Mary gave her a cloak as she had only a shawl. 'She appeared to be very unhappy in her mind and looked very delicate,' Mary recalled.[19]

A week after Ellen's arrival in Pound Street, someone wrote, anonymously, to the *Tipperary Vindicator* to alert the paper to an unnamed 'scandalous matter'. The editor, Maurice Lenihan, although publicly acknowledging receipt of the letter, refused to publish it, stating firmly in his edition of 11 April that the subject it referred to was not suited to the columns of their newspaper. 'We have never at any time,' he wrote, 'permitted this journal to become subservient to the cravings of a vitiated appetite.'[20] Clearly the letter referred to something then on everyone's lips.

Left on her own, Ellen had become fearful of the disease her husband insisted she had contracted. Dr Quin described to the coroner's jury the letters he had received from her during this period.

'I have suffered a good deal of pain in the right loin,' she had written during her first week on Pound Street, 'and am certain you will do anything you can for your affectionate relative.' On Saturday he called on her but she was not at home. 'I feel extremely anxious to see you,' she wrote the following Monday. 'I was greatly disappointed at not seeing you on Saturday, when you so kindly called. God bless you and do come.' When Dr Quin eventually saw her, he found no evidence of any venereal infection but noted her bowel disorder with concern.[21]

'I examined her, and found the lower bowel, called the rectum, protruding from its extreme debility.'

'Were the lodgings comfortable?' asked Mr Dillon.

'I would not say the lodgings were comfortable – certainly they were not. She occupied one room, the dimensions of which were eight feet square, as well as my memory serves me.'

'As small as the black hole of Calcutta,' said Dillon.

Of the 107 properties on the street, records show that the house where Ellen Langley lodged had the cheapest valuation: just £1 10s annually. The landlady was a local grocer, Margaret Meara.[22] The presence of an auxiliary British army barracks made Pound Street a hive for prostitution, and the previous June the manhandling of women by soldiers in public houses on the street had sparked an all-out riot with local residents. The battle cry of the soldiers was 'Split the damnded Hirish [*sic*] like hares!', while the locals, retreating from the bayonets, cried, 'Hurrah for the barricades!' in reference to the revolution of the citizens of Paris the same month.[23]

The members of the coroner's jury were determined to explore the impact of the expulsion from her home on Mrs Langley's state of health.

'Did you ever go to her lodgings?' Mr Harden, one of the jurors, asked Eliza Rohan.

'I did,' she said.

'What kind of lodgings were they?' said Mr Cunningham, another juror.

'Very bad.'

'What was the expense?' he asked.

'One and sixpence a week.'

'What was she allowed for her support?'

'Seven shillings a week, that is a shilling a day, and pay the lodging money out of that.'

There were cries of shock from around the room. Five and a half shillings (or ninepence a day) was a little less than what the paupers working on outdoor famine relief projects earned.[24]

'Had she sheets?' continued Mr Cunningham, again addressing Eliza.

'Only one.'

'Did you ever know her to send for a sheet?'

'Yes, to Solsboro by myself.'

'Did she send to Dr Langley?'

'She did but he would not give it.'

On Tuesday 17 April the weather had changed for the worse; it was described by the *Nenagh Guardian* as 'exceedingly raw and severe' with snow falling heavily in the morning and continuing without break until seven the next morning. The following day, showers of snow and sleet continued before rain and high winds took over and howled through the whole of the following night.[25]

'The weather was very severe when she went there,' Eliza remembered. 'It was a feather bed, but not fit for Mrs Langley; there was no pillow, and the sheet was a canvas one; there was a good pair of blankets and a quilt . . . there was a broken pane in the window near the bed.'[26]

'Were there any other lodgers in the house?' asked Mr O'Brien, another juror.

'Yes,' she said, 'shoemakers in the next room.'

The shoemakers, visible to Mrs Langley through a 'broken partition', were among the many minor tradesmen who inhabited the impoverished street: painters, glaziers, printers, shopkeepers, provision dealers, straw-bonnet makers, tailors, iron merchants, whitesmiths, timber merchants, curriers, turners and publicans.[27] Everyone living here tried to get by through some trade or service, but life was a struggle and the accommodation uniformly poor. It was from this street that Dr Langley had evicted two tenants from a property two years previously, in the harsh winter of 1847. Increasingly, as the famine intensified, the tradesmen who populated this part of the town were being forced to find shelter in the workhouse.[28]

Having given her evidence, Eliza Rohan stepped down, and Mr Dillon once more turned to address the court.

'I might produce other witnesses,' he said, 'but I feel it would be a waste of public time. I feel for the gentlemen here present, and certainly shall not trouble them with other witnesses. I think there is quite enough to send this case to the [grand] jury.'

The Grand Jury was the body of local landowners, largely Protestant, whose job it was to decide whether there was sufficient evidence to bring a case to trial at the county assizes held in Nenagh in March and August every year.

However, Mr Bolton still had his own witnesses to examine.

12

'Every kindness and good treatment'

Mr Bolton began his case in defence of Dr Langley by urging the jury to dismiss from their minds any 'rumours or private stories, which [they] may hear about the town in reference to this proceeding'. 'There is not a country town,' he said, 'and more particularly the town of Nenagh, that does not exaggerate and give impetus to such stories . . . I have made no reference, neither will I now make any allusion to the scandalous rumours and stories that are afloat.'[1]

He set the whole affair against the backdrop of the famine and pestilence that afflicted Nenagh and the country at large.

'I am extremely sorry to see that this inquiry should be protracted to the length it has,' he began. 'There are hundreds of thousands of our fellow-creatures dying around us daily, and no inquiry into the causes of their deaths. You have heard six respectable gentlemen examined, as respectable in their professional and private character as any physicians in Ireland, and each and every one of them concurs in stating that the deceased came by her death from the visitation of God; the disease that produced death being dysentery, a disease which at present is devastating the country.'

It had been improper, he said, to raise every 'little family difference' between husband and wife, going back a number of years, when the medical evidence was so clear. He wished to focus, instead, on Mrs Langley's last days: her sudden return to her husband's home on Barrack Street a week prior to her death, and the treatment she received there.

Dr Langley, having gone to Limerick to fetch his sister, Mrs Jackson, returned to find Ellen back home, complaining of severe illness.

'During the illness of Mrs Langley,' said Bolton, 'she received every kindness and good treatment – nothing was left undone for her. I will produce to you all the persons who were around her, from whose evidence, I am convinced, you will see not the slightest foundation for the charge of ill-treatment, and which, if you believe, a verdict of natural death must be the result. I will say this, that you are imperatively bound to find the cause of death alone, recollecting the oaths you have taken, and you are bound to nothing else.'

He would make his case by questioning two principal witnesses: Dr Langley's sister, Mrs Jackson, and his new servant, Mary Clancy, who had been employed by the doctor to replace Eliza. Miss Clancy, who had previously worked for a Mr Garvey, land agent to Lord Bloomfield, was described harshly in the press as 'a tall strapping wench' and a 'strumpet' – perhaps suggesting she had some previous relationship with the doctor.[2] She recalled the return of Mrs Langley on Saturday 21 April, seventeen days after her departure.[3]

'I am the present servant of Dr Langley,' she testified. 'I entered his service on the 18th of April; on the 20th Dr Langley went to Limerick; he left me in care of the house in his absence; at the time Mrs Langley was at lodgings; while he was in Limerick Mrs Langley knocked at the door which I opened; she said to me, "I am Mrs Langley and I wish to see Miss Jackson."'

Fanny Jackson, Langley's niece, whom he and Ellen had raised, had been left in Nenagh while he went to fetch her mother in Limerick.

'She then came into the parlour,' continued the servant; 'she told me to go upstairs and settle her bed, that she was ill; I had no sheets at the time, as the doctor had them all locked up; she remained in the house until he returned; I then got sheets and prepared the bed for her.'

Mrs Jackson, when she gave evidence, also recorded encountering Mrs Langley at this time, when she and her brother arrived from Limerick.

'We arrived in Nenagh at six in the evening,' she told the court. 'I had heard that in consequence of a family broil, Dr Langley and Mrs Langley had separated; that he had turned her out.'

Mrs Jackson was Dr Langley's only surviving sibling. Her daughter, Fanny, who had lived with the Langleys since she was a young child, was no doubt anxious to see her mother, who might for a period take over the running of the house. But Mrs Jackson and her brother had not expected to find Ellen at Barrack Street.

'I found Mrs Langley in Dr Langley's house when we arrived; we all three remained some time, a half hour, perhaps, in the doctor's bedroom; she had her shawl and bonnet. Dr Langley told her to go upstairs to her garret.'

She said that when her brother had gone out to get her luggage from the carriage, Mrs Langley returned to speak with her, confiding that she felt severely ill. She complained of 'a violent pain in her right side and of a bowel attack'.

'I remained half an hour conversing with her, and she said it was her own fault to be turned out.'

She ordered food to be brought up to her brother's wife, she told the court, including eggs, and attended her sickbed. Mary Clancy also mentioned her role in looking after Ellen's needs that day. 'In the course of the evening I took her up bread, butter, coffee, and an egg,' she said. She later recalled that her employer's wife looked 'puny and delicate'.[4]

'What kind of bread?' asked Bryan Consedine, the most outspoken of the jurors. 'Was it white?'

'Leave her to me,' said Bolton.

'I feared you would leave the brown bread out,' said Consedine.

'What kind of bread did you bring her?' asked Bolton.

'Brown. I got up several times at night to give her a drink; I stayed up two nights entirely without going to bed at all.'

Mrs Jackson told the court that she enquired after Ellen the morning after her arrival in Nenagh.

'I asked the servant the morning after how she spent the night, and she said very bad; I told my brother so, and sent her a breakfast of bread, butter, tea and egg; in consequence of what I told Doctor Langley, he sent for Dr Quin, he saw her on that day, and every day till her death; Dr Kittson also saw her, and attended her.'

Mrs Jackson presented herself as a caring female presence in the house.

'During her entire illness anything she ordered, or that she wished for, or that we thought conducive to her health she got,' she said. 'There was a nurse tender named Judy McCutcheon brought in the day before her death.'

Mr Dillon, when he took over questioning these witnesses, made it clear that he was not convinced by Mrs Jackson's portrayal of the care Ellen received in her last days in Barrack Street.

'How often did you visit Nenagh?' he enquired of Mrs Jackson.

'I was not in Nenagh for four years previous to this visit.

I had no possibility of judging how Dr and Mrs Langley lived heretofore.'

It was an extraordinary admission from a woman whose twelve-year-old daughter had lived so long in the town – and perhaps calls into question the true parentage of Fanny. Was she, in reality, Dr Langley's illegitimate daughter, living undercover as his niece?

Dillon wondered what reason the doctor had for summoning his sister at this time. 'What did Dr Langley say to you when he called at your house?'

She replied that he wanted her to come and spend some time with him, that he was lonely; that Mrs Langley was at lodgings and he had no one to manage his household affairs.

Although living in neighbouring towns just twenty-five miles apart, the last time they had met, she told the court, had been three years earlier when she had visited her brother and his wife at the seaside resort of Kilkee, County Clare. Dr Langley's relationship with Ellen had seemed fine then, she said, though she did note one exception – a quarrel of some sort 'about trivial matters'.

Dillon wondered whether Bolton's claim of his client's good treatment of his wife in her last days was believable.

'Is it not likely that he would put on a fair face before you and treat Mrs Langley better than he had before?' he asked Mrs Jackson.

'I don't know,' she said. 'I was in attendance on her, my daughter was in attendance and the servant.'

Whose idea was it to get a nurse tender? Dillon asked.

'It was Mrs Quin's suggestion,' she said.

Harriet Quin, wife of Dr Quin, was a relation of Ellen's and it was significant that she rather than Dr Langley or his sister thought of providing a nurse at this very late stage of the illness. The nurse would stay a mere twenty-four hours.

He then asked her what she had meant by her remark to Mr Bolton that Mrs Langley had 'said it was her own fault to be turned out'.

Mrs Jackson replied, 'In taking notice of some little matters she had heard, which she ought not, and of which she said, it would have been better had she [taken] no notice.'[5]

Here Mrs Jackson gave some hint as to Ellen's own suspicions regarding her husband's behaviour and the role they may have played in the course of events up to that point. She told Dillon that Ellen claimed to have been happy until October 1848. Despite the testimony of his former groom, John Quigley, regarding earlier periods of incarceration and infidelity on Langley's part, it was becoming apparent that something had happened in the autumn of 1848 that had made Ellen unhappy and set in motion a harsher course of treatment against her. For the moment the exact nature of the rumours that had reached Ellen's ears remained obscure to the jury, and Dillon seemed reluctant to pursue it.

He wondered how much Mrs Jackson really knew about her husband's relationship with his wife.

'You are aware that Mrs Langley was a very innocent lady, and that her husband possessed considerable influence over her?'

'I saw her at all times quite anxious to please him, and he was anxious to please her,' replied Mrs Jackson.

'Don't you think he had very despotic and unlimited influence over her?'

'I can't say, but I know she was always gentle.'

'She was of a confiding, weak temper?'

'Indeed, I think so.'

'Don't you think, on your oath, that he could get her to do anything he pleased?'

'I cannot say.'

Mr Bolton next called on Mrs Jackson's daughter, Fanny, who was examined only very briefly. As a child her testimony was unlikely to be relied upon to any great degree by either party.

'Dr Langley is my uncle,' she told the court, adding that she had been staying with him for the last nine years.

'Do you know the nature of an oath?' asked Dillon.

'I do,' she said.

In response to a question from Mr Bolton, she said, 'I recollect the day my uncle went to Limerick, and returned with my mother.'

'During Mrs Langley's illness was she well- or ill-treated?' he asked.

'No person could be treated better,' she said.

Mr Dillon, given the opportunity to further cross-examine her, declined. 'I shall ask you no questions, Miss Jackson,' he said.[6]

The Rev. Benjamin Bewley, the Protestant curate who had attended Ellen in her final days, gave more puzzling evidence regarding her sentiments during her last illness. He had, he said, attended her solely in the capacity of a clergyman and 'prevented her on several occasions from speaking on various worldly matters'. The young clergyman clearly had not wished to get involved in any unpleasant dispute between the Langleys.

'I was present when she expressed a wish to have an interview with a certain lady; she said she was afraid she would be unable to bear the interview alone. I understood her to wish the interview in the presence of her husband and Mrs Jackson,' he said to Mr Dillon.

Either the newspapers refused to name the person in question or Bewley was being deliberately coy about drawing some hitherto unimplicated figure into the inquest. There is no suggestion in the reports of the inquest that Mr Dillon followed up this line of questioning, or any indication as to how the question came to be asked in the first place. There is some suggestion here of a collective tiptoeing around some unsavoury fact. This silence recalls again the strange request in Dr Langley's letter to the coroner, referred to on the first day of the inquest, that a certain unnamed person should not be called to give evidence. Was this the same person with whom Ellen had wished to speak? Readers of the newspapers were, for the moment, left in ignorance.

Another striking aspect of the testimony is the absence of any indication that Ellen's own family – the Poes of Solsboro and Donnybrook – visited her during the last week of her life. Where were her sisters Frances and Mary Anne? What of her nephew, James Jocelyn Poe? Her niece, Anna? Where were they in her final hours? Why did no member of the Poe family volunteer to give any testimony to the events of this period? As the evidence against Dr Langley grew, the Poes remained silent.

We know that on 1 May 1849 at six o'clock in the morning, nine days after she had returned to her husband's house, Ellen Langley finally died. There is no record of the moment of her death, or of who was there when it occurred, but presumably the nurse Judy McCutcheon was in attendance. Exhausted and emaciated, Ellen had nothing left to fight with.

The exact cause of her death, according to the doctors who compiled her post-mortem report, was 'English cholera', or gastroenteritis. Presumably, she experienced all its dire effects, 'the vomiting and purging of an enormous quantity of bilious fluid matter', the 'burning sensation at the pit of the stomach', the 'severe cramps in the bowels and extremities', the coldness on the surface of the skin, combined with a 'clammy perspiration' and fainting.[7]

Judy McCutcheon, after what must have been a gruelling night, appears to have been dismissed immediately as there is no further mention of her being in the house, and the subsequent treatment of the corpse was left to Dr Langley, his sister and Mary Clancy.

The question of Ellen's treatment following her death was an important one for the members of the jury, who quizzed Mary Clancy on the events of that day.

'In what state was the body brought downstairs after the post-mortem examination?' asked Mr Cunningham.

Mr Bolton, who was wary of where this was leading, objected.

But Mr Dillon was keen that this evidence should come out. 'We have no right to object to anything from a juror,' he said. 'We are here by courtesy. It is Mr Coroner's kindness to allow us to be present at all.'

Cunningham repeated the question.

'She was brought downstairs by the master and me in sheets.'

'Was Mrs Langley put in the coffin in the same state as the doctors left her?' asked Mr Gleeson, another of the jurors.

'No,' she replied, 'I washed her by the doctor's orders.'

'No shrouding?' enquired Consedine.

'No.'

'Was it by the doctor's orders there was no shrouding?'

'It was.'

The jury was also interested to hear about the type of coffin Dr Langley had arranged for his wife, which had arrived at ten o'clock that evening.

'She was put in a coffin: was it a valuable one?' Mr Dillon asked Mrs Jackson directly.

'It was not.'

'A two and tenpenny one,' interjected Mr Consedine.

Mr Bolton protested: 'Really, Mr Dillon, I think this course of proceeding ought to be abandoned.'

'No,' replied Dillon firmly. 'It shows animus, the foregone conclusion.'

The jury wanted to know how the coffin itself was treated. Respectable funeral preparations, rigidly observed by all classes, might tell a lot about the tenor of a relationship.

'After Mrs Langley was put into the coffin where was it brought to?' Mr Nolan, one of the jurors, asked Mary Clancy.

'Into the yard,' she said.

'How long did it remain in the yard?' asked Mr Consedine.

'A day and a night.'

There was a shocked reaction to this news in the schoolroom, and another when a few moments later she corrected this to 'two days and two nights'.

The jury also asked Mary Clancy to explain the events on the day of the funeral. There had been much talk around the town about a mob of women smashing the doctor's windows as Mrs Langley's coffin was being removed from the house, and some details had already crept into the public domain.

'Are you the servant who, the other day, refused to allow the corpse of the lady to pass through the hall door?' asked Consedine.

'No, sir, I did not refuse.'

'Are you the only servant there – is there another servant besides you?' he continued.

'There is not.'

'Then you are the person that did so.'

'No, sir, I opened the hall door the moment they demanded it.'

'No,' Consedine insisted, 'the door was not opened till the people smashed it open.'

'I opened it the moment they asked me,' she said.

Here Mr O'Dell, the police sub-inspector, interjected. 'If you swear me I will depose to an admission made to me by that girl.'

'Yes, we will hear Mr O'Dell,' said Consedine.

'In the presence,' O'Dell said, 'of Mrs Jackson she said it was her master's orders not to open the hall door, but the wicket, and that she did not open the door until they were going to break it.'

'That shows what sort of witness she is,' said Consedine.

Mary Clancy was likely fearful of public opinion and conscious of her own participation in the treatment of Mrs Langley, so her account was perhaps inevitably a jumbled one. However, the jury's insistent extraction of these details from her established in clear terms the bad feeling that Dr Langley harboured towards his wife even after her death.

13

'Thou shalt not escape calumny'

In summing up the case for the prosecution at the end of the third and final day of the inquest, Mr Dillon addressed what he saw as the key facts of the case.

'Gentlemen, with regard to the evidence adduced on the prosecution, it is unnecessary for me to recapitulate it. There is one doctor's testimony I shall allude to – it is Dr Cahalan's – which is very strong. You have heard the cause of his going to see Mrs Langley – he was called on by Dr Langley for the purpose of ascertaining whether she had a certain disease or not. She most unwillingly submitted to his examination, because he felt that natural repugnance, and wished to uphold that respect for the decency of the female sex. Dr Langley endeavoured to extort from Dr Cahalan a certificate that she was in the state he said, he well knowing at the time that she was not. Dr Langley insisted she was, and Dr Cahalan distinctly denied she was, and Dr Quin's evidence states she was not. The evidence of the serving man' – Thomas Pound – 'clearly goes to show the object and intention of Dr Langley. This man confesses he was guilty of the crime in question, and notwithstanding that it had come to the ears of his employer, he kept him in the house more than a week – he was quite familiar with him – he was not displeased with what he had done – and he would have kept him in his service only he was apprehensive that remarks might be made.

'Now, it is evident he made this wretched servant man of

his, by some secret means or other, the ground upon which to found a divorce in the Prerogative Court. That he conspired against this highly respectable, and educated, but at the same time, simple and confiding lady, is apparent, and for doing so it is clear he resorted to means which no man of honour, of integrity and of moral feeling would countenance, and which the basest person in the community would scarcely have used.'

Applause carried him on to his next point: the good treatment Mrs Langley had apparently received during her very last days. This was, he reminded the jury, due to the kindness of Mrs Jackson, not of Dr Langley himself.

'But before that how was she treated?' he enquired. 'She was turned out of her comfortable dwelling, and took refuge in miserable lodgings; she, who was accustomed to the sweets of plenty from her infancy – who was a lady by birth and connection – and who was proverbial for her gentleness of temper and kindness of disposition – was an outcast in society, without pleasure, without happiness, and without peace of mind, owing to the inhuman conduct of her unfeeling husband. To avoid public odium and scorn he may retire from this town and country, and out of the Kingdom, but from henceforth I defy him to show face to human eyes.'

The courtroom erupted again in approval.

'Mr Bewley's evidence . . . shows that if she was permitted to complain she would complain fully; but he, as a clergyman, put a stop to her mouth, and prevented her saying anything about them . . . The insidious tongue of slander is always busy, and few can escape its attacks. Nor is it to be wondered at that the deceased did not escape.' Getting into his stride he now introduced an appropriate theatrical reference. 'Gentlemen, recollect that the immortal Shakespeare has written in his play of *Hamlet* the following, which is addressed to Ophelia – "Be thou pure as ice; or chaster than the driven snow, thou shalt not escape calumny."[1]

Mr Dillon finished with a final encouragement to the jury. 'Gentlemen,' he said, 'I shall keep my word and say no more, leaving my case in the hands of fifteen of my intelligent and upright fellow-townsmen, and confident, that without fear, favour, affection or sympathy you will return a proper verdict; and do justice to the outraged feelings of the public, and to the memory of this persecuted and perhaps murdered lady.'

Loud applause brought his speech to its close.

It was late in the day, with rays from the slowly dipping south-western sun throwing warm light into the school-room, when the jury retired to consider its verdict. The coroner, solicitors, family members and as many of the general public as might fit in the room all waited patiently as the jurors made their deliberations. Half an hour later, when the church bells rang six, the door to the neighbouring room swung open and the fifteen members of the jury filed out.

The head juror, Mr Cantrell, stepped forward and addressed the coroner and assembled crowd:

'We find that Mrs Eleanor Langley came by her death in consequence of a bowel complaint brought on by unnatural and diabolical treatment, received at the hands of her husband, Charles Langley, and of which she died at Nenagh, the 1st of May; we therefore find the said Charles Langley *Guilty of manslaughter*.'[2]

PART TWO

14

'My anxiety to vindicate my character'

The coroner, James Carroll, immediately issued a warrant for the arrest of Dr Langley, including a detailed description of his appearance, which was published in the the *Police Gazette; or, Hue and Cry*: 'He is 42 years of age, 5 feet 10 inches high, slight make, dark complexion, black hair inclining to grey, and black eyes; whiskers shaved off.' He was reportedly dressed in 'a hat, black body coat, dark trousers, dark vest and had a gold watch and chain'. Other details painted him as a storybook villain: his voice 'vulgar', his countenance 'very bad', his teeth 'prominent' and his shoulders 'slightly stooped'.[1]

The description was reprinted widely across Ireland. He was 'far from being a beauty', commented one west of Ireland newspaper when publishing it for their readers. 'A statuary would hardly take him for the model of an Apollo . . .'[2] The editor of the *Tipperary Vindicator*, Maurice Lenihan, described the inquest as 'a flagitious exposition of inhumanity', a 'consummate history of unmanly and brutal guilt', and a 'foul chapter from the chequered pages of family life', the like of which had never before been brought before the reading public. Within days, the story of Dr Langley's cruelty to his wife had reached every corner of the British Isles.[3]

To secure a conviction for manslaughter, the prosecution would not need to show intent to kill but rather a genuine disregard for the life of another. It was not a capital offence, and if convicted Dr Langley might expect a relatively light gaol sentence. It was easier to secure a conviction for man-slaughter than for murder, and yet less than a third of the manslaughter trials during this period ended in conviction.[4] For Langley, the threat to his reputation and career might have been a more fearful prospect than that of being convicted and going to prison.

Given the intensity of the newspapers' interest in the case, the accounts of what happened next are strangely thin, and not entirely consistent. After ten days at large (according to the *Nenagh Guardian*), or twelve days (as stated by the *Tipperary Vindicator*), he was captured at an unspecified location in Dublin, under unspecified circumstances, and committed to Newgate Gaol.[5]

Dr Langley applied successfully for bail and, temporarily free, he retreated to the luxurious Shelbourne Hotel. The *Freeman's Journal* reported on 13 July that he had indicated 'his intention to surrender and take his trial at the next assizes of Nenagh for the manslaughter of his wife' in the first week of August.[6]

He had, it seemed, taken the peculiar decision to return to prison in advance of the trial. He explained his reasoning in a letter to the *Nenagh Guardian* on the following day:

Shelbourne Hotel, Room No. 20,
14th July '49

Sir,

As misrepresentation is the order of the day, I wish to inform you, that before you will have received this, I shall have surrendered myself to the Governor of Nenagh Jail, and will therefore feel obliged by your not inserting that I was arrested, or that I was brought there in the custody of the police, but that I have given myself up of my own

accord, and of my own free will, and that I have been induced to do so
thus early (fourteen days before the Commission [aka Grand Jury]
opens) in order that the Crown may have no reasonable grounds for
postponing my trial, which I am most anxious should take place at
the coming Assizes, when I trust I shall be able to rebut by most
respectable testimony, the horrid and revolting evidence given on the
inquest, at which I was not present. If it were not for my anxiety to
vindicate my character, by having a trial at once, I would not
surrender until the very last day.

Your very obedient humble servant,
C. Langley M.D.[7]

That same day, or very early the following day, Dr Langley
took the train from Dublin to Templemore, the nearest station to Nenagh on the recently completed Great Southern
and Western Railway. On the morning of Sunday 15 July, he
departed from the Queen's Arms posting establishment in a
coach and four accompanied by his brother-in-law, George
Jackson. On arriving in Nenagh, they drove through the
town to the gaol, where the doctor surrendered himself to
the governor, Mr Rock.[8]

The massive gaol, completed seven years earlier, was an
intimidating structure in solid blocks of roughly hewn limestone. At its core, surrounded by seven radiating cell blocks,
was the tall octagonal governor's house, from where there
was 360-degree surveillance over the complex. Here Dr
Langley would be confined until his trial, which was fixed
for two weeks hence. On his arrival a prison officer recorded
his height as 5 feet 9 inches, his hair 'dark' and his complexion 'swarthy'.[9]

Conditions in the prison were poor. Two weeks earlier, at the

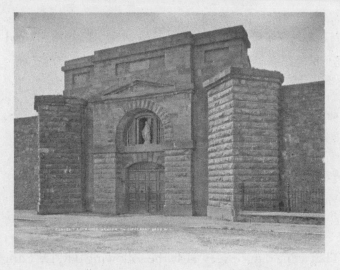

commencement of the most recent quarter sessions in the town, the resident magistrate, John Gore Jones, had addressed the Grand Jury on the difficulty of accommodating new prisoners:

> It is quite right and most desirable that they should not be kept one hour unnecessarily in prison . . . a building originally intended and built to contain 344 persons. At this instant there are confined within its walls 755 individuals . . . [and] pestilence is doing its work. There are several persons dying there at this moment – there are fifty or sixty in Hospital; and within the last few days one of the most meritorious officers of the gaol has fallen a victim to the contagion that prevails there . . . it is little better than a pest house.

A total of 506 people were to stand trial in Nenagh at the forthcoming assizes, most of them guilty of little more than desperation. 'I will not call it crime,' said Gore Jones; 'the cause of the much larger proportion of it may be described by one word – destitution . . . Famine and pestilence have conquered in their struggle against human life and human hopes, and have covered the land with human wreck.'[10]

At the same time that Dr Langley was being investigated under suspicion of poisoning and starving his wife to death, some journalists were accusing the British government of trying to do away with the Irish pauper in a similar manner. Four days after the jury of the coroner's court issued its verdict on the death of Mrs Langley, the *Freeman's Journal* published an attack on the Indian meal being used to feed the hungry in Ireland under the headline THE PROCESS OF SLOW POISONING – DIET OF THE 'MERE IRISH' PAUPER: '. . . the "mere Irish" have prayed for, struggled for, fought for, this loathsome offal – have died of hunger and been eaten by dogs on the mountain roads as they crawled. God help them! after the relieving officers appointed to dole forth this poisonous "meal busk".'[11]

The charge that the British state was deliberately attempting to eradicate the Irish was not uncommon in Ireland's press during these years. 'A fearful murder committed on the mass of the people,' thundered Charles Gavan Duffy, editor of the *Nation*, a radical newspaper that opposed the union with Britain.[12] The previous year, the Catholic archbishop of Tuam, similarly enraged by what he was seeing around him in Connacht, charged that the government had 'promised that none of them should starve and then suffered a million of them to perish'.[13]

These attacks were, in part, a response to English newspaper reports that cast the starving Irish as criminals, requiring the firm hand of the law. In the same month as the Langley inquest, John O'Connell, son of Daniel O'Connell, stood up in the House of Commons to defend the Irish paupers who were being convicted for petty larcenies: 'Look at their wan cheeks – the mournful expression of their countenances – their wasted forms – their eyes starting from their sockets – and their limbs tottering by the slow process of want – look at their ragged garments – their wretched clothing.'[14] He recited grim statistics from various localities. In the Nenagh workhouse, he noted, 941 paupers had died in the preceding four months. In fact, it was widely reported across Britain that Nenagh's coffin maker, James Meara, had sent a bill to the workhouse's Board of Guardians for 1,120 coffins furnished by him between 25 March and 25 July 1849.[15]

In a period when the Langley case and others highlighted the torturous relationships that could exist behind the closed doors of the family home – ultimately leading to new divorce legislation in Britain in 1857 – the political union between England and Ireland was being cast as a bad marriage, wherein the English husband physically and emotionally abused his captive Irish wife. As one-time Irish resident Anthony Trollope complained: ' . . . it was . . . necessary to England's character that the bride thus bound in a compulsory wedlock should be endowed with all the best privileges that a wife can enjoy. Let her at least not be a kept mistress. Let it be bone of my bone and flesh of my flesh, if we are to live together in the married state.'[16]

For those defending the union, the gender inequalities of the Victorian married state were an accepted part of the natural order. Lord Peterborough, in opposing O'Connell's campaign for repeal of the Act of Union, explained: 'Though sometimes there happened a difference between man and wife, yet it did not presently break the marriage; so in like manner, though England, who in this national marriage must be supposed to be the husband, might in some instances be unkind to the *lady*, yet *she* ought not presently to sue for a divorce; the rather because she had very much mended her fortune by this match.'[17]

Others felt that, given Ireland's ongoing famine, her fortune was much diminished. On the morning of Ellen Langley's death, the *Limerick Reporter* bewailed what it saw as a disastrous marriage between the two countries. 'This wasting land sought for English succour, continuously raising the cries of death and despair; but that Godless country to which we had been united in holy bonds of political wedlock heard not the call.'[18] 'Ireland will not remain joined to England except by force,' warned the English radical W. J. Linton in 1848, '. . . [her] own will has pronounced her divorce from England'.[19]

A wave of European revolutions had begun in France in February 1848, and famine-ravaged Ireland came under its influence. In July of that year, the lesser tradesmen of Nenagh had gathered in the town's temperance hall to discuss an uprising. 'We are determined, men of Nenagh, to repeal the union or fall in the effort beneath the sceptre of the tyrant,' declared Dan FitzPatrick, one of the leaders of the group. Mr Holland, a carpenter from Pound Street, also called for action: 'It behoves all of us to come forward to free this country, and to keep in it those crops which have been planted and reared by our hands, and not to permit them to be torn from us and wasted in a foreign land, while we perish of hunger at home.' They appealed for men 'of all creeds' to join them, and every class – 'even the men whose grand lawns fatten cattle for the English market'.[20]

Two weeks later, a group called the Young Irelanders would launch a tiny and ineffectual rebellion in counties

Wexford, Kilkenny and Tipperary. The rebels were quickly arrested and transported to Van Diemen's Land following their trial in the autumn of 1848. But as the mass clearances, emigration and death from disease and starvation continued to take their toll in 1849, fear of further attempts to free Ireland violently from her broken marriage lingered.

The Grand Jury – twenty men, among whom were some of the largest landowners in the North Riding of Tipperary, gathered in Nenagh on Friday 27 July. They were sworn in to adjudicate on a whole range of fiscal and legal issues arising in the northern half of the county, including decisions over which cases should continue to trial and on what terms. Their work would take several days. They might dismiss or alter charges if they thought they did not accurately reflect the evidence that was submitted for their consideration. It was not until the following Wednesday afternoon, the day before Dr Langley's trial was to take place, that they got around to considering the case. And it was evening time before they reached an unexpected conclusion.[21]

If new evidence had been submitted, the public were not made aware of it. All that the people of Nenagh knew at this point was that the Grand Jury thought there were sufficient grounds to alter the charges that had been proposed by the coroner's jury at the inquest months earlier.

The bill against Dr Langley, they decided, should be changed from manslaughter to murder.[22]

15

'The new Bernard Cavanagh'

Dr Langley now faced the prospect of death by hanging. In the long hours of his incarceration, and as the darkness of the night set in upon his cell, he might have recalled a botched execution outside Nenagh Gaol the previous April, when the hangman had failed to draw the cap fully over the condemned man's head. 'All the sufferings and pains of strangulation were plainly visible in the contortions of his countenance,' reported the *Tipperary Vindicator*. 'His eyes shot out some inches beyond their sockets. In a moment the face became blood red; in another instant it assumed a ghastly livid hue, whilst again the facial muscles quivered in every fibre . . . nothing could have been more revolting . . .'[1]

A person in Dr Langley's position might turn to the prison chaplain for solace – but the chaplain in Nenagh Gaol was the Rev. Mr Poe, his late wife's brother-in-law. The one possible sympathizer on the staff was his friend Dr O'Neill Quin, who held the post of prison surgeon. However, just as Dr Langley learned of his new predicament, Quin was removed from the post due to some business irregularities.[2]

Langley had already hired a barrister, Henry Martley, for his defence. (George Bolton, who had represented him at the coroner's inquest, was a solicitor and could not defend him in a capital trial for murder.) Martley, from Dublin, was an older and more experienced lawyer than Bolton. Aged forty-six, he had worked for more than twenty years on the Leinster Circuit – including eight as Queen's Counsel and three as a legal advisor to the government at Dublin Castle.[3] Nine years earlier, he had represented Dr Dempster in his semi-successful libel action against Dr Langley.[4] He had a proven record in both prosecuting and defending murder charges, including cases involving alleged starvation and neglect, and had earned a formidable reputation as a cross-examiner.[5] In 1842 he had unsuccessfully prosecuted a woman charged with murdering her husband.[6]

On Wednesday 1 August, a busy fair day in Nenagh, Langley was taken from his cell and brought into the neighbouring courthouse to hear the new charge against him. The public had already gathered there to glimpse the notorious doctor in the flesh, and the galleries were 'densely crowded with spectators', particularly the Grand Jury gallery, which was 'filled with gentlemen'.[7] The accused was 'fashionably attired in a black dress coat and yellow vest, and wore gold rings on both hands'. He had 'large black whiskers' over his cheeks.[8] According to the *Limerick Reporter*, he was 'in possession of his usual good health, and leaning over the dock rail, with his head and shoulders bent forward, he looked around the crowded court and galleries for a moment, and then looked steadily at the judge'.[9] The paper commented that his 'countenance seemed somewhat dejected, and he appeared to feel strongly the difference in the charge of manslaughter under which he was when he surrendered himself to the custody of the Governor of the Gaol, and the awful charge of the wilful murder of his wife under which he was then arraigned'. The onlookers were reduced to silence as the indictment for murder was formally handed down by the Grand Jury.[10]

Messrs James Scott QC and Matthew Sausse QC appeared for the prosecution. Mr Martley and four other barristers and solicitors, including George Bolton, appeared representing the prisoner.

Mr Carmichael, Clerk of the Crown, addressed the court. 'Charles Langley, are you ready for trial?'

Before he could reply, Mr Martley intervened.

'In this case, My Lord,' he said, 'I have to apply that the prisoner be not put on trial this morning, the bills only having been found last night. The case has assumed a totally different aspect from what we apprehended. I really put it to the Counsel for the Crown whether, considering all the circumstances of the case, they think it expedient to proceed with this trial. Considering also the great change in the nature of the charge against him, I submit, My Lord, that it would more tend to promote the interest of the public and better satisfy the ends of public justice, that this case should be postponed.'[11]

Mr Scott quickly agreed to the proposal. 'The learned counsel of the prisoner ought to be allowed time to consider maturely whatever shape their case may ultimately assume for the defence,' he said.

The judge, Mr Sergeant Stock, agreed. 'Let the prisoner be removed,' he instructed.

Mr Rock, the governor of the gaol, placed his hand on the doctor's shoulder. A turnkey stood on his opposite side, and together they conducted him back down the subterranean passage to the prison next door.[12]

The following Monday, it was reported that the trial was to be postponed until the next assizes, in March the following year.[13]

The Summer Assizes had been unusually quiet, owing to a decline in violent crime in Tipperary. The *Nenagh Guardian* viewed this development as a direct consequence of the famine:

> This is a wonderful change in Tipperary, a county hitherto pre-eminent for its lawlessness and litigation . . . if the wonderful change in the social condition of this county, from being an Aceldama of blood and crime, to what it now is, be attributable to the wise inflictions of the Almighty, who sent forth his messengers spreading pestilence and famine in the land, we should look upon it with gladness rather than with sorrow or regret, when it has brought about a state of things, which the terrors and punishments of the law could never accomplish.[14]

Unable to enjoy the drama of a murder trial, the more prosperous in the town had to content themselves with other entertainments. Some attended the matches between the Nenagh and Templemore cricket clubs at the home of Sir John Carden, the High Sheriff for the county. On the previous Saturday, Templemore had won 'in one innings by several runs', but Nenagh would have a chance to redeem itself the following week.[15] The next month was the Lough Derg Regatta, when day trippers clambered on to a steamer to watch the yacht races under 'a cloudless sky', the lake appearing 'highly pleasing to the eye and charming to the mind'.[16]

There was also the question of the Queen's visit to Ireland that autumn to consider, and Sir John Carden set about arranging an appropriate address from the inhabitants of Tipperary North Riding, ensuring her that 'the strongest attachment is entertained towards your Royal Person, and we trust that you may long live to Reign over a happy, prosperous and United People'.[17]

Those anxious to hear more about the Langley case would

have to wait. For close to four months, there was no news of the notorious doctor. High prison walls had abruptly curtailed the drama.

Then, in late November, a small article appeared in the *Nenagh Guardian*:

> The truth of this paragraph will, no doubt, be questioned by many, but having heard it from a highly respectable source, we ourselves would feel a delicacy in relying on its veracity. Dr Langley, as most of our readers are aware, has been in Nenagh jail on a coroner's warrant and in consequence of some favour which at first he was allowed being withdrawn, he refused to eat and continued without food of any description for a period of thirty-eight days – partaking of nothing except cold water![18]

Langley was much put out by what he viewed as the inaccuracy of the *Guardian*'s report. He wrote a letter of complaint to its rival, the *Tipperary Vindicator*, which promptly published it:

> Sir – In reference to a paragraph in the *Nenagh Guardian*, of this evening relative to Dr Langley, the editor has been misinformed on two points – first, as to the number of days he abstained from food, and next as to the cause. First, as to the number of days (forty) and not thirty-eight, was the number; and next as regards the cause – 'that it was in consequence of some favour which at first was allowed being withdrawn, he refused to eat'. Such is not the fact, as the sole reason for his abstaining from food was a total loss of appetite, nausea, and a disinclination to eat, superinduced altogether by totally different causes from that he has stated. It may be a fact well worth recording for the information of

your physiological readers, that during that time all the organs of the body ceased to perform their functions in the animal economy, with the exception of the heart and lungs. And it is a curious coincidence also, that during that time the loss he sustained in weight was three stone less by two pound, making exactly a loss of 40lb, being a deficiency of 1lb per day for every day he abstained from food. – C. Langley.[19]

Langley was annoyed that his fast had been reported as a petty protest against his gaolers. In insisting on having gone forty days without food, rather than thirty-eight, he might have hoped to join the litany of saints in the Christian tradition who had with pious exactitude measured their worth against Christ's forty days fasting in the wilderness. In entering the fraught enclosure of Nenagh Gaol, exposing himself to disease and assuming the skeletal guise of its half-starved inmates, Langley had assumed the sackcloth of the Christian martyr. The *Nenagh Guardian* reporter John Hallissey, who would later come to loggerheads with Langley over his reporting, had – perhaps knowingly? – robbed the doctor of the fast's intended symbolism by misrepresenting its duration.

Whatever its religious significance, fasting as a means to protest one's innocence had a heroic resonance in the late 1840s. Alexandre Dumas's bestselling *The Count of Monte Cristo* had been published in London three years earlier, its protagonist wrongfully imprisoned through the machinations of a scheming rival. It was Edmond Dantès's willingness to die of starvation for his cause that marked him out as an innocent man. A surviving letter shows that Langley had read Dumas's novel only six months before his arrest, and it had perturbed him deeply – to such an extent that he wished he had never read it. 'It is the most dreadful story of revenge I ever read,' he stated at the time, 'the moral to be deduced from it is certainly bad and dangerous.'[20]

During the long hours of his confinement, his mind must surely have returned to this dramatic story of wrongful imprisonment, perhaps inspiring a new empathy with Dumas's tortured hero.

'Well,' said the jailer, 'are you more reasonable to-day?' Dantès made no reply.

'Come, cheer up; is there anything that I can do for you?'

'I wish to see the governor.'

'I have already told you it was impossible.'

'Why so?'

'Because it is against prison rules, and prisoners must not even ask for it.'

'What is allowed, then?'

'Better fare, if you pay for it, books, and leave to walk about.'

'I do not want books, I am satisfied with my food, and do not care to walk about; but I wish to see the governor.'

'If you worry me by repeating the same thing, I will not bring you any more to eat.'

'Well, then,' said Edmond, 'if you do not, I shall die of hunger – that is all.'

The jailer saw by his tone he would be happy to die . . .[21]

Dantès was resolute in his decision. 'He kept his word; twice a day he cast out, through the barred aperture, the provisions his jailer brought him – at first gayly, then with deliberation, and at last with regret. Nothing but the recollection of his oath gave him strength to proceed.'

But if Langley had intended to appropriate something of the fictional Dantès's defiant attitude, other commentators searched for a more local parallel. The doctor's coldly scientific analysis of his 'animal economy', and his survival on heart and lungs alone, seemed miraculous in the famine-stricken 1840s. Newspapers across Britain hailed him as 'the new Bernard Cavanagh', recalling to many the strange case of the County Mayo man who had claimed, eight years previously, to be able to exist without food.[22]

The earlier case had been a sensational one. In 1842 an English magazine reported: 'Bernard Cavanagh is the name of a person who is now raising considerable sums of money in Dublin by professing to work miracles – the greatest of them all consisting in his ability to live without any food whatever – which he is now said to have done for several months. Crowds flock to him to be cured of their lameness, deafness, &c.'[23]

Cavanagh willingly submitted himself to scientific examination on several occasions. All sorts of tests were carried out, including his confinement in a specially sealed room. The Catholic clergy denounced him as a charlatan but many of the public believed his claims.[24] He was eventually caught attempting to buy food while in disguise. Gaoled for fraud, he began fasting again in prison in an attempt to prove himself innocent, lasting only nine days before collapsing.[25]

Despite these events, some still saw Cavanagh as an injured man. After his imprisonment, one commentator remarked:

> He was, if I may so express it, a pictorial – an ideal representation of a man that fasted: he narrated all the sensations want of food suggests; its dreamy debility, its languid stupor, its painful suffering, its stage of struggle and suspense,

ending in a victory, where the mind, the conqueror over the baser nature, asserts its proud and glorious supremacy in the triumph of volition; and for this beautiful creation of his brain he is sent to the treadmill, as though, instead of a poet, he had been a pickpocket.[26]

Similarly, Langley, accused of mistreating his wife – indeed, of withholding food from her – countered his accusers by asserting his own place in the realm of the spirit, unshackled from the sordid bodily miasma of his marriage.

Although the doctor sought to elicit sympathy for his plight, his action must have shocked and perplexed his fellow inmates, many of whom had committed crimes deliberately in order to get prison rations. Just before he arrived in Nenagh Gaol the *Tipperary Vindicator* reported that 'the destitute condition of the prisoners when committed is, beyond description, painful; they are principally poor wretches whom hunger and sickness have made fit inmates for an hospital, and who commit petty crimes for the sole purpose of gaining the shelter and food of a prison. Many of them on reaching the gaol are scarcely able to crawl, and it is only by the utmost vigilance and care on the part of the excellent governor . . . that they are restored to health.'[27]

In the end, Langley proved no more saintly than Cavanagh and his fast took its toll on him physically.[28] In fact, Henry Martley attempted to get his client released on bail a week before Christmas, citing 'affidavits that the prisoner's health was very bad, and much affected by the confinement'. 'My difficulty,' explained Judge Moore, to whom the application was made, 'is that the Grand Jury have found bills for murder, and the trial was postponed at the instance of the prisoner. When such is the case he cannot complain if he is kept in custody . . . I will take home all the documents and read them over; but as at present advised I do not think I can grant the application – if I do the bail must be very sufficient.'[29]

The application was unsuccessful. Whatever his condition might have been, Dr Langley would have to endure a further three months in prison before his trial at the Spring Assizes.

16

'Allowing for the frailties of our nature'

Nenagh rectory, situated on Summer Hill at the top of the long, rambling main street, was a good place to observe those arriving and leaving the town. Sitting in the drawing room on a chair of crimson damask, Anna Poe – or 'Nanny' to her family – could see past the scarlet moreen curtains to the street beyond; in the early mornings it bustled with the young boys arriving at the academy next door where her father periodically tested them in Latin and arithmetic, and the traffic arriving from the village of Borrisokane, the neighbouring town to the north; the sound of a trumpet at the neighbouring infantry barracks called 500 hardy highlanders of the 79th Regiment in kilts and tartans out to their morning parade. Across the street, the houses extended in a neat undulating row, a series of residences for members of the gentry and well-off tradesmen. Opposite on a flat green, a plot for a new Protestant church was being laid out that would consolidate the area as 'the most desirable part of Nenagh'.[1]

Anna was the last of the Rev. Mr Poe's unmarried daughters. Although she and her parents often stayed with her brother at the family estate at Solsboro, the four-storey Georgian rectory on Summer Hill made a comfortable town house for the clergyman's daughter. When visitors called, they would be ushered into the drawing room by Mrs Poe to receive cups of tea from the handsome vase-like tea urn.[2] Or in the evening, if invited to dine, they would converse across the dark mahogany dining-room table, the service of gold and white china, and glistening cut glass, illuminated by candlelight. But the recent scandal in the family would have cast a pall over social life.[3]

On Sundays, while accounts of her aunt's disastrous marriage lingered unresolved, Anna listened to her father preach Christian virtue in the parish church on Barrack Street. In the nave was the memorial he had erected to his deceased mother, Blanche, a woman who had brought him up alone as an infant, a veritable saint in his eyes, whose 'faith was ardent, her piety sincere, her temper gentle and for tenderness of her heart, it would indeed be difficult to surpass'. This was an ideal for which Anna would have been expected to strive. But her father, clearly aware of the danger of constructing too ideal a notion of womanhood, qualified his mother's 'well spent life' by placing before the latter phrase, in brackets, the words 'allowing for the frailties of our nature'.[4]

It was a wise caution. Wives, mothers and daughters of clergy increasingly assumed active roles in social and charitable institutions, and were held up as exemplars of respectability in Victorian society.[5] Books on religion, domesticity and charity were often publicized as being by 'a clergyman's daughter', a sure indication of wholesome womanly wisdom.[6] Anna sang in the church choir on Barrack Street, under the direction of Dr Quin's wife, Harriet, who was the regular organist in the Rev. Mr Poe's congregation, rehearsing late into the evening on Saturdays to prepare for the following day's service.[7] She raised funds for the Deaf and Dumb Society and regularly joined her parents at meetings in aid of Protestant orphans who might otherwise have found themselves in the workhouse, and likely helped her mother with the Nenagh Poor Clothing Fund.[8] In 1844, before the outbreak of famine, she had visited the new workhouse in Nenagh with her parents. Not anticipating the misery to come, they had left an approving note in the visitor's book remarking on its comfort and cleanliness.[9]

When famine broke out, genteel young ladies rushed to assist local relief committees. Anna was almost certainly one of the 'ladies of the town' involved in running the soup kitchen on Chapel Lane, which her father praised as having saved 'hundreds of our population' and which was feeding a thousand people daily in December 1846.[10]

All indications are that Anna Poe was a model clergy-man's daughter who ought to have had strong marriage prospects. However, in the autumn of 1849, at thirty-two years of age, Anna's situation altered considerably. Her family was enmeshed in a public scandal, and her uncle's estate was in trouble. In a surviving photograph, she has pinned her long brown hair neatly round her head, the eyes large and soft, the chin gently curved. If, in a solitary moment, she caught a glimpse of herself in the large pier glass over the rectory fireplace, in its antique carved and gilt frame, she might have wondered about the purpose of her pretty face.[11]

Before the disaster of the famine, the ruin of her family's estate, and the scandal of her aunt's marriage, her prospects had been more favourable. The summer of 1844 – the last before the arrival of the potato blight – had been relatively carefree for Nenagh's gentry. On a warm August evening, Anna had attended a grand picnic down by the lake at Drom-ineer with 'all the rank and fashion of the neighbourhood'. It had been cloudy that day but a gentle breeze had blown in from the west, driving off the sultry air, as they promenaded by the water. The tables, laid out in a warehouse of the steam company, were fitted up with laurel, bright colours and Union Jacks for a feast. And when after dinner the music began, Anna had joined 'the bright eyed damsels of Tipperary ... the young, and fair, and beautiful receiving and transmitting so much joy and pleasure', dancing to the lively strains of the band of the 35th Regiment. The younger among the dancers even tried out the fashionable polka, eliciting disapproving frowns from the older generation. Only the ominous tones of Bellini's '*Tutto è sciolto*' ('All is lost now') rising softly across the water foreshadowed the tragedy they did not know was yet to come. They danced with abandon till three in the morning.[12]

The coming of famine meant that there was little of this sort of social life for several years. Anna's only viable suitor during this period had been a man whom she could now not possibly countenance: George Bolton. Towards the end of 1848, in the months before her aunt's death, the solicitor had been noticeably attentive. He lived on the same street and was the court-appointed receiver of her uncle's indebted estate at Solsboro. As such he found himself in a peculiarly advantageous position to pursue his suit. It was his job to receive rents from the Poes' tenants, to generally approve and oversee the management of their lands, and periodically to renew the lease of the estate to the highest bidder. So far, he had favoured the bid of Anna's brother James, her uncle John's heir, allowing the Poes to continue to reside in the house despite their indebtedness to a Mr Crofts of Cork, who had pursued his claims against them through the courts.[13] But this courtesy could easily be withdrawn should relations with Bolton sour.

Anna may have found this obligation to Mr Bolton

galling. Estates in receivership were notoriously poorly run, left 'under the care of the worst possible landlord', according to one contemporary critic,[14] and Bolton had dealt with the Poes' tenants harshly, evicting a number of families in the August of 1848. The *Limerick Reporter* decried 'the estate of the Rev. Mr Poe', and 'the appalling number of 104 human beings cast upon the world without the shelter of a roof'.[15]

It wasn't until September 1849, after several years of the potato blight, that Nenagh's gentry ventured out once more – for a subscription ball at the courthouse to dance to the music of the 79th Highland depot band. But by that stage the scandal of her aunt's alleged adultery and death had been widely publicized, and Anna and her family were notable only by their absence. Mr Bolton, perhaps conscious of having offended the Poe ladies in representing the interests of Dr Langley at the coroner's inquest, attended with a Miss Rowan, a daughter of a local solicitor, who was several years younger than Anna. In any case, Anna would have had little polite to say to him should they have met there.[16]

But there was something more to keep Anna Poe enclosed safely behind the door of her father's house and away from the gaze of strangers. She had information she had long tried to conceal, but which she now knew would have to be made public were there to be any justice for her aunt.

17

'How say you, Charles Langley?'

Although so many disastrous years had come and gone, the first three weeks of March 1850 saw the more prosperous farmers busy sowing their potatoes, peas, beans, spring wheat and oats, and slaughtering livestock in hope of a better season ahead. Clear spring weather cast a light frost over the ground, which had, according to the farming news, 'loosed the earth about the roots of the winter-sown wheats and vetches, and in the absence of rain, [settled] the earth about their tender roots'. The solid ground even proved suitable for racing in Galway, and seasonal ploughing matches were organized for 'hale and brawny' farmers attended by great crowds of spectators.[1]

On the morning of Thursday, 21 March 1850, the *Irish Farmers' Gazette* warned of unfavourable hours for the changes of the next moon. Within days a darkening weather front would bring severe frost and a late covering of snow. There was already a chill in the air as the prison officers escorted Charles Langley from his dark cell into the wide, empty space of the exercise courtyard enclosed between the tall radial blocks of the gaol. This place had been his home for eight months. Now, finally, he was to go on trial.[2]

From the courtyard of the gaol, police constables led the doctor down a flight of limestone steps into a dank underground corridor, specially constructed to keep accused persons from the eyes of the curious public prior to a trial. Their footsteps echoed under the brick-vaulted roof, the floor damp and puddled where water seeped through bare stone walls. At the end of the passage, an iron gate swung open and a further flight of steps brought the prisoner and his attendants up to a small holding cell directly beneath the courthouse.[3]

Shortly before ten o'clock, crowds of onlookers began to arrive, climbing the short flight of steps beneath the imposing Ionic portico. Those who pushed past the police constables at the door filed leftwards into the corridor that encircled the principal courtroom, passing through a door to a narrow timber staircase up to the grand gallery overlooking the semi-octagonal space below. They found seats in the tiers of low benches behind the gallery's tall classical columns, which framed perfect views over the panelled theatre with its witness box, judge's bench and jury box.[4]

A few minutes after ten, Dr Langley was led into the dock. He bowed respectfully to Judge Nicholas Ball, sitting behind the high bench under a broad timber canopy. Now fifty-nine years of age, Ball had been educated by Jesuits in England, and elected a Liberal MP for Clonmel in 1836. At Westminster he famously kept his mouth shut sufficiently to be briefly made Attorney General for Ireland and later a judge of the Common Pleas – only the second Catholic to hold such a post since the reign of James II.[5]

Journalists noted that the prisoner appeared physically fit, despite his long incarceration and extended period of fasting. He had crafted his Christ-like image carefully while in gaol, and a month previously the Limerick artist James Worrall had been summoned to his cell to capture it.[6] Just when Dr Langley needed it most, though, prison officials had forced him to shave the enormous beard and moustache that he had cultivated throughout the entire period of his confinement. He retained only his long hair: jet black and parted in the middle, 'falling in long locks over the collar of his coat'.[7] Dressed entirely in black, he stood in the dock, visibly 'excited' and his face 'flushed', according to one witness.[8] Another observed, more sensationally, that 'his face was purple with anxiety, his eyes bloodshot, and the veins in his forehead appeared almost bursting'.[9]

The charges were read out. The indictment, which contained five separate counts, stated that the doctor had 'confined the deceased against her will . . . in a certain cold, unwholesome, and unhealthy lodging', 'gave her food, medicine and drink, which he knew to have been injurious to her body and health', and that 'not having the fear of God before his eyes, knowingly, wilfully, and of his malice prepense, killed and murdered his wife, Eleanor Langley'.

Although the servants had already attested at the coroner's inquest that the doctor's ill-treatment of his wife had begun in October 1848, the indictment framed the murder between two dates: 5 December 1848 and 1 May 1849, the date of her death. The earlier date appears somewhat arbitrary – the inquest evidence showed that the doctor changed his behaviour some months earlier than this – but may reflect an attempt to pinpoint her confinement to her room. During these five months, according to the indictment, 'the said Eleanor Langley became mortally sick, weak, distempered, and diseased in body' and 'lingered' until her death.[10]

'How say you, Charles Langley,' enquired the Clerk of the Crown, 'guilty or not guilty?'[11]

The doctor responded in a tremulous voice, 'Not guilty.'

As he said the words, wrote one journalist, he 'extended his body over the dock, viewing the Judge, Jury, and spectators with wistful glances and deep anxiety'.[12]

The judge explained that, although the Grand Jury had submitted a charge of murder against him, the petty jury hearing the case could still find Dr Langley guilty of the lesser charge of manslaughter if it saw fit.

Mr James Scott QC, for the Crown, addressed the jury next. A wizened figure who had practised on the Leinster Circuit – which in those days included Tipperary – for some forty-four years,[13] he was familiar to the defendant, who had been a medical witness in one of Scott's successful murder prosecutions in the same courtroom five years earlier. Several of the jury members from that trial, part of a select list of property owners, now sat in judgement of Langley.[14]

'Gentlemen,' began Scott, 'this is a most important, awful, unusual charge and trial – a case of a novel, peculiar and appalling character; and most melancholy it indeed is, in its details.'

He rehearsed the charges against the doctor: his expulsion of his wife to poor lodgings; the coldness of her room; the bad quality of her food; 'the brown bread and salt meat while subject to the disease of dysentery', which was 'almost poison to a woman labouring under her complaint'; the suspicious circumstances of her supposed infidelity. All the prosecution had to do, he said, was to prove the doctor's negligence in providing proper care for his wife.

'If Dr Langley accelerated the death of his wife even for one day, one hour, and by anything that was negligent and careless,' he told the jury, 'he is responsible for it; if he did so to shorten her life he is a murderer.'

Scott referred to an earlier case, *The Queen* v. *Marryat*, in which a man had been charged with causing the death of his elderly wife. The judge in that trial had decreed that 'if a man wilfully and grossly neglected to provide for his wife and that by refusing to do so he contemplated her death, he would be guilty of murder, but if her death was only occasioned by culpable neglect he would be only guilty of manslaughter.'[15]

In the earlier case, the defendant had been found guilty of murder and hanged. The present situation was exactly the same, argued Scott. The jury should disregard the notion that because Mrs Langley was ill, her husband could not be held responsible for her death.

There was much evidence, originally heard at the coroner's inquest, that would be grist to Scott's mill in the murder prosecution, but he began by proposing to expose the 'state of the prisoner's mind' at the time of his wife's death, using an entirely new piece of evidence.

He picked up a letter from his desk. The author of the letter was Dr Charles Langley. Its recipient was Edward Nixon, the Dublin wine merchant who was married to Ellen Langley's sister Mary Anne. It was dated 23 April 1849, little more than a week before Ellen's death. Edward Nixon had himself died just days after the inquest, and it would appear that the letter had fallen into the hands of Mary Anne, who submitted it to the Grand Jury as evidence against the doctor.[16]

The letter, Scott argued, revealed Langley's 'deadly hatred' of his wife and callous disregard for her life. Reading it aloud, he brought the courtroom back to the last week of April 1849, when Ellen had just returned to Barrack Street from her lodgings in Pound Street.

Langley began the letter by responding to some advice Nixon had given him on how to settle financial matters between himself and his wife. The doctor was reluctant to allow her any more money than the interest he made on her modest dowry, but had been advised that improving the offer might help induce her to agree to the divorce he wanted. Although Nixon, as Mary Anne's husband, might have been expected to take Ellen's side, it appears that he and Dr Langley were on cordial terms and that he was trying to act as an honest broker. Langley, for his part, seems to have been focused on strengthening his own hand in the financial negotiation, while not bothering to hide his cruel intentions towards his wife. He can't have imagined that the letter would end up being read to the jury at his own trial for murder.

'Dear Nixon,' he wrote, 'As you met me so friendly in this most dreadful unpleasant business, I think it but due to you to inform you how matters are at present. On Friday last, when sending her the weekly sum agreed on, I sent her a message to come up to my office for the purpose of proposing an increase, as you suggested, of £30 a year, and for her to sign a consent of divorce.'

Dr Langley reported that Ellen, under advice from her family at Solsboro and her brother Tom Poe, had rejected the offer as insufficient, looking instead for £60 per annum. He also claimed that, under legal advice the Poes had taken from solicitors in Dublin, Ellen had done something quite unexpected.

Those who had been following the case now heard a possible explanation of why Ellen had gone back to the house where she had been so long incarcerated. Langley told Nixon that it had to do with her financial maintenance. The Poes' solicitor had advised Ellen that only if she was physically *forced* out of the house could she make a legal claim for proper financial support.

On the Friday evening, the doctor's letter continued, after Ellen had rejected the offer of £30 a year,

I went to Limerick to bring my sister to remain with me, and judge of my surprise on Saturday, when we arrived, to find in my absence [Ellen] had come and taken possession. She told us, the poor fool, she had done so under the advice of the Solsboro family, and that as I was a hasty passionate man, I would put her out forcibly, as she went in the first instance quietly, and of her own accord, in which case I would be unable to allow her a good maintenance, which she could not recover without she was made get up out of a sick bed and forcibly expelled from under my roof.

It was brave of Ellen to move back into Barrack Street, but not entirely suprising, given the grimness of her situation in Pound Street. There was, indeed, legal precedent for the view that if a man deserted or ill-treated his wife, a court of equity could compel him to provide for her from her own property.[17]

Ellen, on Langley's account, behaved guilelessly in revealing to her husband the chain of events she hoped to provoke by moving back to Barrack Street. Langley, not lacking in guile, happily thwarted this plan. 'I did not fall into the trap that was laid for me by those wily hypocrites. I at once ordered her up to her garret, where she shall live and die, sooner than I shall allow myself to be so imposed on as to give a bitch of her kind £60 a year, when I draw but £21 17s 6d on her account.'

Relishing the hand he had just played, he said his wife would live a life of misery unto death unless a financial settlement agreeable to himself was reached.

'So you may tell Tom Poe,' he continued, '[that] I will never give her a fraction more than the interest of her own money, which, if she and her friends are not satisfied with, she may stay where she is and drag out a miserable existence during the remainder of her life.'[18]

In Langley's eyes, his wife and her relations – themselves desperately short of funds – were plotting against him. Despite having an annual rental income from the Donnybrook estate of £523, William Poe, like his father before him, owed money to several creditors. The following January, these creditors attempted to force the sale of the estate – though it was so calamitous an economic time no buyer could afford to buy it at a reasonable price and the sale had to be withdrawn.[19] Ellen's surviving brother, Tom, had money problems too. He had owed his father's estate £600 on his death in 1830, and had spent several years in and out of court, battling his wife's family for her marriage settlement.[20]

The Solsboro Poes were also in financial difficulty. Land-owners, unable to acquire rents in a time of mass destitution, were likely defaulting the tithe payments necessary to provide the Rev. Mr Poe's full £600 salary.[21] In May 1849, as the workhouse struggled to gather funds, he applied for a 150 per cent increase in his income as Protestant chaplain there (from £20 to £50 a year). Although only 1 per cent of the 3,000 or so inmates were Protestant, he argued that the risk of having to enter the workhouse at all was so high that it demanded better remuneration.[22]

Although he once had expectations of inheriting Solsboro from his childless older brother, John, much of its value had been squandered. An acquaintance later commented of John, 'Being childless, he lived a careless, thoughtless life, and far beyond his means – as was the fashion of the day – and consequently went to the usual nameless place that spendthrifts generally go to.'[23] Perennially short of money, as early as 1820 he had been listed as one of the largest tithe defaulters in the district – a strange irony given his younger brother's subsequent indebtedness on this count.[24] During the 1840s he was forced to lease Solsboro and its 140-acre demesne to his nephew, James Jocelyn Poe, who earned his living working as a land agent, and would be compelled by his creditors to sell the estate in 1852.[25]

Dr Langley might not have known the full extent of the Poes' financial difficulties, but it is likely that he had a pretty good idea of their situation. 'They had a bad case to extort from me £60 a year, and it was a most infamous trap for them to lay for me to get me in to the power of the law,' he wrote to Nixon. 'They have had their advice from Dublin, I understand, but the horrid old rat has fallen into her own trap, and she would now sooner be back in her lodgings (though bad they were), on her shilling a day.'

In response Langley withdrew the offer of £30. He told Nixon that he would only agree to provide her with a minimal sum.

'If Tom Poe comes down, and her friends, I am satisfied to give no opposition to a divorce, and will sign a deed of separation in a legal form, she will have the interest of her money £21 17s 6d, but not the principal. God knows if it is God's will I should survive her, which I trust I may, I have earned it right well after living with such a prostitute for over 17 years.'

Langley attempted to substantiate this negative view of Ellen by reference to the alleged encounter with Thomas Pound and to two relationships he asserted she had had before marrying him. Langley claimed he had been deceived as to his wife's true character and the Poes should therefore share the financial burden in maintaining her: 'Let them that pawned her on me give her a little assistance,' he wrote, 'towards making her somewhat more comfortable than she can ever expect to be under my roof . . . May his reverence and his wife have the luck they so richly deserve.'

Langley ascribed Ellen's illness not just to the squalor of her lodgings, but to her own moral degeneracy. 'I wonder myself how she can survive her disgrace,' he wrote. 'Her feelings, if she has any, must be in an awful state.'

It was a striking proposition, and one which would resurface later in the trial: the idea that immorality and guilt might manifest themselves in a physical disorder. Langley painted his wife's moral degeneration in rich detail for his correspondent, so there should be no ambiguity about it. Of her liaison with Thomas Pound, he wrote that 'the real truth of her last crime has come to light'. This was the final proof of her depraved character. 'God knows,' he wrote, 'I have been a martyr, and a most deeply injured person . . . She knew that anything she was guilty of before marriage would not enable me to get a divorce, and well knowing that after I had become aware of her acts of prostitution she never could be happy with me, she had recourse to adultery with my servant man, and was the first herself to confess it, in order that I would turn her out and allow a maintenance.'[26]

Regarding her early life, his allegations concerned two men: a George Kingsley and a Dr Keane, 'with whom she was common before I ever saw her'. The papers he had waved in front of the jury on the second day of the inquest – which he claimed contained evidence of his wife's culpability – likely consisted of signed affidavits he had gathered. These papers are only hinted at in the press reports, as they were never entered into evidence; but Eliza Rohan, under questioning from Bolton, had said she was not present when her mistress 'signed any declaration to Dr Langley about her previous life'.[27] It is possible that, having had the declaration formally drawn up, Langley had persuaded his distraught wife to sign it. However, no such document – if it existed – would appear at the trial.

The identities of Ellen's putative premarital lovers are obscure. A Dr Keane was one of several doctors working in Nenagh in the 1830s and is mentioned as taking part in a steeplechase with Ellen's brother in 1834, riding a horse named Impudence. George Kingsley may have been a member of a well-known medical family of that name in north Tipperary during these years, but no clear figure of that name can be identified as her contemporary.[28]

In April, after Ellen's expulsion, the Poes had contested Dr Langley's account of his wife's adultery, claiming privately that he had drugged her and paid Pound to sleep with her. At the coroner's inquest in May this suspicion had led to the cross-examination of medical witnesses by Mr Dillon regarding the possible use of Spanish fly to encourage Ellen's adultery.

The court now heard, in listening to Scott read out the letter to Nixon, Langley's vehement rejections of this accusation:

> It was a most infamous story to invent that I had bribed him and drugged her. She never got anything from me during the time she was upstairs, but a mug of tea in the morning with bread and butter, which I poured out of the tea pot in the presence of the servant maid, and a cut of meat at dinner, which I cut off the joint, also in her presence, and which she took up to the room at once . . .

After this rebuttal, Langley took aim at the various other charges against him, starting with the claim that he had suborned a sexual advance by Thomas Pound on his wife.

Suppose for argument I had bribed him, do you not think as a reasonable man, I would have had witnesses on the watch to catch him in the act, but no, she it was who was the person to confess it to me. Then again suppose I did bribe him, was she not a consenting party – why did she not call out. We were all in bed in the house – could she not have rapped – I slept just under her, and yet Tom Poe [her brother] said it looked very like a trap. Poor woman, if she had been a proper and well conducted person, she would not have been caught in my trap, as she expressed it . . .

Ellen's alleged failure to cry out was an unconvincing point to stress in the face of the charge that he had drugged her, but this does not seem to have occurred to him.

There was another element of the letter that would prove more damning: his account of his treatment of Pound the following day. He wrote, 'as for bribery, the moment I heard of the affair I turned the ruffian out of my house. Does that look like bribery, or that I was in his power?'

This claim of anger towards Pound was of great importance to Scott, as it had already been convincingly contradicted at the coroner's inquest. According to Pound's testimony, the doctor had through various means facilitated an intimacy between his wife and the servant. He dismissed him only after the event due to his fear of gossip, even going as far as to present him with a new suit to show there were no hard feelings between them. Later in the day, Dr Cahalan, under cross-examination, would recall to the court his surprise at finding Pound still in the house, even though Langley had just tried to convince him his wife had slept with the servant. 'I told Dr Langley I wondered he would keep a ruffian like him in the house after such an occurrence as he detailed to me.'[29]

The implication was clear for all to see: Langley had lied in his account of the incident to Nixon. This, in turn, cast doubt over every claim that he made in the Nixon letter, and over his credibility in general.

In the letter, Langley placed the blame for the break-up of his marriage on the suspicions cultivated by his wife's sister, Mary Anne: none other than the wife of his correspondent, Edward Nixon. He added a line addressed as though to her: 'Oh Mary all you have to answer for, but for you we would still be united and happy.' Already in April, while his wife lay in her garret room, Langley was worrying about how these suspicions might develop. 'I am sure if she dies [Mary Anne] and her friends will say I poisoned her,' he wrote to Nixon. He revealed the steps he had taken to counter the idea: '. . . for Mary Anne's peace of mind, I wish to inform you . . . that I got Dr Quin's prescription made up at the apothecary's, and everything she gets as medicine – among which I can't put wine – is given to her through him, and by him alone.'[30]

Langley's concern for 'Mary Anne's peace of mind' does not seem to have run very deep. He was aware of his wife's grave condition and did not pretend that it was a source of worry to him. 'She cannot live long,' he told Nixon. 'On the day before she left her lodgings a child died of cholera opposite to her. She came to my house on Saturday labouring under a very severe bowel complaint and yesterday when I heard of it I sent for Doctor Quin. I could not venture to prescribe for her myself. He saw her again this day, and I would not at all be surprised if it ran into cholera; he is of [the] opinion that she is in a very dangerous state.'

There was, to Dr Langley's mind, no doubting where the blame for this should lie. 'She may thank her sister Poe and her [sister's] son [James Jocelyn Poe] and daughter [Anna] for the awful and terrific end she has come to. If she dies (and to be candid with you I hope she may) she may justly lay her death at their door.'

For the observers in the courtroom, listening in attentive silence, it seems likely that what registered from this passage in the letter was not Dr Langley's disavowal of responsibility for Ellen's condition. What would have come across more memorably was his openly stated desire for her death, an admission which provoked loud hissing from the crowd.[31]

18

'The book of fate'

Mr Scott, prosecuting, had further damning evidence of Langley's attitude towards his wife. He picked up from his desk another letter for the jury to consider.

Written in Langley's own hand, and dated 26 December 1848, it was addressed to a person whose name until this point had not yet appeared in any public notice of the case, a person whose identity had been concealed at every turn from the public.

Mr Scott read the letter aloud.

'"My own still dear and fondly attached Nanny . . ."' he began.

The paper on which Langley had written the letter was edged in funereal black. This was, he wrote, 'emblematic of the deep sorrow and affliction I feel at the unhappy and now uncertain position in which I am placed'. He continued: 'The loss for ever of no friend on earth would cause me to mourn so deeply as I must for ever do, if I lose her to whom I have become so truly, so devotedly attached – her in whom all my hopes centre – her on whose love and affection all my earthly happiness now depends.'[1]

'Nanny' was Anna Poe: Ellen Langley's 32-year-old niece.

The letter charted the dramatic end to their affair and the doctor's deteriorating relationship with his wife. It was almost certainly this sensational new evidence, along with the Nixon letter, that had prompted the Grand Jury in August 1849 to change the charges to murder.

The relationship between Anna Poe and Dr Langley had lasted about a year, from December 1847 to December 1848. The six-page letter, which Mr Scott read aloud in court, was written in the aftermath of its dissolution and charted in detail the doctor's feelings towards both Anna and his wife.

'Twelve months ago if I remember right,' the doctor had written, 'we spent that night at Walker's; we were then only friends; now alas! What are we? What may we be in twelve months again? We may then be one – God grant it. I wish I could look into the book of fate.'[2]

The Walkers were family friends who resided on Summer Hill, close to the rectory. Adam Walker was a prominent land agent and Justice of the Peace; his daughter, Margaret, was engaged to be married to the Rev. Mr Poe's young curate, Benjamin Bewley. The curate was likely a witness to the growing intimacy between Dr Langley and Anna, which may explain his reluctance to hear Ellen speak on 'worldly matters' in the days before her death.[3] Their meeting at the Walkers' that night predated the start of their relationship. Casting his mind back, Langley couldn't quite remember whether Anna had attended the dinner separately or whether she had accompanied him and Ellen, returning afterwards to spend the night at their house on Barrack Street. The arrangement suggested the kind of friendship that might exist between close relatives.

Whenever it began, the court heard that the doctor and his wife's niece had carried on their affair secretly for several months in 1848, finding opportunities to be together. 'We acted our part well,' wrote Langley of their subterfuge.[4]

Initially there had been romantic strolls, and a trip away to Dublin in October 1848, where they found themselves free from the usual constraints. 'My goodness when I do think of the nice walks we have had together,' wrote Langley '– our trip to Dublin – to St Patrick's [Cathedral] – to Jenny Lind [an opera singer] – to Kingstown – to the Mesmeric – and all the happiness of the Shelbourne, and compare my present state, how wretched and dejected I become.'[5]

The Shelbourne was the country's most fashionable hotel. Bright with gas lighting, its private drawing rooms 'warm with conviviality', the Shelbourne was 'rich in associations and possibilities', according to the novelist Elizabeth Bowen, who wrote a short history of the hotel in the following century.[6] Kingstown, a short distance by train from the city centre, was a resort frequented by wealthy visitors to Dublin; afternoon strolls in the sea air offered a welcome retreat from the crowded streets. Its view over Dublin bay had captivated William Thackeray during the 1840s, who observed it in the evening 'rich with a thousand gorgeous hues of sunset, as smiling and delightful as can be conceived . . . brilliant, sunny, enlivening'.[7]

Soon the increasing familiarity between Dr Langley and his wife's niece began to attract attention. Both of them noticed that Anna's father had begun watching them closely, and in December 1848 a plan for another trip to Dublin had been unexpectedly foiled. Although it is hard to be certain of the precise timeline, it appears that on the 17th of that month, a Sunday, they were to dine with a mutual acquaintance, Jane Mundell, in the company of several other friends, including Anna's older brother James.

Jane Mundell was a wealthy young widow recently returned with her infant son from India, where her husband, Captain Mundell, had died from cholera in January 1845.[8] Their wedding in 1843 had been performed in Nenagh parish church by the Rev. Mr Poe.[9] Jane's father, who resided in Nenagh, also owned Killiney Castle, which commanded a view of the stunning coastline just south of Dublin, and it may have been here that the group intended to meet.[10]

An excursion to Dublin, beyond the eyes of Anna's parents, was full of romantic promise. However, it seems that when Langley, who was travelling separately, reached Dublin, he realized Anna had been left behind and would not be joining the party.

Disappointed when she didn't appear, he had gone to St Patrick's Cathedral. There he found the pew where once they had sat side by side at Sunday service. Clutching a locket containing her hair, he thought only of her. 'Your image never left my mind,' he wrote, 'and I opened my shirt and I actually kissed your curl; it was the only thing I had to bring you, as it were, into my presence.'[11]

The letter is vague on the exact dates of his communications with Anna, but he appears to have been staying at the Hibernian Hotel on Dawson Street when he next heard from her. Over the course of a few days, she had written three letters to him, directed to various addresses but eventually catching up with him in Dublin. The first, written on a Saturday morning, a week earlier, was the passionate epistle of a lover, familiar and intimate. The second, written that same day, following a visit by Ellen to Solsboro, was very different, as was the third, written a few days later. Everything had changed. Anna's tone was ice cold. She was, she wrote, breaking off their relationship, and she ordered him not to respond.

Perplexed by the alteration in her affections, he compared the two letters written on the same day.

'I cannot bring myself to think they were written by the same person,' he wrote. 'What in the name of God had occurred during the day, to make you change your mind . . . I am thunderstruck and most wretched.'[12]

He recalled that she had been frosty to him when they had encountered each other out riding in Tipperary the previous Monday. At the time he had attributed her coldness to something he had said to her the day before. But the contents of her letter made clear that this was more than a lovers' tiff. 'You have stated that I treated [Ellen] with the greatest harshness and cruelty; that I am in fact trying to kill her, all of which I deny.' He was horrified to see himself so vilified. 'How dreadfully soon you have turned round to condemn poor unfortunate me.' His worst unkindness to his wife, he protested, was in not speaking to her.[13]

He suspected that Ellen's interference had forced the Rev. Mr Poe to forbid their meeting. 'Are you not afraid to be seen driving with me, or speaking to me,' he asked her, 'and has not your father forbade [you] even to dine with me, tho' accompanied by your brother? These are all the effects of Ellen's talking, and therefore you must try and make some little excuse for my feelings towards her.'[14]

Aware that she possessed some power over him, Anna had sought, in her second and third letters, to improve conditions for her aunt. Langley quoted Anna's stern words back to her. 'If you act in this way [i.e. improve your behaviour],' she had written, 'you will show me I have some influence over you but if not I must give up all intimacy with you . . . I am fully determined that unless I see peace and harmony established, I never will hold any communication with you.'

Dr Langley's response to this plea revealed to the court the extent of his antipathy for his wife, a hatred that surpassed even his passion for her niece:

I would do anything I could to make you happy, but in that instance I cannot comply as you wish. I grieve from the bottom of my heart that such is the case, but I cannot help it. I cannot command my feelings; they have been deeply, vitally, and sorely wounded, and by one who should have been the last to do it. My mind is irrevocably made up – she must be content with the lot she has chosen, so there is no use in ever writing to me again on that subject, or in speaking to me.[15]

Following his receipt of Anna's letters, Langley went to the Theatre Royal, where two months earlier, in October 1848, he and Anna had heard the famous Swedish opera singer Jenny Lind. 'How I did wish for you [there],' he wrote, 'will we ever be there again?' On his return to the theatre he was distracted by these memories throughout the performance. 'I sat in the pit. My attention was divided between the play and the seat in the undress circle where she I loved sat.' He must have recalled the fevered atmosphere of their earlier visit, the ambience heightened by the music of the opera. One Dublin reviewer, present at Lind's performance as Marie in Donizetti's *La figlia del reggimento* the same week, described her 'exquisite soprano notes, so searching and clear, so bell-like and impressive', the crowd 'gay and animated', the rapturous applause and encores.[16]

The courtroom listened in silence as Scott recounted how memories of her singing now pained the doctor. 'I am sometimes almost tempted to curse the day I first heard Jenny Lind; but why should I be so wicked as to do so? . . . There is a fatality over us,' he mused, 'and over which we, poor mortals, have no control.'[17]

The couple's visit to the Theatre Royal in October 1848 was unlikely to have been a spontaneous one. Jenny Lind was an international superstar and tickets for the upper circles at the Theatre Royal that week had cost between £1 and £1 10s – the present-day purchasing power of several hundred pounds – and even in that year of famine, Ireland's urban elite clamoured to buy them up. Some attended on every night she performed, such was the mania she inspired. The takings at the box office were 'never equalled before or since', remarked a historian of the theatre. Lind was paid £500 a night, five times what the doctor had earned in a year at his post in the dispensary. It was the most anticipated series of concerts of the decade.[18]

Believing that Ellen was the source of the Rev. Mr Poe's suspicions, Langley's resentment against his wife only increased. 'My aversion to my poor and unfortunate Ellen,' he confessed to Anna in his letter of 26 December 1848, 'has become now unconquerable. She has brought misery on herself, and what is more she has brought just as great on me . . . She has injured me vitally and deeply.'[19]

In one of her letters Anna had charged Langley's friend William Tuthill, a Nenagh solicitor, with spreading the rumour of their affair. But Langley was keen to prove this wrong. He recounted to Anna, in his reply, a conversation he had had with Tuthill while breakfasting at the solicitor's Dublin residence in Fitzwilliam Place.[20] The Tuthills were closely related to the Langleys and seem to have known something of their difficult marriage. (At the coroner's inquest, Dillon had quizzed Dr Quin about sending Ellen in a carriage to the Tuthill family home at River View, four miles north of Nenagh, after being beaten by her husband.[21]) During this conversation, wrote Langley, William had claimed that it was Ellen who had first told him of her husband's extramarital affair.

'[William] said what a terrible fool Ellen appeared to him to be,' wrote Langley, 'and he went on to detail to me, as a very good joke, a conversation Ellen had with him in the country, and said he could not help laughing at the extreme folly and very great unlikelihood of such a story. He treated it all as most absurd.'[22]

Langley told Anna that when he confronted Ellen angrily about this she denied the accusation of any indiscretion, protesting that it was in fact William Tuthill who had spoken to her first 'and said it was all over the town, and that he had heard it spoken of at Brundley's [Hotel]'.[23]

If it was being discussed at Brundley's, then many of the people in the courtroom would have heard about it long before Dr Langley's letter to Anna was read out. The hotel, on Castle Street in Nenagh, was a meeting place of the local gentry, visiting professionals, and officers of the British regiments stationed in the town. The Ormond Hunt dined together there during the 1840s, enjoying 'wines and viands . . . of the choicest description', and British officers in the new cricket club would gather there in the summer of 1849 to toast the royal family over a sumptuous dinner.[24] It was there that in 1844 the Rev. Mr Poe had presented an address to an outgoing British regiment to express 'sincere and deep regret' at their departure.[25] The hotel's owner, David Brundley, had 'made it famous', according to one of the town's early-twentieth-century historians, who remarked that it was 'well known throughout the south of Ireland'.[26]

Langley informed Anna that when he put Ellen's claim to Tuthill, he denied having heard rumours at Brundley's or mentioning them to Anna, insisting 'it was Ellen who first spoke to him on the subject; and in order to put the saddle on the right horse, and to convince both you and me that

E[llen] had wronged him, he determined to put down on paper the conversation that passed between Ellen and him, in the form of an affidavit, and in my presence, swear before a magistrate in College Green, to the truth of it.' So determined was Langley that Anna should believe her aunt to be the source of the rumour (and potentially her ruin) that he enclosed a copy of this affidavit in his letter to her, insisting that 'there are sentiments which I defy [Tuthill] to have invented if Ellen had not mentioned them to him . . . she ha[s] often thrown the very same words in my face.'[27]

He asked Anna to return the affidavit to him. In his mind it constituted an important part of his defence, just as he would later secure an affidavit from his servant man attesting to his wife's infidelity. Although aware that he and Anna were in reality the guilty parties, he saw himself as a victim of his wife's treachery:

> I solemnly declare that I never mentioned a word to [a] mortal of our unfortunate and fatal attachment, so that any publicity [it] has got has been through her means only and through her alone . . . every word therein expressed is hers not his, as that in my mind, she has been the guilty person, and my Heavens, what a story to go tell a stranger. I am sure the Bennetts, the Bourchiers, and the Burrs, as well as many others in town, have been told the same, and no wonder then that you should hear me spoken of everywhere you go.[28]

The Bennetts, the Bourchiers and the Burrs were among a small group of tight-knit Nenagh families of English derivation, most of whom had intermarried at some point. The Bennetts lived at Riverston on the outskirts of Nenagh. Ellen's nephew James Jocelyn Poe had married John Bennett's sister in 1843, and the family's acquaintance included Tom Lefroy – Jane Austen's one-time romantic hope – who would stay with them when his legal work took him to Nenagh, where he also had an income from a small estate.[29] John Bennett, the head of the family, sat on the board of the dispensary during Langley's years working there.[30] The Bourchiers were Jane Mundell's family. Her father, John Bourchier, was a landowner and treasurer of the Savings Bank, who had also pursued a career in the law, and had houses in Nenagh and Dublin. The Burr family, wealthy merchants and brewers, were Dr Langley's landlords on Barrack Street.[31] Any hint of impropriety threatened the doctor's standing among this close-knit group of local families. Such a rumour, once it got started, could do great damage.

Ellen had crossed a line that, in her husband's eyes, no woman should ever dare to cross. Writing to Anna Poe, he concluded: '... never will I forget such ungrateful and unkind conduct towards one whom she was bound to love and cherish, and over whose faults she should have thrown the cloak of secrecy.'[32]

Scott also read a passage of the letter that showed Dr Langley's desire to rekindle his relationship with Anna. Of his recent trip to the theatre in Dublin, he wrote, 'Had you been there with me you would have liked the acting and the different amusements I think even better than Jenny Lind. They were delightful. If ever we two shall be one, which God grant may be the case, and that soon (I only reiterate an expression in one of your dear letters to me), we will go to the pit, it is by far the best part of the house for seeing and hearing.'

He flaunted other amusements before her in the hope of

reviving the spirit of their former excursions together. The day after his trip to the theatre, a Tuesday, still in pursuit of distraction, Langley had gone to see the magician John Henry Anderson, aka the Wizard of the North: ' . . . never was I more pleased or astonished, but the more wonders I see the more I desire to have my own darling sitting beside me to see them also. He will be in Limerick I understand shortly. O, but for Ellen what a nice little party could we not make up to go and hear him, but that is now like everything else knocked in the head.'[33]

He was accompanied that evening by Edward Tuthill, likely a brother of William's, and his 'nice amiable wife'. He poured out his anger about Ellen's rumours to them. 'Mr Tuthill says, and I perfectly agree with him, what a dreadful thing it is to be married to a fool. Such he considers my poor unfortunate Ellen . . . but she is a dangerous fool moreover, for what mischief has she not caused by her foolish tongue?' He regretted not telling Tuthill that if he came to dine with him in Nenagh, he should not have to see Ellen. 'He will never put his feet in the same house where she is,' he wrote.[34]

He painted a picture of the life they might one day have together in his home town of Limerick, which he tried to measure favourably against Dublin: ' . . . there is Cruise's here that would remind you of the Shelbourne,' he wrote of the city's finest hotel. St Mary's Cathedral, where he attended Christmas service with his sister Lydia, he characterized as 'the St Patrick's of Limerick'. The service and anthem there were 'just as good as in Dublin', he insisted. 'I wish I knew if you were in want of anything that I might bring it to you from here, where there are, I assure you, very nice shops, and quite as good as in Dublin.'[35]

The letter painted a picture of a man distracted by life's

pleasures, superficial and vain in his concerns. While staying in Limerick, from where he wrote to Anna, he had paraded about the streets in a phaeton pulled by liveried ponies.

'You can't think how admired the poneys [*sic*] have been,' he told her. 'Ladies and also gentlemen stopped on the flagway to look at them, and admire them.' He revelled in the attention. 'Perhaps you will say it was me they were admiring; but it was the poneys, I assure you.'

When extravagant facial hair came into vogue, Langley had not been slow in cultivating a new moustache and whiskers. Later he cut them off but had immediately regretted it. 'It is quite astonishing how many people tell me I have spoiled myself very much by cutting off my moustachios; that they would scarcely know me; and that I ought to let them grow again – and they are friends who have said so. I intend, if ever I shall be happy again, to let them grow, and hide my mouth, which is the ugliest feature in my face. The whiskers I shall let grow for your sake, the moustachios for my own.'[36]

During the weeks of their romance he had been flatteringly attentive to her needs, whatever form they took. 'I hope you liked the way your boots were done,' he wrote, 'you need not ask me what they cost, as I won't tell you; if they please I am satisfied. Did Dan do your shoes as well; I sent you soles for them.' Anxious to win back her affections, he promised to go shopping for her in Limerick: 'I will tell my sister I wish to make a young lady of my acquaintance a little present,' he said, and later, having returned from a two-hour jaunt round the town, reassured her that it was Lydia who made the 'few small trifling purchases', which he hoped she would find acceptable. He had previously bought Anna an item of silk – something so feminine he could not even recall the name of it – and had sent it to her as a surprise. 'I have heard you say you would sport it on Christmas Day. Did you wear it, dearest, and did you think of your fond and devoted Charles while putting it on?' Whatever it was, Ellen had noticed her niece wearing it on a former occasion. 'That was one of the causes of [her] jealousy,' he wrote sourly.[37]

He knew they had to be careful now not to arouse further suspicion. His letter outlined his movements over the coming days, and he urged Anna to return Tuthill's affidavit by post or by person, along with a message for him. 'No one save myself opens the hall door,' he assured her, 'the key is always in my room, and the moment the postman knocks I go myself and receive from his hands the letter.'[38] Getting his own letter to her would be more problematic. 'I think I will watch for you going or coming back from the singing on Saturday, and send Thomas after you with it, saying it is a small parcel I brought you from Dublin, and which I forgot to send you.'[39]

He tried to make Anna see that her aunt was 'the author of all [their] unhappiness'. 'Has she not been the cause of it all?' he asked.[40]

Langley assured her that he would provide his wife with all the necessities of life but would do no more. A peace had already been attempted, he said, but it had not lasted. 'When I shook hands before with her and kissed her, that only satisfied her a couple of days. She wanted me to go back with her.'[41] Since then, he suspected that Ellen had driven out to Solsboro and 'worked on' Anna, turning her against him with tales of her mistreatment.

If Anna had begun to resent Langley, it was no more than the resentment she showed towards herself. The Poe family motto was *Malo mori quam foedari* – 'Death rather than disgrace' – and as the affair began to spiral out of control, she struggled with her conscience.[42] Having once declared her desire to marry Langley, she now wished she was dead. Langley chastised her for expressing a wish that she had departed 'this wicked world' three years earlier, when she appears to have contracted a near-fatal disease.[43]

But Anna felt their fate was in higher hands. In words Langley quoted back to her, she wrote to him: 'Neither of us know if it should ever please the Lord who watches over us that we should ever be united, I or you may be taken . . . we know not the hour or the moment.'[44] Now she was breaking off communications – 'a stern and cruel command', he wrote.

Heartbroken by the reversal of her affections, he remonstrated with her for crushing his affection as it reached its full maturity, and confessed the depth of his feelings.

'This shall be my last farewell. But oh! I cannot omit here stating and with the truest sincerity, that never a man loved a human being on this earth, with more devotion, deep, and heartfelt attachment, than I love you. – Alas, it is a fatal love. I now see it when it is too late . . .'[45]

19

'Sweet dear Solsboro'

For those listening to Mr Scott's recitation of Dr Langley's St Stephen's Day letter to Anna Poe, the illicit love affair it depicted may have seemed like something from fiction. There was a novelistic quality to its detailed account of events with which Anna would have been familiar, and at one point Langley wrote that he believed their affair was 'quite a subject for a romance'.[1] The letter also revealed his fondness for G. P. R. James, a prolific writer of second-rate, multi-volume historical novels.[2] 'How did you like *Arrah Neil*?' he asked Anna of the writer's 1845 work. 'There was a namesake of mine a very prominent character in it, Mrs Margaret Langley, a good creature. I fancy you took an interest in the book on that account.'[3]

He gave their last fleeting encounters a characteristically dramatic tint. On 23 December, three days before he wrote the letter, word had arrived at Barrack Street that Anna's nephew, Johnny, needed a doctor. Johnny and his brother, Hill, were three and four years old respectively, the sons of Anna's brother James, who was leasing the Poe family mansion at Solsboro from his spendthrift uncle John. The Poes had actually sent for Dr Frith, the dispensary doctor, who, deciding it was too cold to venture out, had asked Dr Langley to take the call. 'When I heard it was a summons to go to sweet dear Solsboro,' he confessed to Anna, 'I leaped out of bed, and was dressed and in the gig in about five minutes. I thought I might have seen you.'[4]

As an unmarried woman, Anna remained in the care of her family, moving between her father's rectory on Summer Hill and the family seat at Solsboro, where she helped with the children. Her nephew Johnny would remain sickly into his adulthood, a sufferer, like his grand-aunt Ellen, from tuberculosis. 'I can't tell you how fond I have become of those little fellows,' Langley told Anna. 'Johnny is the best patient I ever met for taking medicine. My dear Nannie is also very fond of them, which I suppose is an additional reason for my being so too – there is such sympathy between us that I love whatever my dearest loves.'[5]

Visits to Solsboro, two miles from Nenagh, had become a habitual part of the doctor's life since he had come to live in the town in 1831. It was likely that Langley first set eyes on Anna there, when she was a girl in her teens and he a young doctor in his mid-twenties. His marriage to her aunt

made him part of the extended family, a regular guest at lunches, dinners and Christmases.

Although his sister-in-law Frances Poe, Anna's mother, later came to abhor Langley, their relationship had once been one of easy familiarity. As the frequency of his visits increased, he had even playfully begun to refer to her as 'mother', echoing Anna's own affection, as he had done with her two nephews. 'I commenced it in joke,' he wrote in his letter. 'Does it not now look like doating?'[6]

The very early stages of his relationship with Anna are unclear. A few details in Langley's St Stephen's Day letter suggest that after some initial acquaintance, she had gone away for a time before returning to live with her brother James and her parents at Solsboro. Where exactly she went is unclear, but possibly to nurse her uncle John's wife, Barbara, who died of an illness at Avranches in Normandy in July 1845.[7] In his letter to Anna, Langley mused that it was 'destiny that brought us together, after being separated so many years'. He painted a picture of a period, before their affair began, when he was quite unguarded about his affection for her. 'Did I not tell you in the presence of your mother when I kissed you on the steps, that I always loved you,' he wrote, 'oh! At that time it was only friendship, which, alas, has grown into a warmer love, a love that now consumes me.'[8]

One possibility is that Anna's near-fatal illness, which had struck in 1845, may well have allowed a mutual attraction to increase beyond the confines of friendship. His letter showed that in the early months of 1848 Langley was still 'most uneasy' about her health, enquiring whether she had taken the pill and draught he had made up for her.[9] Their meetings had assumed a regular pattern. As he recounted, it was to 'sweet dear Solsboro' that Langley had gone every Saturday to see Anna, 'the day [he] used to look forward to with so much pleasure'. At the time of their going to dinner at the Walkers' the previous Christmas their romantic intimacy had not yet begun. After that, their relationship had changed dramatically. In his letter, he mentions 'the time of our sleeping together at Solsboro' as something of a milestone in the relationship, though it is unclear when this took place.[10] The affair, clearly, was carried on under the noses of the Rev. Mr Poe and his wife.

The Poe estate was approached down a narrow road lined on each side with a hundred beech trees, which Anna's uncle, John Poe, had planted many years before. The road cut through an old fairy fort – a sacrilegious and ill-fated act in the eyes of the Irish peasantry – and then swung to the left over a cattle grid, before passing a small square gatehouse.[11] Here the landscape opened up into spacious parkland, grazed by short-horned Devon cattle; and in the centre was a large Georgian block rising three storeys over a basement.[12] At the front a handsome porch with solid Tuscan columns, atop a flight of lichen-covered steps, projected out to shelter arriving guests. There they were greeted by Mara, the butler, whose fondness for whiskey would eventually see him dismissed from his post.[13] Windows continued around the sides of the house in regular bays to capture views over the surrounding park.

The best part of Solsboro was hidden away. A pathway led to a wilderness at the rear before finding the great expanse of the walled garden stretching to the north-west. In summer its sheltering walls and neat parterres invited slow, lingering walks in still, richly scented air; the flowers here were said to be matched in their beauty only by those at Riverston and Richmond, the homes of the Poes' relations, the Bennetts and

Gasons. A writer during the 1870s recalled these gardens at their peak during the 1830s and '40s, stating that visiting gentry 'freely acknowledge[d] that three such places in one locality could not be found in any part of the three kingdoms . . . no places would better repay the pilgrimage of the florist or horticulturist.'[14] It was here that sickly young Johnny, unable to participate in the rough-and-tumble of boyish sports, developed his lifelong love of gardening. '[He] could hardly pass any plant without having an illuminating discussion on its ways and wants, its merits and use in garden practice,' recalled his friend Gertrude Jekyll when he died in 1926.[15]

On 23 December 1848, as Langley set off in the gig to Solsboro to attend to young Johnny, he was going to revisit a world that was slipping away from him, seeking, as he had done in Dublin, a chance to retrace his steps over the familiar haunts of their secret courtship – and perhaps, less consciously, some reassurance of his place in the family circle to which he had grown so accustomed. It was this that drove him back there on 'the coldest night [he] ever was out'.[16]

His route took him into the centre of the town, crossing the junction of Castle Street and Silver Street, passing up Queen Street and then turning the sharp corner on to Pound Street. Here, where four months later he would exile his wife, terraces of poor, single-bay houses lined his route, with rows of greasy tallow candles flickering in their windows. As he turned the corner, he caught sight of the Poes' carriage at the top of the street, coming in from the Limerick road. It contained Anna and her father. They were late, on the way to rehearse carols for the Christmas service, and evidently in a hurry. Langley immediately halted his gig and darted into a shop doorway to watch them pass by unseen. As he hid in the shadows, he thought Anna turned to glimpse him momentarily as they rode by. 'I fancied you looked in,' he later wrote, 'as if you had seen me leave the coach.'[17]

He continued to Solsboro, attending to Johnny and hoping to encounter Anna later that evening. But she returned late, and to his dismay retired immediately without seeing him. He lingered, retreating to the warmth of the kitchen fire in the basement, and attempted to distract himself by reading a twopenny romance; but his mind returned to her continually. 'I could not bring myself to see you,' he wrote, but 'during the night I actually stole up from the kitchen where I was reading to your door three times to listen to hear you breathing; and then obliged to run away, fearing to see you, after reading your cruel letters to me, was, indeed, dreadful.'[18]

Having spent the night slumbering before the kitchen fire at Solsboro, he breakfasted the next morning with Anna's brother James, with whom he was friendly. But, much to his chagrin, there was no sign of Anna, who, having retired later than usual, slept long into the morning – or was perhaps hiding from the man who was now her ex-lover. In her absence, Langley had a tête-à-tête with her mother, Frances, who arrived downstairs in her dressing gown. She questioned him about his recent trip to Dublin. 'In the course of the conversation,' wrote Langley, 'she asked me in a very sly way if I had seen Jane Mundell when in Dublin. I burst out laughing, and would not say; but I said it was not a fair question, and that I could not answer it. I believe she thought, from my manner, I had seen her. I don't know what her motive was in asking me the question.'[19]

Frances was evidently keen to let Langley know that she was keeping an eye on him. She attempted to turn the conversation towards Ellen's welfare, but he stopped her, saying he would arrange an early opportunity to speak to her and the Rev. Mr Poe on the subject when the three of them could be alone. He admitted to Anna that he had no intention of having any such a conversation with them, but if 'forced into any explanation', he would be sure to find out what claims Ellen had made against him.[20]

The court heard how the conversation with Frances Poe was useful to him in another way: he quizzed her on guests she had invited to dine for Christmas dinner the following day. Would he and Ellen be asked to join them, he wondered. But the mood at Solsboro had turned against him. 'I waited for the last moment to see if we would be invited before I made up my mind to leave home [for Christmas],' he said. Only for Ellen's talking, he was sure, they would have been included in the party.[21]

Not daring to remain any longer for fear it would create further suspicion, Langley left soon after breakfast. Later that day, when the Poes called to see Ellen at Barrack Street, he disappeared upstairs 'to remove any suspicion of our attachment'. He recalled the incident later with pain. 'Oh, will I ever forget Sunday,' he wrote, 'when I shut myself up in my room and you in the same house with me; but I could not resist looking at you from the window – it was a moment of sunshine; but it was too much for me and I cannot describe to you how I passed the remainder of the day.'[22]

The intensity of his passion for Anna Poe must have alarmed those listening in court. Later in his letter he wrote: 'I have no fancy to meet you only but gaze on you with pleasure and delight for hours by stealth, unknown to you.'[23]

Faced with the prospect of spending Christmas with his wife in Barrack Street, Langley felt a desperate desire to get away.

Leaving Ellen and his young niece, Fanny, in the gloomy town house on Barrack Street, he travelled alone to Limerick on Christmas morning, making no secret of his destination before his departure. He hoped word would get through to Anna, should she wish to send him a note of reconciliation, and left instructions with a servant (probably Thomas Pound) that the last volume of the G. P. R. James novel he had been reading at Solsboro – and which he had taken away with him to finish at Barrack Street – should be returned.[24]

In his absence, his small family were not left in total isolation. The Rev. Mr Poe, perhaps uncomfortable over Ellen's exclusion from Christmas dinner, joined her and Fanny for breakfast, and must have wondered at the doctor's sudden flight.[25] The gathering was likely a cheerless one: the elderly clergyman, his spurned sister-in-law and Langley's twelve-year-old niece, no doubt all politely avoiding any reference to the drama unfolding around them. But it was, in any case, no time for joy. The homily in the Christmas service they attended that morning would have echoed the sombre tone struck by the *Nenagh Guardian*'s seasonal editorial, which spoke of the harrowing events of the year gone by, of those 'mown down by the unsparing scythe of Death', of 'friends now in their "narrow home"' and tenants of the cold and silent tomb'. To wish anyone 'Merry Christmas', it warned, was to make a mockery of sorrow.[26]

Langley's depression was of another kind. It had been a fine and bright morning when he left home, but the following day, when he picked up his pen to write to Anna from Limerick, a gloom had descended on the city.[27] His low spirits at his sister's house chimed with his chosen distraction – Charles Dickens's new novel, *Dombey and Son*, a family drama set in a morose London home. One of the principal characters, a

disregarded child, seeks intimacy with an aloof father by listening to his breathing through a bedroom door, a solace
Langley claimed to have sought from Anna only days earlier
when creeping round the bedroom corridors at Solsboro.

The novel was a pioneering exposé of domestic abuse
within the middle-class home, a subject until then confined in
fiction to the murky underclass world of the same author's
Oliver Twist.[28] To Langley, it was 'a most amusing book', and in
his conciliatory way he promised Anna that she should have it
once he was finished. But his breezy assessment may have
concealed his absorption of a darker thread in its narrative.

Dombey's cold-heartedness towards his wife, and his
determination to bend her to his will, was the catalyst for her
eventual adultery; and perhaps it was here, consciously or
otherwise, that Langley first began to formulate a pretext for
his own course of ill-treatment. Mrs Dombey's elopement
with one of his employees on their wedding anniversary, at
the climax of the novel, must have been suggestive to the
doctor as he sought an escape plan from his own marriage:

When the door yielded, and [Dombey] rushed in, what did
he see there? No one knew. But thrown down in a costly
mass upon the ground, was every ornament she had had,
since she had been his wife; every dress she had worn; and
everything she had possessed . . . Heaping them back into
the drawers, and locking them up in a rage of haste, he saw
some papers on the table. The deed of settlement he had
executed on their marriage, and a letter. He read that she
was gone. He read that he was dishonoured. He read that
she had fled, upon her shameful wedding-day, with the man
he had chosen for her humiliation; and he tore out of the
room, and out of the house, with a frantic idea of finding

her yet, at the place to which she had been taken, and beating all trace of beauty out of the triumphant face with his bare hand.[29]

As it turned out, Mrs Dombey was innocent and had fabricated her elopement merely to escape from her husband. For Langley, a similar disgrace cast on to his wife would give him the grounds he needed to divorce her.

That the doctor was planning, in December 1848, to extract himself from his marriage was apparent from his repeated references in his letter to the hope that he would be married to Anna within twelve months. Such a union between uncle and niece, even if not consanguineous, was still regarded as incestuous and illegal, but he was clearly aware of the ongoing campaign to have the law changed.[30] Since June 1847 a commission had been investigating the matter and a new marriage bill was due its first reading in the House of Commons in February 1849. The debate had been strenuously argued on both sides, opponents warning that it would 'turn the home into a sexual laboratory, in which husbands would be forever contemplating marriage with the woman who stood next in line'.[31] Horrified evangelicals declared it would pave the way for 'the coming of the Antichrist'.[32] Dickens himself would wrestle with the question in *David Copperfield*, published the same year as the Langley trial, drawing on his own ambiguous feelings towards his wife's sister.[33] In his last and unfinished novel, *The Mystery of Edwin Drood*, he explored the darkest side of the theme, describing an uncle stooping to murder in pursuit of his nephew's fiancée.

This controversial subject hung over the trial of Dr Langley. As the prospect of a more liberal marriage law came into view, the doctor had been confronted with the problem that he was not yet a widower; he had also been aware that, as time moved on, Anna might come under pressure to accept a proposal from a more viable suitor. Towards the end of his letter to her, he wrote: 'I am sure I hope Mr B[olton] won't lose his heart to you. He is latterly a good deal at Solsboro, and you are so agreeable to everybody that I begin to fear for the result.'[34]

Unable to propose to her himself, Langley must have known how this new and controversial legislation – should it be passed – could change his life. Could it have been a coincidence that in early December 1848, as news of the impending bill surfaced, his ill-treatment of his wife intensified and he began again to confine her to her room? As one journalist later put it: 'From the moment that thought [of marriage] found harbour in his breast, he began to hate his wife.'[35]

20

'God grant I may never again dream such a dream as I dreamed last night'

In December 1848 Langley wrote his long, rambling letter to Anna from 37 William Street, Limerick, a house which survives at the junction with Wickham Street, a busy precinct a quarter mile east of the city's main thoroughfare. The home of his sister, Lydia, and her husband, George Jackson, a former Royal Navy man who had taken a job as the city's harbourmaster, it was only a short walk from the docks. In the late-night candlelight, Langley's feelings of loss chimed with the deeper sorrow that had marked the lives of his hosts.

Only six months earlier his sister's youngest daughter, Louisa, had died there aged seven.[1] Six years before that, in 1842, another daughter, Lydia, and a son, Jeremiah, had died within two months of each other.[2] Their daughter Bessie accidentally drowned five years earlier, aged ten.[3] They also lost a son, Thomas, in 1838.[4] Nevertheless, despite all this personal tragedy, of a sort that often puts terrible pressure on a marriage, Langley was conscious that the Jacksons retained a strong affection for each other, and he remarked on it to Anna in his letter. Their deep bond contrasted with the alienation in his own marriage, and he looked to them for comfort: 'I cannot tell you how kind she is to me and so is her husband . . . she commiserates with me very much.'[5]

Sitting there, in the quiet Georgian town house, hearing only the dim clatter of the retiring city, he complained of sleeplessness: 'I wrote three sheets of this letter today, and it is now have [*sic*] past 12 o'clock as I am writing this part, and I feel no inclination to go to bed. Everyone in this house is gone long since.' He lingered until the clock struck one, writing another ten lines, assuring her that all his 'earthly happiness' depended upon her, before finally signing off – at least for that day. 'I will bid my dearest love good night, and go to my lonely bed, leaving her to imagine who I should like to be with on Wednesday.'[6]

As he dozed off, with Anna's lock of hair strung closely round his neck, he may well have reflected on the course of action he had chosen. He had insisted that he could not change his behaviour towards his wife, even should it mean the total loss of Anna's affection. In the darkness of the night the weight of this decision crept in upon his sleep, as he recounted the next morning in an addendum to his letter:

Wednesday [27 December 1848]

Good morning to you, my sweetest pet. I slept well, but I was so troubled all night with horrible dreams about blood and shots and death, that it was a relief to me when I awoke. My own dearest love, though last in my mind when going to sleep you never once appeared to me in my dream of fancy. I thought your father and Ellen came and tore the sweet relic from my neck, which lay on my breast, and I thought that in the fierce struggle maintained to keep it, that Ellen burst a blood vessel and spat up in a basin her heart's blood – and then the funeral and all the sad obsequies gave food to my imagination. And then I thought there was a warrant for my apprehension for murder, and that I was in the Railway train going to Dublin, and was intended to set sail for America, leaving behind me all I held most dear on earth. I thought the first thing I would do

*on arriving in Dublin was to transfer my money in the funds for my
own dear and beloved Nanny.*

*I pictured to myself how soon she had forgotten her own devoted
Charles, and how happy she had been with all his money, which with
her own dear self she would transfer to Mr Bolton. But as I was going
into the Bank I thought I was arrested and brought back under a
strong escort to Nenagh Gaol. I thought your father came to me to
induce me to repent, and that he handed me a small parcel, which, he
said, I would find to comfort me in my sad affliction, which when I
opened, contained a large dose of poison, which you recommended me to
take in order to avoid the odium of a public trial at the assizes, which
were just at hand, that you were afraid your name would be brought
on, in some way, which would be most injurious to your character, and
might prevent Mr Bolton, your affianced husband, marrying you. Just
as I was mixing the bitter draught which was to consign me to eternity,
I awoke and thanked my God it was only a dream.*

*Was it not a frightful one, my darling? I don't know when I dreamed
before – never since that memorable night in which I dreamed – a
happy dream, in which you were with me, an account of which I gave
you, in which I described the thrill of joy and happiness I felt. God
grant I may never again dream such a dream as I dreamed last night.
I was most unhappy while it lasted.*

Mr Scott, having read aloud Dr Langley's long letter almost
in its entirety, came to its end. The doctor's nightmare, to the
astonishment of the court, had actually foreseen the dreadful events of the following year: Ellen's death, and his own
arrest and incarceration in Nenagh Gaol.

In writing at such length, he had delayed facing the fact
that it might be his last communication with Anna. When no
letter from her arrived the following morning, he reluctantly
brought his own to a close.

My entertained opinion of hearing from you, my love, this morning, ha[s] vanished into thin air . . . I have only to say my dearest, my loveliest, farewell. Farewell, my darling Nanny, and may you enjoy every comfort in this world, and everlasting bliss in the next, is the devoted and sincere wish of your attached and devoted, but now unhappy

Charles

As he sat in the dock listening to his own words, Dr Langley knew that they were perhaps even more prophetic than the crowd realized. Unknown to the court he had somehow got his hands on arsenic pills, and sewn several of them into the lining of his coat. Should the verdict be a negative one, he intended to kill himself there in front of them all.[7]

'Mrs Langley's constitution'

At the start of the day, Mr Scott had instructed the jury that all that was required of the prosecution was that they show Dr Langley had accelerated his wife's death. He had then read the accused's letters to Edward Nixon and Anna Poe, which had demonstrated conclusively Dr Langley's hostile intentions towards his wife, including his wish that she would die. The remaining witnesses, almost without exception, were doctors and domestic servants who had already testified at the coroner's inquest, and who largely recapitulated their testimony for Mr Scott.

Thomas Pound – who had reportedly absconded in advance of the first day of the abortive trial the previous August – had been detained by the police as an important witness for the prosecution.[1] He and his wife were living in the constabulary barracks, and he was given work 'burnishing their cartouche boxes [ammunition pouches] and accoutrements'.[2] He repeated the evidence he had given in the coroner's court, as did the housemaid Eliza Rohan.

Several of Dr Langley's medical colleagues stated that they believed his treatment of his wife had had a negative impact on her health. 'Knowing Mrs Langley's constitution,' said Dr Kittson, 'I consider [that] brown bread and salt beef was totally unfit for her . . . brown bread was calculated to bring on bowel complaint; salt beef would have accelerated death if she was suffering under bowel complaint.' Kittson concluded: 'I am of [the] opinion that the death of the deceased was accelerated by the bad treatment, and being placed in inferior lodgings, &c.'[3]

Dr Quin, who had defended Langley at the coroner's inquest, was now more ambivalent. Although he could see no evidence in the post-mortem that Mrs Langley had suffered want of food, he agreed with Kittson on the dangers of brown bread and salt beef. And, like Kittson, he acknowledged the damaging effect her expulsion from home had had on her. The lodgings Langley had sent his wife to were 'not a fit or proper place for a person in her situation', he said. 'I am of [the] opinion,' he told the court, 'that her removal to this lodging would aggravate a bowel complaint and think it would accelerate her death.'[4]

Evidently, Quin's view of the case – perhaps influenced by popular revulsion at Dr Langley's behaviour – had changed in the ten months since the inquest. However, he was to qualify his statements in a very particular way before the hearing had finished.

Dr Finucane concurred that a diet of brown bread and salt beef was 'injurious'. Dr Cahalan, who had been called to Mrs Langley's room to examine her for venereal disease, reprised his account of her husband's unsuccessful attempt to extract a medical certificate to prove her adultery and his apparent complicity in his manservant's behaviour.[5]

The trial witnesses who had not appeared at the inquest did not add anything dramatically new to the jury's sense of Ellen Langley's last days, but three of them conveyed notable details. James Kilkelly, a solicitor in the town, described Mrs Langley's want of food during this period. 'About a month before her death she came to my house to get something to eat,' he testified. 'She appeared to have been very weak and much exhausted. She came three or four times to my house for the same purpose.'[6]

This was during a time, Kilkelly said, that Dr Langley was at home in Nenagh. Kilkelly, who lived around the corner on Castle Street, had fallen out with the doctor, which may explain why his wife had sought his aid. 'I had a quarrel with Dr Langley about 2s 6d; I then thought it better to discontinue my acquaintance with him, as he was a person that was not well liked, or whose society was not appreciated.'[7]

Dr Kittson recalled once more Ellen's visits to his house 'in a very weakly state' to ask for food; but he added that Dr Langley had then written to his wife, Mrs Kittson, to put a stop to them. 'After the receipt of that letter she was forbid the house,' he said.[8] He also remembered calling on Ellen days before her death. 'When I saw her on the 24th [of April] I expected she'd die she was so far gone; her hand and feet were cold, and her frame in an emaciated state.'[9]

James Magrath, a servant at Donnybrook, told the courtroom that he had come across Mrs Langley in the rain one day, wearing only a light pair of slippers, and she had asked him for sixpence. He had spent a year working for Dr Langley as a groom, in the period before the doctor hired Thomas Pound in 1848, and recalled that even then Mrs Langley was frequently turned out of the parlour by her husband and left to eat her dinner with the servants in the kitchen.[10]

Margaret Meara, who had been Ellen's landlady in Pound Street, testified that, shortly before Ellen died, she called to Barrack Street and asked to see her to discuss the return of her clothes from the lodgings on Pound Street. 'The doctor and Miss Jackson brought me up; we met Mrs Langley on the stairs [and] on meeting her the doctor seemed displeased, and in a very angry way desired her to go up to her room; she went to the garret.' When Mrs Meara wished her former lodger 'joy at getting home to her house', Dr Langley interjected that his wife would 'prefer going back with her again'. Mrs Meara returned the following day when the doctor was 'at prayers', and managed to see Ellen one last time: 'she was in bed in the garret room; . . . appeared very delicate and said she would not live long.'[11]

When Meara asked to see Mrs Langley again, the doctor refused her.

Mr Bewley testified that Ellen had requested to see her sister Frances in the days before her death, but that Dr Langley – clearly fearful of what she might say – would only allow it if he was present. As a result of the stand-off, the visit never took place and Ellen never saw any of her family again.[12]

When Ellen Langley died in May 1849, the cause of her death had been decided by a jury largely made up of local Catholic merchants and tradesmen who had no compunction about seeing her husband prosecuted. Only the foreman and one other were classed as gentry.[13]

Coroner's juries, which were assembled quickly, were not subjected to the same property qualifications as those in criminal trials.[14] Under the terms of an act of 1833, a whole series of property restrictions determined who could sit on petty juries. A townsman must own a house at an annual valuation of £20, or personal estates of £100. In the country-side, he had to have a freehold worth £10 or leasehold of land worth £15 annually.[15] Although farmers and shopkeepers could in theory sit on these juries if they owned property of sufficient value, their inclusion on an annual list of jury candidates depended on the discretion of the county sheriff.[16] He had to ensure that such lists were arranged according to rank and property, and that those chosen as foremen were of high social status.[17]

In Tipperary, the religious composition of juries had been an issue of grievance throughout the 1840s. At the Nenagh Spring Assizes of 1840, for example, of the 200 men selected, none was below the rank of 'esquire', indicating that they were men of greater economic means than those merely acknowledged as 'gent'.[18] The privileging of property meant that wealthy Protestants often dominated juries on high-profile cases. In 1844 Maurice Lenihan, editor of the *Tipperary Vindicator*, expressed his 'feeling of intense dissatisfaction' at the small number of Catholics on the long panel from which jurors might be selected.[19] In 1848 the rebel MP William Smith O'Brien – a Protestant himself – complained that only a tiny fraction of the special jury panel arranged for his treason trial were Catholic.[20]

Langley's fate now depended not on the Catholic shopkeepers of the town, but on the judgement of a jury of Protestant landowners.

The selection process was an arduous one. Langley's defence team had been thorough, objecting to no fewer than twenty candidates – the maximum number of objections that the law permitted. Five further men – Mr B. White, Mr D. E. Young, Mr William Waller, and John and Thomas Harden – were excused on the grounds that they were relatives of the deceased. The prosecution objected to three candidates, perhaps considering them too close to the defendant.[21]

The chief constituency excluded from the jury were women. Sixty years into the future, Ellen's great-grand-nieces would all become active members of the women's suffrage movement, attending lectures and raising funds, but in 1850 the idea of women serving on juries was a very distant prospect.[22] Of course, in the absence of any official voice, local townswomen had already given their verdict on the morning of Ellen's burial by smashing all the windows in the doctor's house. Now all they could do was watch.

The twelve jurymen were some of the most notable landowners in the district. Almost all were of Anglo-Irish stock. Several of them were connected to the late Mrs Langley. John Bennett of Riverston, the head juror, was brother-in-law to her nephew, James Jocelyn Poe, and uncle to young Johnny at Solsboro. He was also the new employer of Eliza Rohan, a key witness against Dr Langley – and a member of the Board of Superintendence of Nenagh Gaol, which had been the defendant's place of residence for the best part of a year.[23] James Willington, the squire of Castle Willington, was a neighbour of Ellen's from her childhood at Donnybrook and was connected with the Poes of Solsboro through marriage.[24] He was of the same generation as Ellen and must have known her well when they were young, attending hunt balls and paying neighbourly visits. William Crawford, another neighbour of Ellen's family, was married to a cousin of the Willingtons.[25] Richard Short was a 'gentleman farmer' who lived south of the town. His sister had recently married Dr Kittson, who had helped conduct the post-mortem on Ellen's body.[26] Nine years later he would attempt to marry off his 18-year-old daughter to a 55-year-old farmer; when the farmer broke off the engagement, Short sued him for breach of promise. At the time of that trial, the *Freeman's Journal* wrote that Short 'had great influence amongst the jurors of Tipperary as a popular resident gentleman of extensive connections'.[27]

Richard Nash of Borrisokane was a member of the Nenagh Board of Guardians with Ellen's nephew James.[28] Ralph Smith was the owner of a fine mansion at Milford, north of Nenagh, though unable to occupy it due to debt; he had a family connection with Ellen, through the marriage of his cousin William Smith to her aunt Abigail.[29] Thomas Doolan was probably the man of that name whose family had owned the Wingfield estate near Ballingarry, north of Nenagh, and who later lived at Whitehall in the same region. Ellen's first cousin, Aquilla Smith, had married a Miss Doolan, suggesting a further family link.[30]

The jurors listened to the prosecution evidence on the trial's first day – the letters, the medical evidence and all the curious circumstances of Langley's deteriorating relationship with his wife. When the case for the Crown concluded at seven in the evening, after nine arduous hours, the men were locked into the jurors' room for the night.[31] It was a small rectangular space, windowless to prevent communication with the outside world, and they would have had to find what comfort they could on the stiff timber chairs. The only light was that provided by hissing gas fittings on the wall and a slow-burning timber fire along one side. The stifling heat of the airless chamber would not have improved tempers already frayed by a long day.[32] Here they had plenty of time to reflect quietly on all they had heard. The next day they would be called upon to weigh up the case for the defence, and, finally, to consider whether the doctor deserved to go free, face imprisonment, or die.

22

'Who would not have done similarly?'

At ten o'clock the following morning, the sheriff escorted the jury into the courtroom once more, this time to hear the arguments of Mr Martley, counsel for the defence.[1] He began by paying his respects to Mr Scott's case for the prosecution and telling the jury that they already had sufficient evidence to make an intelligent judgement. Mr Martley was so sure of the jury's ability, he told them, that he would not call a single witness.

What more could be said? His client, he suggested, had already been 'shipwrecked' by the notoriety of the case and would be 'an unhappy man for the rest of his life'. 'It is impossible,' he said, 'to conceive the anguish, the pain of mind, and feelings that that unfortunate man possesses by the torture inflicted on him, which this investigation created and gave rise to.'[2] Respectable people were involved, he reminded them. Names had been sullied by the 'disgusting' details of the case.

Mr Martley's strategy was a straightforward one. He downplayed Langley's maltreatment of his wife and focused on the medical evidence, which had been unable to demonstrate the exact cause of the stomach and bowel ailment that had led to Mrs Langley's death. The jury already knew from the coroner's inquest that the doctors had not been able to establish whether poison had been administered, and all agreed that Mrs Langley was already suffering from several serious ailments. There was no need to recall the doctors,

Martley said, as the jury had heard their evidence. The case was now a matter of interpretation alone.

Martley urged the jury not to consider the causes that had led to the estrangement between Langley and his wife – then proceeded to dwell on the subject for some time. Referring to Dr Langley's letter to Edward Nixon, he centred his argument on the supposedly compromised virtue of Mrs Langley. The course of treatment Dr Langley adopted towards his wife, Martley suggested, was due to 'wrongs done to him' and 'some impropriety on her part, spreading abroad reports and other indiscretion'. He did not remark on the fact that these indiscreet reports related to Langley's own adultery; nor did he mention that Mrs Langley had denied spreading any such rumours, regardless of their truth, and that Dr Langley was the sole source of the accusation. He repeatedly returned to the subject of her alleged infidelity, attempting to extract some advantage from the contents of the Nixon letter:

> I now approach a revolting part of the case. Indeed I hardly know how to approach it. That letter which has been read from beginning to end, suppressing no name – concealing no abominable fact – proves that about this time disclosures had been made that led this most unfortunate man to the conviction that the person to whom he had been united so many years had been criminally intimate with other men before he married her.[3]

Martley admitted that he did not know the origin of these charges against Ellen – whether they came from Mrs Langley or from another source (in the letter they came from her husband) – but he did not for a moment question the veracity of his client's account. He argued that once the doctor had ascertained this extraordinary information regarding his wife's past, his behaviour towards her quite naturally changed. The incident with the servant man Thomas Pound merely confirmed her bad nature.

'And now, gentlemen,' he said, 'conceive what must have been the state of mind of the prisoner thinking that a woman of light and improper character had been pawned upon him in marriage by her family! The horrible fact had just come to his ears at the time; but was not there something more? Was not there something indiscreet in the deceased, or why should the unfortunate woman invite to her bed that unprincipled villain . . . ?'

He was building up to his point, inviting the male jury to see through Langley's eyes something of the dishonour and shame his adulterous wife had cast upon him. And it was in the context of this that he framed Mrs Langley's exile to the miserable lodgings in Pound Street.

'I cannot gloss over the fact that any female accustomed to genteel society should be sent to such a place as that lodging house was described; but let me ask you, are those things true? Had he reason to believe that a person of bad character had been put off upon him in marriage? Are not these great palliatives for what he did? He acted harshly no doubt in sending her away: but who would not have done similarly?'

Martley's argument was a passionate invocation of a man's supremacy in marriage; of his right to punish his wife for sins he had committed himself. Public morality, he knew, took a much dimmer view of sexual misdemeanours by women. Lord Brougham, debating a 'bastardy clause' for a Poor Law bill in the House of Lords a few years earlier, had stated the case most clearly: 'Although a want of chastity was a sin in a man,' he argued, 'yet it was a greater sin in a woman.

In a woman, it went to corrupt society at its very root.' If women behaved as men, he suggested, the bonds of society would 'burst asunder' and 'man would be driven back into a state of savage and uncivilized life'.[4] Langley articulated a striking corollary of this viewpoint in his letter to Anna, when he wrote that his wife had failed in her duty to throw 'a cloak of secrecy' around his own failings.[5]

A contemporary legal treatise summed up the general view: 'The wife, it is said, may and ought to forgive an unfaithful husband; but no husband can forgive an unfaithful wife.'[6] This double standard meant that almost all the divorces granted through Act of Parliament between 1700 and 1857 were at the husband's petition.[7] To the contemporary Irish writer Lady Morgan, the situation was the result of 'an insidious, ignorant tyranny that . . . injures the best interests of society and retards its progress towards reform'.[8]

The degree of subservience expected of Victorian women was laid out in clear terms in a popular domestic guidebook of the day:

> . . . she must not think that any thing will do for her husband, – that any room is good enough for her husband, – that it is not worthwhile to be agreeable, when there is only her husband, – that she may close her piano, or lay aside her brush, for why should she play or paint merely to amuse her husband? No! she must consider all these little arts of pleasing chiefly valuable on his account, – as means of perpetuating her attractions, and giving permanence to his affection.[9]

Within this context, Martley would have felt confident that he could mitigate the actions of Dr Langley before an all-male jury, even though the evidence of Ellen's alleged misdeeds was far from conclusive. The *Dublin Weekly Register*, picking up on his line of argument, emphasized Ellen's own culpability in its report: 'It would appear that Mrs Langley was not a person of strong mind, and that she committed adultery, on her own confession, with her man servant, in order to lay ground for a divorce.'[10] The paper also recounted another part of Dr Quin's assessment of her from the previous day. 'I considered her always to be a woman of very weak mind,' he said, 'and I considered that her mind and body had been sinking for three months before death . . . I think her mind certainly aggravated her disease and accelerated her death.'[11] On its own, we might read this as an unexceptionable statement that Mrs Langley had been suffering from what we would today call depression, and that this had exacerbated her physical illness. But Quin did not attribute her state of mind to the troubles in her marriage or her mistreatment at the hands of her husband; he attributed it to what he called 'her shame'. 'It was,' he said, 'a matter of public notoriety which caused her uneasiness of mind.'[12]

When Mr Martley finished his defence, Judge Ball addressed the members of the jury, outlining how they should proceed to make their decision. A trial like the present one, he said, had never before taken place in Ireland, and he was sorry to observe that it exhibited 'a frightful amount of depravity and immorality'.[13]

If the jury believed that the disease of which Mrs Langley had died was induced by the wilful ill-treatment and neglect of her by the prisoner, they should find him guilty of murder.

If they were of the view that the decease of the unfortunate lady had been accelerated by the treatment she had received through non-wilful neglect on the part of the prisoner, they should convict him of manslaughter.

If they should come to the conclusion that her death had not been occasioned or in any way accelerated by the conduct of the prisoner, notwithstanding however unkindly he might have treated her, they were unquestionably bound to acquit him.[14]

The jury adjourned at two o'clock to consider their verdict.

23

'Suppressio veri'

At five o'clock, three hours after they had retired, the members of the jury returned to the courtroom. Dr Langley was asleep and had to be woken to hear the verdict. The *Freeman's Journal* reported that he slept in the dock for half an hour, 'and it was only by laying a hand on his shoulder that his slumbers were broken'.[1]

The head juror, John Bennett, stepped forward with the issue paper on which was written the verdict. A dour man in early middle age with a bulbous nose, heavy eyelids and whiskers that extended in wisps down fattened cheeks, he was a grandson of a Justice of the King's Bench and nephew of the Father of the Munster Circuit.[2] The outcome of the trial would directly affect the family of his younger sister, Jane, a sister-in-law of Anna Poe. An acquittal would bring an end to the affair; a murder conviction would see more newspaper reports, the horrors of a public hanging, and further notoriety for the extended family. He now faced Dr Langley across the courtroom, his fate gripped between his fingers. He handed the issue paper to the clerk of the court to read.

Silence descended over the room.

'Not guilty,' said the clerk.

There is no record of Dr Langley's immediate response, or indeed that of the courtroom as a whole. The *Freeman's Journal* reported what happened next: 'After the verdict of acquittal had been pronounced [the doctor] exhibited a number of arsenic pills which he had concealed in the lining of his waistcoat, and with the utmost composure said that had the verdict been an adverse one he would have swallowed the poison, and thus realise in almost every particular the strange and startling foreshadowings of his extraordinary dream.'

Here Langley the narcissist came once more to the fore, a tragic hero robbed of his compelling final act, and eager to let everyone know what he had planned. In the absence of so dramatic an ending, the best he could do was play the part of the wronged man. As he left the courthouse, he leaned for support on Dr Quin and his friend Mr Francis Byron, a Nenagh merchant – though the *Freeman's Journal* noted sceptically that 'he evinced no sign of having suffered in bodily vigour' from his imprisonment and fasting.[3]

Rumours circulated in the days that followed. Some said that Langley had been remanded in his cell by Judge Ball until the end of the assizes. The *Nenagh Guardian* stated that he had not yet been released from custody as he was still in the gaol's hospital.[4] Another newspaper reported that he proceeded to 'a suite of apartments at Brundley's Hotel, Nenagh' where he spent 'a very gay evening' with his close acquaintances.[5] The paper noted that he had no design to leave the locality but rather intended defiantly to continue his residence in Nenagh. Another report suggested he left Nenagh for a period, going 'on a tour' to Dublin and London, but had apparently returned to Nenagh by the end of April, a month after the trial.[6]

At the end of March, Colonel James Chatterton, an MP from County Cork, raised the issue of Langley's brutality to his wife in a Westminster debate on the new marriage bill.

The bill would grant a widower the legal right to marry his wife's sister or niece, and Chatterton proposed that it was this that had encouraged Langley to hope that he might make such a marriage as soon as the law was amended. 'How many uncles and brothers-in-law would transfer their affections in a similar manner,' he asked, 'if the law should open the way towards the gratification of their illicit fancies? This case of Dr Langley's should not be lost sight of by the defenders of Christian morality in Parliament when Mr Wortley's Bill comes again to be considered.'[7] Such fears would continue to pervade debates around the issue, and the law against such marriages would not be repealed until 1907.[8]

Three weeks after the trial – possibly having returned from a trip abroad, if those reports were true – Langley was defiant in spirit, and intent on reclaiming his reputation. The *Freeman's Journal* reported: 'He wears a conical shaped hat with a huge cloak, and is shorn altogether of the moustache and whiskers which contributed to give him so formidable an appearance.' He assumed an 'unconcerned air' and was rumoured to be taking action in the courts against certain newspapers in the Thurles petty sessions that would begin the following week.[9] He was also said to be intent on pursuing his 'pound of flesh' from those debtors to his loan fund who had defaulted while he was in prison.[10] He could be seen 'either smoking a long pipe, under the portico of the hotel in morning gown and conical hat, or walking through the streets, occasionally, with shoulders rather stooped, and cane in hand'.[11]

Dressed in this bizarre costume, the keen reader of romances may have been attempting once again to slip into the guise of Alexandre Dumas's injured hero, Edmond Dantès, a man who on his return to society assumes the manner and mystique of a magician – 'an enchanter of the Arabian Nights, a wizard of the Middle Ages' and 'a dealer in magical arts'. He reveals his identity to those who wronged him, 'enveloped in a cloak, half lost in the shadow[s]'.

The excitement of Dr Langley's trial paralleled the sensational novels of the day, differing only in its far more salacious detail. The *Belfast Newsletter*, giving just a short account of the trial, titillated its readers by declaring the circumstances of the case 'totally unfit for publication', so much so that 'we cannot even fairly allude to them.'[12] To further tease its readership, it cited the opinion of a Tipperary newspaper, which was even more emphatic on this point:

> The circumstances form so abominable a history, if we may be allowed to use the expression, that we could not – in fact we *dare* not, having regard for morality – report them. In good truth our readers may rely on this: – Our reporter tells us that although he has been 27 years connected with public proceedings of all kinds, he never heard, until this case came before him, so much depravity detailed to a court, a jury, and a gaping public.[13]

Unsurprisingly, six weeks after the trial, the *Nenagh Guardian* announced that it was receiving requests from 'distant quarters' for extra copies of its reports. In order to satisfy this demand, the editor said that they were in the process of printing a special pamphlet to be entitled *The Extraordinary Trial of Charles Langley, M.R.C.S.I.*, to be available for one shilling in all booksellers in Dublin, London, Glasgow, Edinburgh, and the principal towns in all the provinces.[14] It would bring together all their original reporting on the case, allowing the reader to consume the narrative from start to finish.

Many newspapers had reported the prosecution evidence but not the arguments of Mr Martley's defence, with all their calumnies against Mrs Langley. The reporter for the *Freeman's Journal*, for example, simply remarked: 'After a most able and impressive speech, which occupied upwards of three hours in its delivery, the learned gentleman concluded his case without calling any witnesses.'[15] The *Nenagh Guardian* reported a little more detail yet stopped short of giving the full account. Only the *Tipperary Vindicator* had dared to publish it, but its readership was largely Catholic, and not of the class with whom Dr Langley most sought to have his reputation restored.

On 27 March he complained to the editor of the *Limerick Chronicle* that had Mr Martley's speech been published and 'fairly laid before the public', it 'might have had the effect of retrieving my unfortunate and deeply injured character'. Those involved in such censorship, he argued, would have to answer for this before 'a higher tribunal'. [16]

The Limerick paper, perhaps more sympathetic given that Langley was a native of that city, eventually agreed to publish the full speech. John Hallissey, the *Nenagh Guardian* reporter whom Langley had attacked in his letter to the *Limerick Chronicle*, hit back on 6 April. Responding to the doctor's charge that he had suppressed the defence case, Hallissey retorted: 'I beg to inform this unenviable disciple of Esculapius, where the *suppressio veri* did occur, namely, on the part of the Crown, who omitted bringing forward material facts, which were sworn to at the inquest, and but for which omission (I don't know whether it was intentional or otherwise) he probably would now be the occupant of gloomy apartments.'[17]

It is unclear what evidence Hallissey was referring to, but

it may have been the lack of any further questioning on the subject of poisoning, something which had proved inconclusive at the coroner's inquest.

The disagreement manifested itself in other ways. Hallissey and his editor sued Langley for non-payment of his subscription to the *Nenagh Guardian*, which had been delivered to him throughout his time in gaol. The sum of money owed was a pittance and though the editor, Mr Kempston, claimed to act on 'a matter of principle, justice and of fair play', the affair provided more content for the newspaper to sell to a greedy readership – and he promised that any debt they retrieved would go to charity.

Rather wickedly, the paper hired George Bolton to prosecute his former client, reporting the case gleefully in its own pages and recounting the multitude of humorous digs and jibes that were customary between opposing counsels in frivolous disputes; unsurprisingly, they referenced at every turn the more ridiculous aspects of the murder trial, and even Mr Dillon appeared, seemingly in an informal capacity, to contribute further mockery from the sidelines.[18]

Other commentators poked fun at Langley's literary failings. The *Cork Examiner* described his long love letter as the 'miserable production of a diseased fancy'. The author of such an epistle, mused the paper, represented a particular class of 'long haired' letter writer that plagued society, of which it claimed 'there were hundreds', who had to be kept in check. They were 'part educated, part sentimental, with a mixture of pride and idleness, meanness and gentility'. There should be no mercy, argued the journal, for such 'sentimentalisms and werterisms'.[19]

The latter was a reference to Goethe's epistolary novel *The Sorrows of Young Werther*, published in 1774, a series of indulgent reflections on life by a self-absorbed youth which became synonymous with maudlin letter writing, giving rise to a period when (according to the critic Thomas Carlyle), 'literature lay all puking and sprawling in Werterism, Byronism, and other Sentimentalism'. This was, he said, the 'fruit of internal *wind*'.[20]

For the *Cork Examiner*, Langley's indulgent prose was the product not of a distracted mind, but of an indolent lifestyle and an acquisitive character: ' . . . knowing nothing of industry, and the independence of useful labour, he perhaps married a woman older than himself for advantageous reasons.' In doing so, he had perverted the course of nature: 'An unnatural union brought infamous results.'[21]

But the wider import of the murder trial was not forgotten, and John Hallissey was not alone in questioning the acquittal of Charles Langley. Three days after Dr Langley walked free from court, under the heading IS MURDER BY TORTURE A CRIME?, a correspondent to the London *Times* expressed disgust over three much-publicized cases of domestic abuse, including the Langley trial, in which the perpetrators had been fully acquitted. The other cases involved the deaths of a servant girl, routinely beaten by her employers, and that of an old woman similarly abused by her daughter. The correspondent complained that the failure of prosecutors to attribute death to one specific instance of abuse had led to acquittals in all three cases: 'I ask whether it is not most revolting to moral feeling that such cases should be decided only with reference to that point, and not a word of condemnation for proven cruelties be heard either from judge or jury, if the report is correct.'[22]

The letter, which was also sent to *Lloyds Weekly London Newspaper*, was signed simply 'A. B.' The writer was almost certainly John Stuart Mill, the renowned philosopher and campaigner for women's rights, who frequently published correspondence under these initials.[23] Moved by the account of a wife 'kept in a garret without fire . . . only allowed weak tea, brown bread, and salt meat, turned out the house, and shut up in a small dark room, where she died', he reminded the public of the 'strongly criminative' nature of the evidence against Dr Langley.[24] He said he was 'greatly struck by the want of some provision for the detention and prosecution on a lower count of wretches who, though not absolutely proved to be guilty of wilful murder, have, by the strongest evidence, been shown guilty of barbarity such as in a Christian and civilized land cannot be contemplated without horror'.[25] Other British newspaper editorials expressed similar concern about these three trials, 'distinguished . . . by great deficiency of tact and discernment on the part of the professional gentlemen who prepared the endictments [sic]'. Langley, it was argued, 'was acquitted notwithstanding the strong evidence against him'.[26]

That same year, Mill and his partner Harriet Taylor published a series of articles in the English press highlighting the plight of women as victims of domestic violence, leading to wider debate on the issue in Parliament and forming a prelude to their influential essay 'The Subjection of Women' of 1861 (published 1869).[27] The experiences of Ellen Langley, and other women like her, had roused public indignation against domestic abuse and raised serious questions about the inequality of marriage. Driven by these injustices, Mill would later become the first MP to argue in Parliament for female suffrage, helping to set in train the fraught political campaign of the ensuing decades.

24

'Woman's frailty and sinful passion'

In 1906, Ellen Langley's grand-nephew, Colonel Sir William Hutcheson-Poe, commissioned the genealogist Sir Edmund Bewley to trace the 'history and origin' of his lineage.[1]

Bewley found certain details hard to come by. Diligently searching through the Nenagh parish records for every member of the family he could find, each of whom he scrupulously recorded in his notebook, he catalogued births, marriages and deaths to form a largely accurate family tree stretching back to the arrival in Ireland of Thomas Poe, with Cromwell, in the late seventeenth century. The Donnybrook line had died out by the 1890s, but Bewley, in sketching out their pedigree, found the name of Ellen and all her siblings listed in the will of her father, William, and then consulted local records to establish the dates of their births, marriages and deaths. He did this successfully for all of them, with one exception.

For Ellen he found no details in the parish register, and as a result her name appears on the family tree without any date of birth. According to the pedigree, her marriage never happened, and her controversial death, so conspicuous a feature of 1849, took place in 1853. In the near-absence of information on her, Bewley had confused her with another woman named Ellen Poe, a poor dressmaker who had lived around the same time, on the same street, and who had died four years after her.[2]

That so little evidence should survive of a woman whose life had been so publicly scrutinized suggests some wilful attempt to suppress the scandal of her death. The churchyard where she was buried in Nenagh has no trace of any head-stone, suggesting that none was ever erected.[3]

The voicelessness of Ellen is a poignant feature of the case. She passed into oblivion without leaving any statement of her own perspective on her marriage and the events leading to her death. The inquest and trial, which threw up such a detailed picture of the character of the doctor, failed to produce a full picture of the woman whose death occasioned them.

A possible response to this frustrating silence appears in a short story attributed to Joseph Sheridan Le Fanu, published some eighteen years after Ellen Langley's death. By virtue of his wife's close kinship with the Bennetts of Nenagh, Le Fanu must have been familiar with the case, and feasibly drew upon it.[4] In the story, the principal protagonist is led, by means of a ghostly whisper, to discover the diary of a woman poisoned by her unfaithful husband:

'Read!' muttered the voice. I read. There were long entries by poor Julia of her daily life; complaints of her husband's unkind-ness, neglect, then cruelty. I turned to the last pages: her hand had grown very feeble now, and she was very ill. 'George seems kinder now,' she wrote; 'he brings me all my medicines with his own hand.' Later on: 'I am dying; I know I am dying: he has poisoned me. I saw him last night through the curtains pour something in my cup; I saw it in his evil eye. I would not drink; I will drink no more; but I feel that I must die.'

These were the last words. Below were written, in a man's bold hand, the words 'Poor fool!'[5]

In his letter to Nixon, Langley had used the same contemp-tuous words – 'poor fool' – to describe his ailing wife just days before her death. Other details provide a similar echo. The murderer is eventually arrested but avoids the gallows by swallowing poison concealed on his person, just as Langley had been prepared to do in the event of his conviction.

Unlike that of the diarist in Le Fanu's story, the voice of Ellen Langley remains silent, except for its occasional refraction through the accounts of others in the murder trial, or her hastily scribbled lines to Dr Quin from Pound Street. The latter are polite, affectionate and warm, but they tell us little beyond what we know of her character from the testimony of the servants. About much more we are ignorant.

The silence of the Poes of Solsboro during the inquest and trial suggests a family torn between a wish for justice and a fear of exposure. Remarkably, Mr Bolton, who had so vigorously defended Dr Langley, retained the confidence of the men in the family, acting for Percy Jocelyn Poe in a land dispute of 1853, and in the select vestry the Rev. Mr Poe convened for the rebuilding of the Anglican church in Nenagh in 1857.[6] James Jocelyn Poe even entrusted him with drafting his will several years later.[7]

His subsequent life revealed Bolton to be a man at war with the world. In his role of Crown Solicitor for Tipperary, he became infamous for his brutal dealings with Fenian suspects. As prosecutor in the famous Maamtrasna murder trial of 1882, he was widely thought to have contrived the execution of several innocent men. 'Speaking of this case as coolly as I can,' said the Irish Parliamentary Party leader Charles Stewart Parnell in the House of Commons, 'I believe that if ever a murderer deserved to be placed on trial and sentenced to death that man was Bolton!'[8]

He sank into further ignominy in a controversy that

mimicked that of Dr Langley to an extraordinary degree. Following the premature death of his first wife, he had married in 1863 a wealthy widow sixteen years his senior, and was accused of attempting to get his hands on her £60,000 fortune through a devious marriage settlement. His wife's action against him, and a challenge to the will that followed her death, revealed to the world his adulterous behaviour with two separate women, and the pregnancy of one of them.[9] He was labelled by one prominent nationalist MP as 'a self-convicted thief, fraudulent bankrupt, wife-cheater, and heartless debauchee', and by another as a 'forger, adulterer and wife-swindler'.[10]

The damage to Anna Poe's reputation was more immediate. Once her affair with Dr Langley had been made public, she had no hope of acceptance within polite society. The American novelist Nathaniel Hawthorne, who published *The Scarlet Letter* just five days before the Langley murder trial, described how a fallen woman in a small town 'would become the general symbol at which the preacher and moralist might point, and in which they might vivify and embody their images of woman's frailty and sinful passion'.[11]

In their attempts to supress investigation beyond the medical evidence at the inquest, both her father and eldest brother had tried to keep her name out of the public eye. In his strange premonition, Langley had even dreamed of her father giving him poison to consume in gaol as a means of preventing his daughter's shame. No doubt with the same concern in mind, he had asked that 'a person whose name it may be well not to mention' should not be called to testify at the coroner's inquest. But rumours of the affair likely made any continued anonymity for Anna impossible as the murder trial loomed. We do not know by what means Langley's letter found its way to the Grand Jury in the summer of 1849. While it may well have saved Anna from a traumatic public cross-examination in court, and served to demonstrate her determined opposition to her former lover in the months before her aunt's death, the admission of her involvement in his extramarital affair nevertheless condemned her to disgrace.

Anna Poe disappeared from Nenagh in the aftermath of the trial. Surviving family papers make no reference to her after 1850 and there is no mention of her in the local newspapers attending any public event over the next fifty years, nor any public notice of her death. Burke's *Genealogical and Heraldic Dictionary*, published in a new edition in 1863, omitted her name from its account of the Poe family, though it included all her siblings.[12] Her brother James's will, drafted years later by George Bolton, would similarly make no reference to the name that had once been so widely publicized. Sir Edmund Bewley, in compiling his pedigree for her nephew forty years later, drew a discreet veil over her existence. She was wiped from the record.

Similarly, Dr Langley disappeared entirely from view. Although he had vowed to make his residence in Nenagh after the trial, there is no mention of him in Ireland after 1850. The hostility against him was such that it would have been impossible to settle back into his old way of life. As Mr Martley had told the jury, regardless of the outcome of the trial, Langley was already 'shipwrecked' by the damage to his reputation and had little to hope for in the future.

If there was anything of his life to be salvaged, he would have to look beyond Ireland.

25

'The interposition of a kind Providence'

In the papers passed down through the Poe family in Nenagh, there is nothing to recall the scandal of the late 1840s – with the possible exception of two small photographs that hint at the final fate of Anna Poe. Among a collection of Victorian *cartes de visite*, dating largely to the 1860s and '70s, and taken in photographers' studios in Dublin, they stand out from the rest, principally because the dress of the sitters is of an earlier style than all the others, suggesting a date in the 1850s.

The figures are evidently a couple – a man and a woman, each sitting on an identical armchair, and, when set side by side, facing towards each other. The woman's right hand hangs delicately downwards from the arm of the chair, displaying a ring on her third finger. The photographic technique of the period reversed the image, indicating that this was actually her *left* hand, and the ring on the wedding finger, suggesting the portrait was made in the aftermath of a marriage. Another feature of these two photographs distinguishes them from the others: they were made not in Dublin but in Liverpool.[1]

A two-line newspaper report reveals the course of action Anna Poe took in the summer of 1850 in the aftermath of the trial. Unable to continue her life in Nenagh, her options were limited. Her affair with Charles Langley had become the defining experience in her life, and perhaps realizing

this, she decided to accept the path that she had set out upon two and a half years earlier. The *Freeman's Journal* announced her marriage to Charles Langley in the June of 1850.[2]

> At Chester, Charles LANGLEY Esq to Anne Matlida [*sic*], daughter of the Rev James Hill POE, rector of Nenagh, co Tipperary

The ceremony took place in the church of St Oswald's, Chester, on 4 June, less than three months after the doctor's acquittal for the murder of his wife. The publication of a notice in an Irish national newspaper no doubt reflected Langley's continued determination to retrieve what he regarded as his rightful status in the world; but the couple were alone on the day of their marriage and the only persons present as witnesses were an illiterate servant woman and the parish clerk.[3] Proposals to amend the Marriage Act had been rejected by Parliament, so their union was an illegal one: they must have lied either about Dr Langley's marriage to Ellen or about Anna's kinship to Ellen. From here, it was not far to Liverpool, a bustling international port, where sometime later they had their photographs taken at Keith's Photographic Studio on Castle Street.[4]

Given her distaste at his treatment of her aunt and their period of enmity, the marriage forms a remarkable conclusion to their affair. For Langley, at least, it was the fulfilment of his greatest desire, and his final triumph over adversity. He had long prepared for such a day. When Anna had first expressed horror at his behaviour towards her aunt in the winter of 1848, he had rushed to reassure her that he would never treat *her* like that, should they ever be married:

> Don't imagine I can ever be a bad husband to you, my love. You know how good and kind I am capable of being, and how kind and good and generous I have been for many, many years, until I have been deeply and irrevocably cut to the quick, and injured and wounded in a most vital point. If we were, through the interposition of a kind Providence, [to] become one, you may calculate on my unalterable, unchanging love.

In a hint at his true motivation in marrying Ellen seventeen years earlier, he had written: 'It will not be for money I shall unite my fate with yours, but for love – the most devoted, the most deeply attached.' In contrast to the fate he felt had befallen him as a result of his ill-judged first marriage, he idealized an alliance contracted on the basis of mutual attraction: '. . . where a union takes place under such circumstances happiness supreme must follow.'[5]

Liverpool in 1850 was a global crossroads, its docks 'full of life and commotion . . . an epitome of the world, where all the nations of Christendom, and even those of Heathendom, are represented'.[6] Within the whirling, shifting population of the port city, Langley set up a medical surgery in relative anonymity, finding a home for his new wife on Norton Street in the suburbs to the east of the city centre. It was here that their first child, Jeremiah, named after Langley's father, was born on 10 May 1851, and baptized at the church of St Peter's.[7]

Ten years later, the census records them living at Ross Villa on Newlands Street in the prosperous township of Everton on the outskirts of Liverpool, a large house with a drawing room, a dining room and six bedrooms.[8] Their neighbours were affluent members of the middle class: cotton brokers, fundholders, merchants, building contractors and bankers – a mixture of English, Scottish and Irish.[9] Everton was described by a guidebook of the 1840s as having 'some of the most fashionable residences of the Liverpool merchants'.[10]

By 1861 Jeremiah had acquired a younger sister, Annetta, aged seven, who suffered from a long-term spinal disease. A brother, Charles, born in 1858, had died from whooping cough aged only one year and eight months.[11] His parents remembered him on a gravestone in Toxteth as their 'sweet and lovely flower'. Their daughter, Annetta, whom they may have realized would not live a long life due to her spinal illness, followed her little brother to the grave in 1862, aged only eight.[12]

Only the eldest, Jeremiah, would survive. Whether Charles and Anna ever revealed to him the truth behind their marriage is uncertain. Whatever the case, the young boy must have known Ireland only as a distant and unfamiliar part of his parents' early lives. It was easy to conceal the past here.

Liverpool was full of unspeakable memories of Ireland in the second half of the nineteenth century and even more affluent families had reason not to speak of the circumstances that had driven them there. For the poor, silence was often the only response. In 1847 alone some 300,000 Irish had crowded into the city, 'the scum of Ireland', according to the hostile *Liverpool Mail*, almost half of whom continued on to America to join the migrant underclass in the cities of the east coast and Canada.[13]

By 1876 Jeremiah was twenty-five years old and working as a ship and insurance broker at the Queen's Insurance chambers on Dale Street. That he had inherited something of his father's character is suggested by an account of a court case in the Liverpool press that year. He had, according to the prosecution, been introduced to a young woman named Elizabeth McCarthy by a mutual acquaintance three years earlier at a concert in Liverpool's Philharmonic Hall. She was then nineteen years old and had just returned to Liverpool to live with her mother, having completed her convent education with the Sisters of Mercy in Birmingham. Adopting a false identity, he introduced himself to her as Harry Montagu, the name of a well-known 'vocal comedian, mimic, instrumentalist and author', and claimed to be a professor of music. According to the report in the *Liverpool Mercury*, 'Their conversations were warm and attached, [but] he carefully abstained from committing himself in the letters he wrote to her. Over and over again he refused to be introduced to her family.' He told her to address her letters to Hugh Montagu, care of J. C. Langley, White Star Company, Liverpool.[14]

The prosecution claimed that after six to eight months, Jeremiah said he wished to introduce her to his cousin, a lady who lived at Erskine Street on the outskirts of the city. 'She went there, and there, unfortunately, he seduced her.' She subsequently discovered she was pregnant but he refused to marry her 'and gradually grew colder and colder'. When her physical state could no longer be concealed, he sent her to Manchester 'to escape the notice of her family'. After a premature confinement she discovered she 'was suffering from a shocking disease', probably syphilis, and had to go to hospital. 'There she remained for six weeks or more . . . now a mere wreck, without a home, without friends, and with every prospect blasted.' An attorney offered to bring a case on her behalf against her seducer. When she informed Jeremiah of this, he said he knew all about it and that her attorney was now working for him and would not represent her. Claiming that he was poor and going abroad, he and the attorney persuaded her to accept £5 and to sign a document relinquishing any further claim against him.

This was the story according to the prosecution, who described it as 'a case unparalleled in the history of deception'. For their part, the defence attacked Miss McCarthy's moral integrity, claiming she had immediately accompanied Langley to a 'house of ill-fame' the first time they had met, imputing that she was a common prostitute.[15] The assessor for the case, Mr Pickering, decided that 'in point of law' there was insufficient evidence against Jeremiah Langley and the action was terminated. There is little reference to the child, though the papers make clear that a child was born.[16]

In 1881, Charles and Anna, now in the twilight of their lives, were still living at 44 Newlands Street, with their only surviving child, Jeremiah, who by then was a 29-year-old insurance broker. Also living with them was a middle-aged Irish servant named Ann Ryan – perhaps from Tipperary, where that name was very common.[17] Jeremiah had established himself as part of Nodder and Langley & Co., a firm of accountants and shipping insurance agents on Fenwick Street, in the commercial district close to the docks.[18] Charles, then seventy-five years of age, had retired but retained a keen sense of his professional identity, describing himself in the census of that year as 'Charles Langley, Surgeon F.R.C.S.I.'.

On 22 August 1882, thirty-two years after he had been acquitted of his first wife's murder, Charles Langley died. The death certificate gave the cause of death as 'white softening of [the] brain'. He passed his last moments in the house where he had spent his new life with Anna, and was buried with his younger children in the elegant garden cemetery at Toxteth, where his grave can still be seen today. He left an estate of £2,273, a substantial sum that set his family apart from the vast majority of emigrant Irish in nineteenth-century Britain.[19]

Ten days before his father's death, Jeremiah, at the age of thirty-three, married Elizabeth Pitts Lake, the daughter of a farmer and miller from Okehampton in Devon. She lived nearby in Everton, worked as a draper and was some ten years his senior – though she admitted to being only thirty-five.[20] Elizabeth died in 1893, and by 1898 Jeremiah had taken a second wife: Barbara Burton, the daughter of a plumber from Liverpool.[21] His social circle was far removed from that of his first cousin in Ireland, Edmund Poe, almost the same age, a naval officer on his way to becoming commander-in-chief of the Mediterranean fleet and aide-de-camp to the future king.[22]

Following her husband's death, Anna moved with her son and his first wife to a large semi-detached house on Woodhey Road, in an affluent suburb of Liverpool on the edge of Rock

Ferry on the Wirral peninsula.[23] Jeremiah's firm had been dissolved in 1886 when his partner went bankrupt, and this may have prompted the move.[24] For the 1891 census Jeremiah, aged thirty-nine, described himself as an 'insurance manager'; when serving on the Cheshire Grand Jury the same year, he said he was a 'merchant'.[25]

Rock Ferry was a pleasant place for Anna to spend her remaining years – a 'delightful neighbourhood, thickly studded with elegant villas and mansions' overlooking the river Mersey, with the smog of Liverpool only a distant haze, and steamers constantly moving between the two.[26] It was a popular retreat for day trippers from the city's factories, keen to breathe the fresher air across the river.

A short walk from Anna's home in Woodhey Road was the former residence of the celebrated author of *The Scarlet Letter*, Nathaniel Hawthorne, who had moved here in 1853 while working as a US consul in Liverpool. His presence still lingered at his white-stuccoed Gothic villa that looked out on to the Mersey, and when Anna arrived in the area a committee was busy arranging for a bronze plaque to be erected 'for the benefit of pilgrims'. His sympathetic story of a fallen woman had resonated with outsiders everywhere, inviting many to seek him out, his son recalled, 'attracted . . . out of the void by the fame of the book'.[27]

On 9 January 1893 Anna suffered an attack of acute pleurisy – an inflammation of the membrane around the lungs – followed by cardiac weakness, which sent her into unconsciousness. After lingering for two days, she died with her son at her side.[28] Jeremiah died eight years later without leaving any legitimate children, by which time there were few alive to directly recall Anna and the scandal in which she played so large a part in the years of 1849 and 1850.[29]

Nathaniel Hawthorne, who had rambled around many of the churchyards in the surrounding locality, had observed the quick decay of memorials to the dead in the damp English climate. 'So soon do lichens creep over the surface,' he remarked, 'so soon does it blacken, so soon do the edges lose their sharpness, so soon does Time gnaw away the records.'[30]

Acknowledgements

I would like to thank many people for their kind assistance during the course of writing this book. Thanks to my wife, Sarah, for commenting on the text in its earliest form and for lending a hand in digging through papers in the National Archives and the National Library of Ireland. My parents, John and Fedelma, and my siblings, Stephen, Veronica and Simon, all gave insightful feedback at important junctures. Mary Stanley provided useful comments at a later stage. My thanks in particular to Brendan Barrington at Penguin Ireland for his enthusiastic support and his judicious editing of the final drafts; and also to all the Penguin staff who helped produce the finished work. I am grateful to Charles and Susie Poë and Emma Poë, for their hospitality in Dorset and for kindly allowing me to look through their collections of Poe family documents and portraits; and to my McCutcheon cousins for access to Poë documents at Kilmore. My thanks also to Nancy Murphy for sharing her rich knowledge of Nenagh. To my former colleague Dr Diane Urquhart at the Institute of Irish Studies, Liverpool, for her generous advice in matters relating to nineteenth-century divorce. To Dr Menno Bouma for his expert advice on cholera. To Mary O'Doherty for her guidance in searching the archives of the Mercer Library at the Royal College of Surgeons. To Tony Canning, caretaker of Nenagh Courthouse, for helping me retrace Dr Langley's steps on the day of the trial. Any mistakes are, of course, my own.

ACKNOWLEDGEMENTS

My grandmother Maura, to whose memory this book is dedicated, was a great source of local knowledge about Nenagh and its old families, though unfortunately I never had the chance to discuss the Langley case with her. She carefully kept many family documents and photographs that were passed on to her from her mother Ida Poë and aunt Blanche Poë, the last surviving members of that family to live in Nenagh. Her grandfather, whom she remembered well, was one of the two little boys Dr Langley regularly encountered on his visits to Solsboro in the 1840s.

Note on sources

The destruction of Ireland's Public Record Office in 1922 saw the loss of many of the official files relating to the case of Dr Langley, including most of the nineteenth-century Crown files for the Nenagh assizes. As a result, newspaper accounts provide the principal source material for the coroner's inquest and subsequent trial. The *Nenagh Guardian*, established by John Kempston in 1838, and the *Tipperary Vindicator*, established by Maurice Lenihan in 1844, represented the respective Tory and Liberal interests in the town. Reporters from both newspapers attended the inquest and trial hearings and their accounts largely agree in substance, though not always in detail. Another important source is *The Trial of Charles Langley, Esq., F.R.C.S.I.* (Dublin: J. M'Glashan, 1850), a pamphlet in the National Library of Ireland's Joly Collection. It comprises the collected reports of the *Nenagh Guardian*, and contains the full reproduction of Dr Langley's letter to Anna Poe of 26 December 1848. I also drew on a range of regional and national newspapers from across Britain and Ireland whose coverage of the trial gives some sense of the broader interest the case inspired.

In transcribing speech and dialogue, I have tried to do justice to the rich contemporary detail and language while remaining true to the source material. Where sources differ on precisely what was said, I have attempted to reconstruct the exchanges as coherently as possible. I have silently trimmed repetitions, tidied punctuation and standardized the spellings of names. I have spelled the name Poe without the diaeresis over the 'e', as the form Poë (reflecting the disyllabic pronunciation of the name) was not adopted by the family until the latter half of the nineteenth century. The name Solsboro is a contraction of Solsborough or, sometimes, Salsborough (normally indicated by an apostrophe at the end – i.e. Solsboro'). For simplicity, I have omitted the apostrophe throughout.

Notes

Prologue: Nenagh, Co. Tipperary, 3 May 1849

1 'Records Court', *Nenagh Guardian*, 21 March 1840, p. 3.
2 'Attack on Dr Langley's house, Nenagh', *Freeman's Journal*, 7 May 1849, p. 4. The address of Dr Langley is given as 52 Barrack Street by E. H. Sheehan, but a comparison of *Slater's National Commercial Directory of Ireland* of 1846 and 1856, and Griffith's Valuation, indicates that the Langleys (and the Kittsons, who Sheehan tells us later lived in their house) lived at no. 50. Griffith's Valuation shows that this house (marked 41 on the accompanying map) is identifiable with the current no. 52. The ground floor is now divided into two commercial premises. See Sheehan's *Nenagh and Its Neighbourhood* (Dublin and Bray: Record Press, 1948), p. 13.
3 These scarves, along with black crêpe on the hats of undertakers, derived from medieval mourning practices; see Trevor May, *The Victorian Undertaker* (Oxford: Shire, 2008), p. 7.
4 Mr William Keane was contracted to supply coffins and shrouding (at 3d per yard) for the workhouse in Nenagh in September 1847; see Daniel Grace, *The Great Famine in Nenagh Poor Law Union, Co. Tipperary* (Nenagh: Relay Books, 2000), p. 174.

1. 'My poor unfortunate wife'

1 For Dr Langley's letter, see *Nenagh Guardian*, 2 May 1849, p. 3; *Tipperary Vindicator*, 2 May 1849, p. 3. Mr Carroll lived at 49 Barrack Street; see *Slater's National Commercial Directory of Ireland* (Manchester and London: Slater, 1846), p. 295.
2 James W. Hurst, 'Disturbed Tipperary: 1831–1860', *Eire-Ireland*, 9:3 (1974), 44–59.
3 See 'Remuneration of medical witnesses', *Nenagh Guardian*, 8 December 1838, p. 1; 'Petition from Ireland for remuneration at inquests', *Lancet*, 2 (1838–9), 174.

4 'Destitution', *Nenagh Guardian*, 7 April 1849, p. 2; 'Nenagh Union – Tuesday', *Nenagh Guardian*, 19 May 1849, p. 2.

5 'Pauperism', *Nenagh Guardian*, 12 May 1849, p. 2.

6 For Nenagh's rising population between 1841 and 1851, see Daniel Grace, *The Great Famine in Nenagh Poor Law Union, Co. Tipperary* (Nenagh: Relay Books, 2000), pp. 21 and 180–81.

7 'Another murder in North Tipperary – the inquest', *Nenagh Guardian*, 7 May 1845, p. 2.

8 'Another murder in North Tipperary – inquest on the body', *Nenagh Guardian*, 11 March 1846, p. 4.

9 Judith Flanders, *The Invention of Murder: How the Victorians Revelled in Death and Dectection and Created Modern Crime* (London: HarperCollins, 2011), p. 147; see also Kate Summerscale, *The Suspicions of Mr Whicher: Or the Murder at Road Hill House* (London: Bloomsbury, 2008).

10 Two men were subsequently charged with his murder. 'Crown Court, Tuesday – murder', *Nenagh Guardian*, 2 August 1845, p. 4.

11 Mercer Library, Copy Letter Book Box 27, Oct 1838, 143 RCSI/LET/2, p. 138.

2. 'Sworn to find a verdict'

1 For his description, see *Hue and Cry*, cited in *The Trial of Charles Langley, Esq., F.R.C.S.I.* (Dublin: J. M'Glashan, 1850), p. 25. He was described as 'a gentleman of substance and good social position' in the *Spectator*, 23 (1850), 295; the photograph survives in the papers of Blanche Poë, private collection.

2 'Deaths from exposure to cold on board a steam packet', *Advocate: or, Irish Industrial Journal*, 2 May 1849, p. 4; 'The swallows', *Freeman's Journal*, 3 May 1849, p. 3; 'The weather', *Dublin Evening Mail*, 2 May 1849, p. 4.

3 'Coroner's inquest', *Nenagh Guardian*, 2 May 1849, p. 3; 'Coroner's inquest', *Tipperary Vindicator*, 2 May 1849, p. 3.

4 Trevor May, *The Victorian Undertaker* (Shire: Oxford, 2008), p. 16.

5 The property qualification for coroner's juries had been long established at 40 shillings. A Barrister, *The Juror's Guide, or, the Spirit of the Jury Laws, pointing out the qualifications, duties, powers and liabilities of jurors in general* (London: T. Hurst, 1833), p. 9.

6 Newspaper reports show almost all of these men appearing on juries in Nenagh during the 1840s. Their various trades can be traced in

newspaper advertisements and in *Slater's Directory* of 1846. The religious affiliations of the jurors can be traced in local newspaper sources, particularly 'Address to the Rev Telford McDonagh', *Nenagh Guardian*, 7 September 1844, p. 3; 'Nailing the chapel doors', *Nenagh Guardian*, 6 October 1849, p. 2; and 'Catholic feeling in Nenagh', *Tipperary Vindicator*, 6 October 1849, p. 2. The social aspirations of this class are a subject of commentary in the press. Already in 1834, a satirical Dublin newspaper had lampooned those Nenagh Catholics who ventured on to the water for the regatta of the newly formed Lough Derg Yacht Club, giving them boats with made-up names such as the *Plunderer*, *Starvation* and *Conservative* (the latter described as 'a condemned shallop'). Bryan Considine had been placed in the brig *Impertinent*; see 'Nenagh personalities of a century ago', *Nenagh Guardian*, 16 February 1935, p. 4, extracted from the *Dublin Weekly Satirist*, 30 August 1834.

7   Names and dates of baptisms of George and Lydia Jackson's children from St Munchin's parish records, Limerick: William Marcus (2 March 1822); Frances (18 January 1823); Lydia (8 March 1824); Lydia Taylor (29 June 1826); Jeremiah Langley (3 May 1828); Charles (26 October 1829); Henry (29 January 1833); Elizabeth (4 July 1834); Thomas Jackson (24 February 1836); Thomas Villiers (3 October 1838). Note: Fanny's age does not correspond with that of the Frances mentioned above. Her age is given as twelve later in the inquest, indicating that she was born in 1837 – likely named after a deceased elder sister. This would also explain the repetition of the name Lydia among the children. There is no record of Fanny's birth in 1837 in the parish of St Munchin's, Limerick.

8   He is recorded as coroner for Nenagh as early as 1830; see *Treble Almanack for the Year 1830*, p. 90. At his death he is recorded as being of 'a very advanced age'; see 'Died', *Tipperary Vindicator*, 17 October 1849, p. 3, and *Slater's National Commercial Directory of Ireland* (Manchester and London: Slater, 1846), pp. 295–6. The election of a new coroner in November 1849 shows how hotly contested such an election could be; see 'Election of coroner', *Tipperary Vindicator*, 24 November 1849, p. 2.

9   For Quin's professional background, see 'Nenagh Union', *Nenagh Guardian*, 14 April 1849, p. 3.

10 Quin briefly mentions his wife's kinship with Mrs Langley; see 'Coroner's inquest on Mrs Eleanor Langley', *Tipperary Vindicator*, 9 May 1849, p. 1. Miss Harriet Harding of Beechwood, daughter of William Harding, was married in 1824 to Dr O'Neill Quin. She was related to Sir

Francis Osborne of Beechwood and the Holmes family, according to
E. H. Sheehan, *Nenagh and Its Neighbourhood* (Dublin and Bray: Record
Press, 1948), p. 16.

11 'Coroner's inquest', *Nenagh Guardian*, 5 May 1849, p. 1.

12 Peter Vinter-Johansen et al., *Cholera, Chloroform and the Science of Medicine*
(Oxford University Press, 2003), p. 168.

13 G. H. Barlow, 'Remarks on the pathology of cholera', *Medical Times
and Gazette: A Journal of Medical Science, Literature, Criticism and News*,
2 (1866), 114.

14 My thanks to Dr Menno Bouma for his help in interpreting the
post-mortem report.

15 'Inquest on the body of Mrs Eleanor Langley', *Tipperary Vindicator*,
5 May 1849, p. 1.

16 James S. Donnelly Jnr, *The Great Irish Potato Famine* (Stroud: Sutton,
2002), pp. 174–5; Dennis Pringle, 'The resurgence of tuberculosis in
the Republic of Ireland: Perceptions and reality', *Social Science & Medicine*, 68 (2009), 620–24 at 621.

17 John Hughes Bennett, *The Pathology and Treatment of Pulmonary Tuberculosis* (London: Simpkin, Marshall & Co., 1853), p. 36.

18 W. E. Vaughan, *Murder Trials in Ireland, 1836–1914* (Dublin: Four Courts
Press, 2009), pp. 46–7.

19 'Inquest on the body of Mrs Eleanor Langley', *Tipperary Vindicator*,
5 May 1849, p. 1.

20 'Coroner's inquest', *Nenagh Guardian*, 2 May 1849, p. 3.

21 The rumour of Dr Langley's arrest was later attested to by his clerk,
Mr Gabriel Prior; see 'Trial of Dr Langley', *Nenagh Guardian*, 23 March
1850, p. 2.

22 In January 1849 he was among those who attacked the Poor Law Guardians for not doing enough to prevent the death of a pauper named
Michael Collins; see 'Extraordinary proceedings', *Nenagh Guardian*, 17
January 1849, p. 1. He was also part of the group that barricaded the
church in protest against the hierarchy's treatment of the Rev. Mr Power;
see 'Nailing the chapel doors', *Nenagh Guardian*, 6 October 1849, p. 2.

23 'Inquest on the body of Mrs Eleanor Langley', *Tipperary Vindicator*,
5 May 1849, p. 1; 'Coroner's inquest', *Nenagh Guardian*, 5 May 1849, p. 1.

24 He had contributed funds towards the construction of a Catholic chapel
in his former parish of Hacketstown, Co. Carlow, but later become a
founder member of the local Brunswick Club established to oppose
Catholic emancipation; see 'Protestant liberality', *Freeman's Journal*,

9 April 1824, p. 3; 'From the Evening Mail', *Freeman's Journal*, 20 September 1828, p. 3.

25 'Coroner's inquest', *Nenagh Guardian*, 5 May 1849, p. 1; 'Inquest on the body of Mrs Eleanor Langley', *Tipperary Vindicator*, 5 May 1849, p. 1.

3. 'Things that ought to be buried in oblivion'

1 'Extraordinary proceedings', *Nenagh Guardian*, 17 January 1849, p. 1; 'Inquest at the Nenagh poorhouse', *Tipperary Vindicator*, 17 January 1849, p. 2.
2 'Inquest on the body of Mrs Eleanor Langley', *Tipperary Vindicator*, 5 May 1849, p. 1.
3 'Public meeting', *Nenagh Guardian*, 5 May 1849, p. 3.
4 'Public meeting at the Temperance Hall', *Nenagh Guardian*, 9 May 1849, p. 2.
5 'Inquest on the body of Mrs Eleanor Langley', *Tipperary Vindicator*, 5 May 1849, p. 1.
6 For Nenagh's market day, see *Slater's National Commercial Directory of Ireland* (Manchester and London: Slater, 1846), p. 295.
7 'Inquest on the body of Mrs Eleanor Langley', *Tipperary Vindicator*, 5 May 1849, p. 1.
8 Kenyon Street graveyard contains the graves of many of her contemporaries and close family members but there is no record of Mrs Eleanor Langley or Eleanor Poe (her maiden name) on any gravestone; see Nancy Murphy, *Gravestone Inscriptions, Co. Tipperary: Section B: Barony of Upper Ormond, Vol. 5: Parish of Nenagh, Kenyon Street Graveyard, St Mary's Church of Ireland* (Nenagh: Ormond Historical Society, 1992). There is also no record of her at Ballymackey; see Denise Foulkes, *Gravestone Inscriptions, Co. Tipperary: Section B, Barony of Upper Ormond, Vol. 8: Parish of Ballymackey* (Nenagh: Ormond Historical Society, 1984).

4. 'A handsome mansion, pleasantly situated'

1 For the early history of the Poe family, see Sir Edmund Bewley, *The Origin and Early History of the Family of Poe* (Dublin: Ponsonby & Gibbs, 1906). The grant to Thomas Poe of 2 March 1667/8 lists the lands of 'Killownine', 'Lislane' (*sic*), and 'Knockgilty-granane', which

correspond to those lands later mentioned in the particulars of sale for the Poe estate in the Landed Estates Court Rentals, available on www. findmypast.ie: 'Fee simple lands of Knockilligrane, Lisbane, and Killounine, now called Donnybrook', as listed in the sale of 6 August 1850.

2 Map of Donnybrook, Tipperary County Library, Thurles; Bewley, *The Origin and Early History of the Family of Poe*, p. 69.

3 NLI, Genealogical Office, MS 512, Bewley notebooks (R), pp. 166–9. The Hardens were minor gentry of English stock, who had originally settled in Borrisoleigh, a small town fifteen miles south-east of Nenagh, and whose social standing was sufficiently respectable for them to have a short entry in 'Burke's Guide', a social register of landed families, later in the century. See John Burke, *A Genealogical and Heraldic Dictionary of the Landed Gentry of Great Britain and Ireland*, vol. 1 (London: Henry Colburn, 1847), p. 536.

4 The map of 1810 shows that the Poe freehold amounted to only 264 acres, with a further 5 acres leased from the Minchin family in Knockillegrenane. A more extensive holding recorded in the Encumbered Estates papers, 1850, likely reflects the true extent of their lands during this period. Several of the leases of the lands making up the Donnybrook estate refer to George Harden, William Poe's father-in-law.

5 Samuel Lewis, *Topographical Dictionary of Ireland* (London: S. Lewis, 1837), p. 144.

6 The architectural style of the house would indicate a date in the 1770s, which would suggest the builder was Parsons Poe, the first of the family to be mentioned in reference to Donnybrook in documentary sources, or his son William Parsons Poe; see Bewley, *The Origin and Early History of the Family of Poe*, Pedigree B.

7 Private collection, Co. Tipperary. It may have been originally commissioned to advertise the sale of the estate in response to the Encumbered Estates Act.

8 These gardens appear clearly on the 6-inch Ordnance Survey map of the area for the late 1830s. See www.osi.ie.

9 He died in 1829; see E. H. Sheehan, *Nenagh and Its Neighbourhood* (Dublin and Bray: Record Press, 1948), p. 53. Later it came into the ownership of the Bowens of Bowen's Court, Co. Cork, the family of the Anglo-Irish novelist Elizabeth Bowen. Their Tipperary home at Camira, the neighbouring house to Donnybrook, was where the novelist's father would 'run wild' in his childhood during the 1870s – a

place of 'delighted surprises' and 'delighted friends', where the church during harvest time was 'decorated with apples, melons, vegetable marrows, potatoes and wreaths of berries'; see Elizabeth Bowen, *Bowen's Court and Seven Winters* (London: Vintage, 1999), pp. 325–42.

10 These houses all appear on the estate map of 1805.

11 Cited in M. Perceval Maxwell, *Outbreak of the Irish Rebellion of 1641* (Montreal: McGill-Queen's University Press, 1994), p. 18.

12 Ellen's older brother William is listed as one of the magistrates for the county of Tipperary in *Thom's Directory*; see, for example, 1834, p. 205, and 1836, p. 236.

13 Bewley, *The Origin and Early History of the Family of Poe*, Pedigree B. Her father, William, was only forty-four years old when Anne died, and he would live for a further thirty-five years. Frances Harden's birth date is given by Bewley as 16 May 1757; her date of death is found in Denise Foulkes, *Gravestone Inscriptions, Co. Tipperary: Section B, Barony of Upper Ormond, Vol. 8: Parish of Ballymackey* (Nenagh: Ormond Historical Society, 1984), p. 12. There was possibly a further sister, Jane: 'On the 17th inst, at Phibsborough, Jane wife of Robert A TIGHE Esq and daughter of the late William POE Esq of Donnybrook, co Tipperary'; see 'Deaths', *Freeman's Journal*, 22 September 1842. She is not mentioned in her father's will of 1819 and her baptism was not found by Bewley among the parish records, which throws some doubt over the accuracy of this notice. My thanks to Diane Gray, Sydney, Australia, for her correspondence on this issue.

14 A Late Professional Gentleman [R. Maunsell], *Recollections of Ireland* (Windsor Printing Works, 1865), p. 59.

15 She was out in a jaunting car with a friend, Miss Archer, when their horse took fright, overturning the vehicle. Frances escaped with only a broken leg, but Miss Archer, a doctor's daughter, was killed. *Annual Register* of 1805, p. 504.

16 *Traveller's Guide through Ireland* (Dublin: John Cumming, 1815), p. 266. The provincial regiments, including the Tipperary Militia, moved around the country as required; see *Finn's Leinster Journal*, 25 September 1805, p. 2.

17 Untitled, *Finn's Leinster Journal*, 9 July 1806, p. 2; 'The Army', *Freeman's Journal*, 6 January 1812, p. 4.

18 A Late Professional Gentleman, *Recollections of Ireland*, p. 59.

19 Sydney Owenson, *Lady Morgan's Memoirs: Autobiography, Diaries and Correspondence* (London: William H. Allen & Co., 1862), vol. 1, pp. 224–6.

20 The Rev. Mr Poe became rector of Hacketstown, Co. Carlow, in October 1815; see *HC Accounts and Papers 1, Relating to Churches, First Fruits; Civil and Military Offices; Reduction of Salary and Offices; Vice-Treasurer of Ireland*; Session 26 October 1830–22 April 1831, vol. 7, p. 60. In the parish church of St Peter in Dublin, close to the fashionable area of St Stephen's Green, Thomas Parsons Poe married the daughter of Major Faviere Maximilian, 'an old military gentleman', Parish Records for the Church of St Peter, 30 June 1815, record identifier: DU-CI-MA-48177; see churchrecords.irishgenealogy.ie; see also *A Full Report of the Trial at Bar, in the Court of King's Bench: In which the Right Hon. Arthur Wolfe, His Majesty's Attorney General, Prosecuted and A. H. Rowan, Esq. Was Defendant* (Dublin: Mackenzie, 1794), p. 5. Margery was married to Matthew Minchin; Bewley, *The Origin and Early History of the Family of Poe*, Pedigree B.

21 Bewley, *The Origin and Early History of the Family of Poe*, Pedigree B. According to Bewley, Mary Anne married a man named George Chiswell in 1819, though no further particulars are given and no more can be found. Her elder sister Martha died sometime after 1819 and it is unclear whether she had married or not. She is mentioned in the will her father made in 1819; see Bewley notebooks (R), pp. 166–9.

22 In 1808 William had married a young woman from a neighbouring county in a ceremony conducted by their brother-in-law, the Rev. Mr Poe. She was Bryanna, daughter of Thomas Gabbett of Castle Lake, Co. Clare. See Bewley, *The Origin and Early History of the Family of Poe*, Pedigree B. In the newspapers he is called John Gabbett of Rutland Street, Limerick: 'Married', *Freeman's Journal*, 13 January 1807, p. 3.

23 Bewley, *The Origin and Early History of the Family of Poe*, Pedigree B; via http://churchrecords.irishgenealogy.ie.

5. 'A very subtle thing'

1 'Coroner's inquest on Mrs Eleanor Langley', *Nenagh Guardian*, 9 May 1849, p. 1.

2 'The Lord Lieutenant in Ireland', *Nenagh Guardian*, 5 September 1838, p. 2.

3 E. H. Sheehan, *Nenagh and Its Neighbourhood* (Dublin and Bray: Record Press, 1948), p. 69.

4 Donal Murphy, *The Two Tipperarys: The National and Local Politics – Devolution and Determination of the Unique 1838 Division into Two Ridings* (Nenagh: Relay Books, 1995), p. 164.

5 Sheehan, *Nenagh and Its Neighbourhood*, p. 33.

6 Legal documents relating to the Poe family were drawn up by George Bolton – papers of Blanche Poë, private collection; House of Commons papers, no. 517: *Abstract Return of Notices Served on Relieving Officers of Poor Law Districts in Ireland, by Land-Owners under Act for Protection and Relief of Destitute Poor Evicted from Their Dwellings*, vol. 49 (London: HMSO, 1849), p. 27.

7 'Epistle from Phil Fickle to Solomon Crab, gent', *Dublin Weekly Satirist*, 23 August 1834, reproduced in 'Nenagh personalities of a century ago', *Nenagh Guardian*, 30 March 1935, p. 4.

8 Public Record Office of Northern Ireland, D971/34/G/6/2 (1841).

9 William O'Brien, *Evening Memories* (Dublin: Maunsel & Co., 1920), p. 24.

10 Jarlath Waldron, *Maamtrasna: The Murders and Mystery* (Dublin: Edmund Burke, 1992), p. 31.

11 A photograph of this portrait can be found in the papers of Blanche Poë and the original is in the possession of Charles Poë of Dorset.

12 For Bloomfield's involvement in the creation of the north and south ridings of Tipperary, see Murphy, *The Two Tipperarys*.

13 The Bishop of Clogher died in Edinburgh in 1843, having lived out his days in service as a butler; see *Gentleman's Magazine*, 175 (1844), 314. The bishop's sister wrote to the Rev. Mr Poe in 1826, four years after the scandal broke, assuring him that she had 'perfected the papers according to your directions and I trust, that happens what may, those I so tenderly love are safe from a possibility of further persecution or insult'. Public Record Office of Northern Ireland, MIC147/10 [August 1826]. [S. Arbuckle, Donaghadee] to the Rev. Mr Poe, Hacketstown. The bishop left the Rev. Mr Poe £300 in his will 'for all the kindness and attention which my beloved sisters and myself have uniformly experienced from him for many years past during a period of extreme calamity and misfortune'. Cited in Rictor Norton, 'The Bishop of Clogher', *Gay History and Literature*, via http://rictornorton.co.uk.

14 Rictor Norton (ed.), 'The Bishop of Clogher vs. James Byrne', *Homosexuality in Eighteenth-Century England: A Sourcebook*, 5 April 2010, via http://rictornorton.co.uk.

15 'Election of Guardians', *Nenagh Guardian*, 7 April 1849, p. 3.

16 'Coroner's inquest on Mrs Eleanor Langley', *Nenagh Guardian*, 9 May 1849, p. 1. There were three William Poes of Donnybrook: Ellen Langley's father (d. 1830), her elder brother (d. 1840) and her nephew (d. 1852).

17 The *Nenagh Guardian* reporter took these names down incorrectly as 'Biera' and 'Majennie'; see M. Magendie, *Formulary for the Preparation*

and Employment of Several New Remedies, trans. from 8th edn (London: E. Cox, 1835).

18 This dialogue is reconstructed from the reports of both the *Tipperary Vindicator* and the *Nenagh Guardian* of 9 May 1849.

19 'Coroner's inquest on Mrs Eleanor Langley', *Nenagh Guardian*, 9 May 1849, p. 1.

20 For the poison panic of the mid-nineteenth century, see Judith Flanders, *The Invention of Murder: How the Victorians Revelled in Death and Dectection and Created Modern Crime* (London: HarperCollins, 2011), pp. 183–247.

21 'Shocking attempt to poison a family', *Nenagh Guardian*, 11 April 1849, p. 1; 'Aberdeen – sentence of death for murder', *Nenagh Guardian*, 5 May 1849, p. 1.

22 'Analyses and notices of books', *London Medical Gazette*, 35 (1845), 861.

23 David Skae, M.D., F.R.C.S., 'Trial of John Tawell for the murder of Sarah Hart by prussic acid', *Northern Journal of Medicine*, 2 (May 1845), 396.

24 'Coroner's inquest on Mrs Eleanor Langley', *Tipperary Vindicator*, 9 May 1849, p. 1.

25 'Coroner's inquest', *Nenagh Guardian*, 9 May 1849, p. 1.

26 James S. Donnelly Jnr, *The Great Irish Potato Famine* (Stroud: Sutton, 2002), p. 174.

27 'Coroner's inquest', *Nenagh Guardian*, 9 May 1849, p. 1.

28 'Coroner's inquest on Mrs Eleanor Langley', *Tipperary Vindicator*, 9 May 1849, p. 1.

29 'Coroner's inquest', *Nenagh Guardian*, 9 May 1849, p. 1.

6. *'Ellen Poe of the city of Dublin, Spinster'*

1 'To the Editor of the Dublin Inquisitor', in *The Dublin Inquisitor for 1821*, vol. 1 (Dublin: C. P. Archer, 1821), pp. 271–2.

2 'Curious case in the Insolvent Court, Dublin', *Morning Chronicle*, 4 January 1830, p. 3; 'Insolvent debtors', *Freeman's Journal*, 7 February 1827, p. 4.

3 See Marriage Settlement of Ellen Poe and Charles Langley, National Archives, M5631 (2).

4 NLI, Genealogical Office, MS 512, Bewley notebooks (S), pp. 117–18; for the income from the Donnybrook estate, see the Landed Estates Court Rental of 1850, Lots 1 and 2.

5 The will stated that the £1,000 be divided in three, but his daughter Martha's early death meant that it was divided between Ellen and her sister Mary Anne.

6 National Archives M5631(2). This document shows that in 1831 Donnybrook was being leased to William's sister Margery and her husband, Matthew Minchin.

7 Probably the same Edward Nixon listed as 'merchant' living on Denzille Street on the voters' register of 1832 and at 60 Abbey Street in 1835: see transcriptions on www.findmypast.ie. An Edward Nixon is recorded as operating a loan fund in Dublin – see *Freeman's Journal*, 21 March 1844, p. 1; and an Edward Nixon, Esq., lived at 6 Erne Street, Dublin, in 1842, *Dublin Directory*, p. 501. The death was recorded of an Edward Nixon of Cornish Terrace, Rathmines, Dublin, in the *Nenagh Guardian*, 23 May 1849, p. 3.

8 Marriage of Philip Robert Adam Despard of 32 Upper Merrion Street, St Peter's, and Anna Poe of St Peter's on 28 May 1829; baptism of Elizabeth Frances Despard of 32 Upper Merrion Street on 26 May 1830: see parish register of St Peter's Church, Dublin, Book no. 9, p. 27, entry no. 235, via http://churchrecords.irishgenealogy.ie.

9 *Metropolitan Magazine*, 41 (1844), 141.

10 For Dublin's season, see Sarah Drumm, '"None but Persons of Fashion Need Apply": Dublin Townhouses of the Irish MPs 1750–1800' (MLitt dissertation, School of Art History and Social Policy, University College Dublin, March 2007), pp. 12–42.

11 See *The Treble Almanack for the Year 1830* (Dublin: C. Hope, 1830), pp. 86–7; J. S. Scott, King's Counsel, is listed among the residents here.

12 Thomas Parsons Poe is 'of Lucan' in Ellen's marriage settlement of 1831. He is listed as Capt. T. P. Poe of Lucan Lodge in Samuel Lewis's *Topographical Dictionary* (London: Lewis, 1837), vol. 1, pp. 321–2.

13 Ibid., p. 321.

14 The Taylors were seated at Noan, south of Thurles in Tipperary, close to the Langleys of Lisnamrock in the same county, and prominent in the same provincial society; see Sir Bernard Burke, *A Genealogical and Heraldic History of the Landed Gentry of Ireland* (London: Harrison & Sons, 1912), p. 684. For the marriage of Jeremiah Langley, see *Freeman's Journal*, 23 July 1798, from 'Nick Reddan's Newspaper Extracts', via members.iinet.net.au; 'Parish Records St Munchin, Co. Limerick', www.ancestry.com, FHL Film Number 924505.

15 'Died', *Waterford Mail*, 22 December 1841, p. 3.

16 'Mr Langley', *Limerick Chronicle*, 6 November 1811, p. 3. For the development of Richmond Place East from 1805 to 1809, see James McMahon, *The Perry Square Tontine* (Limerick: Limerick Civic Trust, 1999).

17 'Royal College of Surgeons in Ireland', *Saunders's News-letter*, 29 September 1830, p. 3.

18 These comments were made when the college was on the cusp of reform and had drafted new regulations – see 'Medical literature', *Freeman's Journal*, 10 March 1830, p. 3.

19 Cited in J. D. H. Widdess, *The Royal College of Surgeons in Ireland and Its Medical School* (Edinburgh and London: E. & S. Livingstone, 1967), pp. 48–9.

20 'Deaths', *Freeman's Journal*, 12 October 1819, p. 3.

21 For the relationship between the Langleys and the Tuthills, see Burke, *A Genealogical and Heraldic History of the Landed Gentry of Ireland*, pp. 383 and 708.

22 For the history of nineteenth-century dispensaries in Ireland, see Laurence M. Geary, *Medicine and Charity in Ireland 1718–1851* (University College Dublin Press, 2005), pp. 54–69.

23 Daniel Madden, *Ireland and Its Rulers: Since 1829*, 2nd edn, vol. 2 (London: T. C. Newby, 1844), p. 29.

24 *Tipperary Free Press*, 9 April 1831, p. 2. Dr Langley refers to the starting date of his dispensary post as April 1831 in a letter to the *Nenagh Guardian*, 16 December 1840, p. 4.

25 *Tipperary Free Press*, 13 April 1831, p. 2; *Waterford Mail*, 20 April 1831, p. 1.

26 According to his obituary in 1859, the Rev. Mr Poe had served as rector of Nenagh for twenty-eight years, i.e. from 1831. See 'Death of the Rev James Hill Poe, rector of Nenagh', *Nenagh Guardian*, 9 February 1859, p. 2.

7. 'The quietest creature in the world'

1 'Theatre Royal', *Freeman's Journal*, 13 December 1831, p. 3.

2 In their marriage settlement of 10 December 1831, Charles is described as 'of Nenagh'. Ellen is described as 'Ellen Poe of the city of Dublin, Spinster'; see National Archives M5631 (2); and *Limerick Evening Post and Clare Sentinel*, 16 December 1831, 'Nick Reddan's Newspaper Extracts', via members.iinet.net.au/~nickred/newspaper/.

3 Marriage settlement: National Archives M5631 (2).

4 'Coroner's inquest', *Nenagh Guardian*, 9 May 1849, p. 1.

5 'Coroner's inquest on Mrs Eleanor Langley', *Tipperary Vindicator*, 9 May 1849, p. 2.

6 'Coroner's inquest', *Nenagh Guardian*, 9 May 1849, p. 1.

7 'Coroner's inquest on Mrs Eleanor Langley', *Tipperary Vindicator*, 9 May 1849, p. 2.

8 River View appears incorrectly in the newspapers as 'Riverstown' and 'Riverlawn', both of which were names of other houses in the neighbourhood. For River View, see http://landedestates.nuigalway.ie.

9 Margaret Leeson, *Memoirs of Mrs Margaret Leeson* (Dublin: 1797), vol. 3, p. 213.

10 See Lisa Surridge, 'On the Offenses Against the Person Act, 1828', in *BRANCH: Britain, Representation and Nineteenth-Century History*, ed. Dino Franco Felluga, extension of *Romanticism and Victorianism on the Net*, www.branchcollective.org. For the 1853 legislation (Act for the Better Prevention and Punishment of Aggravated Assaults upon Women and Children), see Ben Griffin, *The Politics of Gender in Victorian Britain: Masculinity, Political Culture and the Struggle for Women's Rights* (Cambridge University Press, 2012), p. 70; for the full text of the 1853 Act, see www. legislation.gov.uk.

8. 'Private and pecuniary affairs'

1 'Thurles Quarter Sessions', *Tipperary Free Press*, 28 October 1837, pp. 2–3.

2 'Nenagh Dispensary', *Nenagh Guardian*, 8 January 1840, p. 4.

3 'Wanted', *Nenagh Guardian*, 4 January 1840, p. 3.

4 For an overview of the size and value of the estates in north Tipperary, see Griffith's Valuation, via www.askaboutireland.ie.

5 For the date of his commencement at the dispensary, see 'Nenagh Dispensary', *Nenagh Guardian*, 23 December 1840, p. 3.

6 'Record Court', *Nenagh Guardian*, 21 March 1840, p. 3.

7 'Nenagh Dispensary', *Nenagh Guardian*, 23 December 1840, p. 3.

8 'Nenagh Dispensary – Annual Meeting', *Nenagh Guardian*, 13 January 1841, p. 4.

9 'Nenagh Dispensary', *Nenagh Guardian*, 23 December 1840, p. 3.

10 'Nenagh Dispensary – Annual Meeting', *Nenagh Guardian*, 13 January 1841, p. 4.

11 'Nenagh Loan Fund Society', *Nenagh Guardian*, 4 January 1840, p. 3.

12 'Nenagh Loan Fund Society', *Nenagh Guardian*, 6 January 1841, p. 1. Langley was a committee member of this loan fund and like many fellow members lent some of his own money for profit. The accounts for the year show he made £20, a 6 per cent return on his investment. The sum was equal to almost four times the annual salary paid to the porter who worked in the dispensary and represented a 20 per cent boost to Langley's annual income. For Langley's salary and other annual expenses of the dispensary, see the accounts for 1841 published in the *Nenagh Guardian* on 22 January 1842, p. 3.

13 An office on William Street was leased by Dr Langley to John Bennett, treasurer of the loan fund, at an annual rate of £5 5s – see Griffith's Valuation, Nenagh North, p. 146: www.askaboutireland.ie.

14 HCP, *Fifth Annual Report of the Commissioners of the Loan Fund Board of Ireland*, vol. 28 (1843), p. 39.

15 'The usury laws – Nenagh petition', *Nenagh Guardian*, 14 May 1842, p. 3.

16 'Glorious news for the usurers!', *Nenagh Guardian*, 18 February 1843, p. 3.

17 'Nenagh Dispensary – Annual Meeting', *Nenagh Guardian*, 13 January 1841, p. 4.

18 Captain Gason also joined Dillon in leading the opposition to Langley; see 'Nenagh Dispensary – Annual Meeting', *Nenagh Guardian*, 13 January 1841, p. 4.

19 That Langley's moneylending activity continued until 1849 is clear from the testimony of Gabriel Prior at the inquest, who is described as a clerk working on his loan fund. See *The Trial of Charles Langley, Esq., F.R.C.S.I.* (Dublin: J. M'Glashan, 1850), p. 51.

20 National Archives of Ireland, *Register of debtors committed to the County Gaol, Nenagh, during the year ended 31st December 1847*, no. 158.

21 Cited in Ciarán Ó Murchadha, *The Great Famine: Ireland's Agony 1845–52* (London: Continuum, 2011), p. 103.

22 'Assault', *Nenagh Guardian*, 23 May 1847, p. 3; National Archives of Ireland, Prison Register, Nenagh Gaol, May 1847, pp. 447–8.

23 'Meeting of the Nenagh Poor Relief Committee', *Tipperary Vindicator*, 9 May 1846, p. 3; 'Poor Relief Meeting', *Nenagh Guardian*, 6 June 1846, p. 3.

24 'To the governors of the Nenagh Dispensary', *Nenagh Guardian*, 5 January 1842, p. 3.

25 'Deaths', *Waterford Mail*, 22 December 1841, p. 3.

26 *Dublin Medical Press*, 7 (1842), 96. Immediately under his resignation letter, as it appeared in the *Nenagh Guardian*, was a letter from his

friend Dr George Frith to the governors of the Nenagh Dispensary, seeking their support for his candidacy to replace Langley. This prompted an anonymous letter from one of these governors accusing Langley of having 'an understanding' with Frith or a quid pro quo of some sort. The editor of the newspaper also came under attack: 'The transaction smells rankly of jobbing, or a disposition to job. You, Sir, as the conductor of a highly respectable Public Journal, are called upon to get out of this matter with "clean hands" if you can. Surgeon Langley may despise public opinion, and refuse to explain; – but, Sir, your reputation as an Editor should be like that of Caesar's wife – not only pure, but above suspicion'; see 'To the governors of the Nenagh Dispensary', *Nenagh Guardian*, 5 January 1842, p. 3. That Langley and Frith were in collusion there can be little doubt, as the editor admitted that both letters had arrived in his office within half an hour of each other and he had simply printed them without any further communication with either party. Despite the controversy, Frith was successfully appointed in Langley's place; see 'Nenagh Dispensary', *Nenagh Guardian*, 12 January 1842, p. 3.

27 'Nenagh Fever Hospital', *Tipperary Vindicator*, 22 January 1845, p. 3; 'United Kingdom Life Assurance Company', *Tipperary Vindicator*, 23 November 1844, p. 4; 'United Kingdom Life Assurance Company', *Tipperary Vindicator*, 8 January 1845, p. 3.

28 See the testimony of Eliza Rohan, *The Trial*, p. 51.

9. 'A very bad room'

1 *The Trial of Charles Langley, Esq., F.R.C.S.I.* (Dublin: J. M'Glashan, 1850), p. 49.

2 'Coroner's inquest', *Nenagh Guardian*, 9 May 1849, p. 1.

3 Ibid., p. 2.

4 Ibid., p. 1.

5 Ibid., p. 2.

6 Ibid., p. 1.

7 John Hughes Bennett, *The Pathology and Treatment of Pulmonary Tuberculosis* (Edinburgh and London: Sutherland and Knox, 1853), pp. 88–9.

8 'Coroner's inquest', *Nenagh Guardian*, 9 May 1849, p. 1.

9 'Coroner's inquest on Mrs Eleanor Langley', *Tipperary Vindicator*, 9 May 1849, p. 2.

10 False hair allowed women to preserve the formality of their appearance without hours of unnecessary labour. The hair was acquired by dealers from poor women and sold on at high prices. See Galia Ofek, *Representations of Hair in Victorian Literature and Culture* (Farnham: Ashgate, 2009), pp. 9–10.

11 'Coroner's inquest', *Nenagh Guardian*, 9 May 1849, p. 1.

12 'Suicides', *Westmorland Gazette*, 23 June 1849, p. 1. 'Suicides by poison', *Worcestershire Chronicle*, 31 January 1849, p. 4. 'Suicide by laudanum', *Pharmaceutical Journal and Transactions*, 16 (1856–7), 340.

13 'Coroner's inquest on Mrs Eleanor Langley', *Tipperary Vindicator*, 9 May 1849, pp. 1–2.

14 Ibid., p. 1.

15 'Afflicting and fatal accident', *Tipperary Vindicator*, 23 March 1844, p. 3. By 1844 the Tuthills had moved to Rapla House on the north-east side of Nenagh. See 'The Packet's libel on the Rev. A. Nolan, P. P. Monsea', *Tipperary Vindicator*, 1 March 1848, p. 2.

16 'Coroner's inquest', *Nenagh Guardian*, 9 May 1849, p. 2; 'Coroner's inquest on Mrs Eleanor Langley', *Tipperary Vindicator*, 9 May 1849, p. 2.

17 'Coroner's inquest', *Nenagh Guardian*, 9 May 1849, p. 2.

10. 'By the doctor's orders'

1 For Dr Cahalan, see 'Public meeting', *Nenagh Guardian*, 5 May 1849, p. 3; 'The Catholics of Nenagh', *Nenagh Guardian*, 8 December 1849, p. 3; *Nenagh Guardian*, 3 October 1849, p. 3.

2 'Coroner's inquest', *Nenagh Guardian*, 9 May 1849, p. 1.

3 For the double standards in divorce law, see Diane Urquhart, 'Ireland and the Divorce and Matrimonial Causes Act of 1857', *Journal of Family History*, 38:3 (2013), 301–20 at 302.

4 Mary Lyndon Shanley, *Feminism, Marriage, and the Law in Victorian England* (Princeton University Press, 1989), pp. 36–7; see also Urquhart, 'Ireland and the Divorce and Matrimonial Causes Act', p. 302.

5 'Coroner's inquest on Mrs Eleanor Langley', *Tipperary Vindicator*, 9 May 1849, p. 1.

6 'Coroner's inquest', *Nenagh Guardian*, 9 May 1849, p. 1.

7 For the poverty at Toomevara, see Helen O'Brien, *Famine Clearances in Toomevara* (Dublin: Four Courts, 2010). The whole village was evicted just two weeks after the coroner's inquest.

8 'Declaration' [by Thomas and Nicholas Pound], *Nenagh Guardian*, 12 March 1845, p. 3.

9 Register of Nenagh Gaol for 1847, www.findmypast.com, pp. 415–16.

10 He used to 'drive out' with Eliza Rohan, but had since married a woman who worked in the Victoria Mill outside Toomevara. Much of the information on Pound comes from his later testimony; see 'The Trial of Dr Langley', *Nenagh Guardian*, 23 March 1850, p. 2. On 22 April 1842 the London *Times* recorded an attack on a woman by a 'notorious character named Pound' in the Toomevara area in that year.

11 On physical disqualifications, generative incapacity, and impediments to marriage: 'The silent friend', *Nenagh Guardian*, 30 December 1848, p. 3. *Tipperary Vindicator*, 9 May 1849, p. 1. The remedy, conveniently available through local sales reps, was the cordial balm of syriacum, priced at 11s per bottle, or four bottles for 33s. The cure for venereal disease was Perry's Purifying Specific Pills, which could be had for 3s 9d, or 11s per box.

12 'Coroner's inquest on Mrs Eleanor Langley', *Tipperary Vindicator*, 9 May 1849, p. 1.

13 'Coroner's inquest', *Nenagh Guardian*, 9 May 1849, p. 1.

14 'Coroner's inquest on Mrs Eleanor Langley', *Tipperary Vindicator*, 9 May 1849, p. 2.

15 'Coroner's inquest', *Nenagh Guardian*, 9 May 1849, p. 1.

16 Ibid.; 'Coroner's inquest on Mrs Eleanor Langley', *Tipperary Vindicator*, 9 May 1849, p. 2.

17 'Coroner's inquest on Mrs Eleanor Langley', *Tipperary Vindicator*, 9 May 1849, p. 2.

18 Ibid.

19 Ibid., p. 1.

20 John Davies, *A Manual of Materia Medica and Pharmacy, from the Fr. of H. M. Edwards and P. Vavasseur* (London: Whittaker, Treacher & Co., 1831), p. 54; John L. Capinera, *Encyclopedia of Entomology*, 2nd edn (New York: Springer, 2008), vol. 4, pp. 2008–9. Robert Edmund Scoresby-Jackson, *Note-book of Materia Medica, Pharmacology, and Therapeutics* (London: Simpkin, Marshall & Co., 1871), p. 558.

21 'Coroner's inquest', *Nenagh Guardian*, 9 May 1849, p. 1. For Abbott's appointment as a commissioner of affadavits, see 'Court of Queen's Bench', *Nenagh Guardian*, 10 June 1840, p. 2.

11. 'As small as the black hole of Calcutta'

1 Quoted in Daniel Grace, *The Great Famine in Nenagh Poor Law Union, Co. Tipperary* (Nenagh: Relay Books, 2000), p. 156.
2 Ibid., p. 161.
3 Ibid., p. 157.
4 *Nenagh Guardian*, 11 April 1849, p. 2.
5 For paupers fleeing the workhouse at the beginning of April 1849, see Grace, *The Great Famine*, p. 157.
6 Ciarán Ó Murchadha, *The Great Famine: Ireland's Agony 1845–52* (London: Continuum, 2011), p. 168.
7 'State of the country', *Nenagh Guardian*, 17 March 1849, p. 6.
8 Grace, *The Great Famine*, p. 156.
9 *Nenagh Guardian*, 14 April 1849, p. 2.
10 Bruce Elliott, *Irish Migrants in Canada: New Approach* (Montreal: McGill-Queen's University Press, 2004), p. 50.
11 'The cholera', *Nenagh Guardian*, 18 April 1849, p. 2.
12 'Doctors' salaries', *Nenagh Guardian*, 21 April 1849, p. 2.
13 'Meeting of the town commissioners', *Nenagh Guardian*, 25 April 1849, p. 2.
14 'A melancholy picture', *Nenagh Guardian*, 25 April 1849, p. 3.
15 *The Trial of Charles Langley, Esq., F.R.C.S.I.* (Dublin: J. M'Glashan, 1850), pp. 51–2.
16 She would have gone even sooner had he not insisted that she give sufficient notice. Some of her friends, she said, came and demanded she be released. Soon afterwards she got a job at Riverston, the home of the Bennetts, on the east side of the town, where the gardener, Edward Rohan, was likely a relation of hers. For the reference to Edward Rohan as the gardener at Riverston, see 'Nenagh Quarter Sessions – Tuesday', *Nenagh Guardian*, 18 July 1846, p. 1.
17 'Coroner's inquest on Mrs Eleanor Langley', *Tipperary Vindicator*, 9 May 1849, p. 1.
18 Anonymous, *The Female's Friend under the Sanction of the Associate Institution for Improving and Enforcing the Laws for the Protection of Women* (London: Houlston and Stoneman, 1846), p. 61.
19 *The Trial*, p. 51.
20 'To correspondents', *Tipperary Vindicator*, 11 April 1849, p. 2; *Tipperary Vindicator*, 14 April 1849, p. 2.

21 'Coroner's inquest on Mrs Eleanor Langley', *Tipperary Vindicator*, 9 May 1849, p. 1.

22 The two-storey house (no. 37) where Ellen lodged still stands today on the south side of the street, like many of its neighbours only one bay wide, testimony to the cramped conditions routine among the working classes in provincial Irish towns. See Griffith's Valuation of 1851, Parish of Nenagh, p. 141, via www.askaboutireland.ie. The house is no. 93 on the accompanying valuation map.

23 'Military outrage in Nenagh', *Tipperary Vindicator*, 7 June 1848, cited in the *Tuam Herald*, 10 June 1848, p. 2.

24 See Cormac Ó Grada, *Black '47 and Beyond* (Princeton University Press, 2000), p. 64; Grace, *The Great Famine*, p. 84.

25 'The weather', *Nenagh Guardian*, 25 April 1849, p. 4.

26 'Coroner's inquest', *Nenagh Guardian*, 9 May 1849, p. 2.

27 *Slater's Directory* of 1846, pp. 295–8.

28 'A sign of the times', *Nenagh Guardian*, 30 December 1848, p. 2.

12. 'Every kindness and good treatment'

1 'Coroner's inquest', *Nenagh Guardian*, 9 May 1849, p. 2.

2 'Coroner's inquest on Mrs Eleanor Langley', *Tipperary Vindicator*, 9 May 1849, p. 2.

3 The length of her stay was given as a fortnight and three days in the testimony of Margaret Meara, her landlord in Pound Street; see 'The trial of Dr Langley', *Nenagh Guardian*, 23 March 1850, p. 2.

4 'Coroner's inquest', *Nenagh Guardian*, 9 May 1849, p. 2; *The Trial of Charles Langley, Esq., F.R.C.S.I.,* (Dublin: J. M'Glashan, 1850), p. 58.

5 'Coroner's inquest', *Nenagh Guardian*, 9 May 1849, p. 2; 'Coroner's inquest on Mrs Eleanor Langley', *Tipperary Vindicator*, 9 May 1849, p. 2.

6 Ibid.

7 F. W. Richardson, *The Successful Treatment of Asiatic and English Cholera with Brief Remarks on the Various Forms of Diarrhoea* (London: Simpkin, Marshall & Co., 1853), p. 12.

13. 'Thou shalt not escape calumny'

1 Dillon slightly misquotes Shakespeare. Act 3, Scene I of *Hamlet* contains the following lines: 'Be thou as chaste as ice, pure as snow, thou shalt not escape calumny.' A reference to 'as white as driven snow' appears in Act 4, Scene II of *A Winter's Tale*.

2 'Coroner's inquest', *Nenagh Guardian*, 9 May 1849, p. 2; 'Coroner's inquest on Mrs Eleanor Langley', *Tipperary Vindicator*, 9 May 1849, p. 2.

14. 'My anxiety to vindicate my character'

1 *Trial of Charles Langley, Esq., F.R.C.S.I.* (Dublin: J. M'Glashan, 1850), p. 25; also reproduced in London's *Morning Post*, 14 May 1849, p. 2.

2 *Limerick and Clare Examiner*, 19 May 1849, p. 4.

3 See for example 'Serious charge against a medical doctor' in London's *Lloyd's Weekly Newspaper*, 13 May 1849, p. 9; 'Ireland', *Morning Post*, 10 May 1849, p. 6; 'Coroner's verdict of manslaughter against Dr Langley', *Standard*, 10 May 1849, p. 3; 'Ireland', *Daily News*, 11 May 1849, p. 7; 'Coroner's verdict of manslaughter against Dr Langley', *Hampshire Telegraph and Sussex Chronicle*, 12 May 1849, p. 8; 'Cruelty of a husband', *Blackburn Standard*, 16 May 1849, p. 4; 'Ireland', *Trewman's Exeter Flying Post or Plymouth and Cornish Advertiser*, 24 May 1849, p. 2.

4 Martin J. Wiener, *Men of Blood: Violence, Manliness, and Criminal Justice in Victorian England* (Cambridge University Press, 2004), pp. 26–7.

5 'Dr Langley', *Nenagh Guardian*, 19 May 1849, p. 2; 'Dr Langley', *Tipperary Vindicator*, 20 June 1849, p. 2.

6 *Freeman's Journal*, 13 July 1849, p. 2, citing *Limerick Chronicle*.

7 'To the editor of the *Nenagh Guardian*', *Nenagh Guardian*, 18 July 1849, p. 3.

8 'Dr Langley', *Tipperary Vindicator*, 18 July 1849, p. 3.

9 Prison Register for Nenagh Gaol, 15 July 1849, prison number 2672, www.findmypast.ie.

10 'Nenagh Quarter Sessions', *Nenagh Guardian*, 14 July 1849, p. 2.

11 'The process of slow poisoning', *Freeman's Journal*, 9 May 1849, p. 4.

12 D. G. Boyce, *Nineteenth-Century Ireland* (Dublin: Gill and Macmillan, 1990), p. 116.

13 Cited in James S. Donnelly Jnr, *The Great Irish Potato Famine* (Sutton: Stroud, 2002), p. 143.

14 'Emigration from Ireland', Parl. Deb. (series 3), vol. 105, cols. 500–532 (15 May 1849), via hansard.millbanksystems.com.

15 'A coffin maker's bill', *Observer*, 9 September 1849, p. 7.

16 Cited in Mary Jean Corbett, *Allegories of Union in Irish and English Writing, 1790–1870* (Cambridge University Press, 2004), p. 149.

17 William Bullen, *A Memoir of the Union and the Agitations for Its Repeal* (Dublin: William Curray, Jun. & Co.; London: Brown & Co., 1843), p. 39.

18 *Limerick Reporter*, 1 May 1849, p. 2.

19 W. J. Linton, 'Ireland and Repeal' in *The Republican: A Magazine Advocating the Sovereignty of the People* (London: J. Watson, 1848), p. 83.

20 'The O'Meara and Fulton Club', *Nenagh Guardian*, 12 July 1848, p. 2.

21 For details of the Grand Jury at the Summer Assizes in Nenagh in 1849, see 'Tipperary North Riding Summer Assizes', *Tipperary Vindicator*, 28 July 1849, p. 2. For the timing of their judgement, see 'Dr Langley's trial', *Limerick Reporter*, 7 August 1849, p. 4.

22 'Dr Langley', *Nenagh Guardian*, 1 August 1849, p. 3.

15. 'The new Bernard Cavanagh'

1 'Another horrible scene at a public execution', *Tuam Herald*, 29 April 1848, p. 2, cited by the *Tipperary Vindicator*.

2 Poe and Quin are listed in these respective roles for the county prison in Nenagh in *Slater's Directory* of 1846, p. 298. Quin was removed from the post because he was also acting as a supplier of milk to the gaol, which was against regulations. See 'Nenagh County Prison', *Tipperary Vindicator*, 4 August 1849, p. 3.

3 *Annual Register* of 1859, vol. 101, p. 457; *Gentleman's Magazine*, 179 (1846), 306; 'Mr Martley, Q.C. was on Friday appointed to the office of counsel to the chief secretary, in the room of Mr Brewster', *Law Times* (1846), 423.

4 'Dempster vs Langley', *Tipperary Free Press*, 25 March 1840, p. 2.

5 For his role in the case against O'Connell, see William Charles Townsend, *Modern State Trials: Revised and Illustrated with Essays and Notes* (London: Longman, Brown, Green and Longmans, 1850), vol. 2, p. 392; 'Trial of John Delahunt', *Freeman's Journal*, 15 January 1842, p. 3; 'Charge of murder', *Freeman's Journal*, 13 August 1842, p. 4.

6 'Trial of Mrs Ellen Byrne', *Nenagh Guardian*, 20 August 1842, p. 4.

7 'Nenagh Assizes – County Court – Thursday, Dr Langley's case', *Limerick Reporter*, 7 August 1849, p. 4.

8 'Nenagh Assizes – Thursday, 2nd August', *Dublin Evening Mail*, 6 August 1849, p. 4.

9 'Nenagh Assizes – County Court – Thursday, Dr Langley's case', *Limerick Reporter*, 7 August 1849, p. 4.

10 'Arraignment of Dr Langley', *Nenagh Guardian*, 1 August 1849, p. 2.

11 'Dr Langley's trial', *Limerick Reporter*, 7 August 1849, p. 4.

12 Ibid.

13 'Our assizes', *Nenagh Guardian*, 4 August 1849, p. 3; 'Tipperary Assizes', *Freeman's Journal*, 6 August 1849, p. 4.

14 'Our assizes', *Nenagh Guardian*, 4 August 1849, p. 3.

15 'Cricket match', *Nenagh Guardian*, 1 August 1849, p. 3.

16 'Lough Derg Regatta', *Nenagh Guardian*, 12 September 1849, p. 2.

17 'The Queen's visit', *Nenagh Guardian*, 1 August 1849, p. 3.

18 'Bernard Cavanagh in the shade', *Nenagh Guardian*, 28 November 1849, p. 2.

19 'Extraordinary fasting', *Tipperary Vindicator*, 1 December 1849, p. 2. This letter was widely reported in the Irish and British press; see, for example, 'Fasting extraordinary', *Newcastle Courant*, 14 December 1849, p. 2; 'Facts and scraps', *Berrow's Worcester Journal*, 13 December 1849, p. 1; 'The Tipperary Vindicator says', *Morning Post*, 6 December 1849, p. 6.

20 *The Trial of Charles Langley, Esq., F.R.C.S.I.* (Dublin: J. M'Glashan, 1850), p. 42.

21 Alexandre Dumas, *The Count of Monte Cristo*, vol. 1 (London: Chapman and Hall, 1846), p. 56.

22 'Bernard Cavanagh in the shade', *Nenagh Guardian*, 28 November 1849, p. 2; 'The new Bernard Cavanagh', *The Times*, 7 December 1849, p. 3; 'Bernard Cavanagh outdone', *Era*, 9 December 1849; 'Another Bernard Cavanagh', *Dundee Courier*, 12 December 1849, p. 1; 'A new Cavanagh', *Caledonian Mercury*, 10 December 1849, p. 1.

23 L. Blanchard (ed.), *George Cruikshank's Omnibus* (1842), p. 53.

24 'Quackery and total abstinence', *Medical Times*, 4 (1842), 115.

25 For a full account of Cavanagh's career, see Jimmy Kavanagh 'The Man Who Lived on the Word of God', www.kavanaghfamily.com.

26 'Nuts and nutcrackers – no. 1', *Dublin University Magazine*, 19 (1842), 114.

27 'Nenagh Gaol', *Tipperary Vindicator*, 28 April 1849, p. 2.

28 *Reports from Commissioners, Vol. 16: Prisons (Scotland); Prisons (Ireland); Factories*, Session 2 February–24 August 1843, vol. XXVII, p. 77.

29 'The Queen vs Dr Charles Langley', *Nenagh Guardian*, 19 December 1849, p. 4.

16. 'Allowing for the frailties of our nature'

1 For the academy next door, see 'Nenagh School', *Nenagh Guardian*, 22 July 1843, p. 3. For a description of the 79th Highland Regiment at Nenagh Barracks under Captain Monroe, see 'Another insurrection – Bella! – Horrida bella!', *Tipperary Vindicator*, 9 December 1848, p. 2; 'Most desirable residence', *Tipperary Vindicator*, 23 July 1845, p. 3.

2 The tea urn, mentioned in the rectory inventory (see note 3 below), was a common feature of Victorian drawing rooms. It was designed as 'the most elegant mode of supplying water for tea ... made in the form of a vase, but in a great variety of patterns'. See Andrea Broomfield, *Food and Cooking in Victorian England: A History* (Westport: Praeger, 2007), p. 70.

3 A full list of the contents of the rectory during the Rev. Mr Poe's tenure is given in 'Auctions', *Nenagh Guardian*, 23 March 1859, p. 2.

4 The monument is on the north wall of St Mary's Church, Nenagh:

It would ill suit the meekness of those Christian doctrines, her veneration for which constituted the true and lasting glory of the deceased, to celebrate on this marble those intellectual endowments, which conferred on her a higher distinction than rank, or titles of mere human contrivance can bestow, but it may be recorded with strict propriety and perfect truth, that her faith was ardent, her piety sincere, her temper gentle and for tenderness of her heart, it would indeed be difficult to surpass. It is accordingly hoped that through the mercies of her God and the merits of her redeemer, in which she ever firmly trusted, and devoutly believed, she is now reaping the eternal fruits of (allowing for the frailties of our nature) a well spent life. Her son James Hill Poe, Rector of this parish, left (in deploring his loss) to imitate her example has erected this plain memorial of a mother's virtues and a son's regret.

5 See Midori Yamaguchi, *Daughters of the Anglican Clergy: Religion, Gender and Identity in Victorian Britain* (Basingstoke: Palgrave Macmillan, 2014), pp. 74–130.

6 *The Female Visitor to the Poor: or Records of Female Parochial Visiting. By a Clergyman's Daughter* (London: Seeley, Burnside and Seeley, 1846); *Female Examples Selected from Holy Scriptures. For Young Persons. By a Clergyman's Daughter* (London: J. Hatchard and Son, 1848); *The Young Cook's Assistant: Being a Selection of Economical Receipts and Directions, Adapted to the Use of Families in the Middle Rank of Life. Edited by a Clergyman's Daughter* (London and Edinburgh: John Johnstone, 1848); A Clergyman's Daughter, *The Battles of the Bible* (Edinburgh: Patton & Richie, 1852).

7 *The Trial of Charles Langley, Esq., F.R.C.S.I.* (Dublin: J. M'Glashan, 1850), p. 43; 'Presentation to Mrs Quin', *Nenagh Guardian*, 13 May 1846, p. 3.

8 'County Tipperary Protestant Orphan Society', *Nenagh Guardian*, 10 September 1845, p. 3. Her subscription card for the Deaf and Dumb Society in 1835, when she was just eighteen, shows that Dr Langley and his wife had been enthusiastic supporters of their niece's cause, each contributing 2s 6d. For Mrs Poe's involvement in the Nenagh Poor Clothing Fund, see *Tipperary Vindicator*, 2 August 1845, p. 3.

9 'Poor Law intelligence – Nenagh Union', *Tipperary Vindicator*, 8 July 1844, p. 3.

10 Daniel Grace, *The Great Famine in Nenagh Poor Law Union, Co. Tipperary* (Nenagh: Relay Books, 2000), p. 96; 'Nenagh soup kitchen', *Tipperary Vindicator*, 30 December 1846, p. 1.

11 Blanche Poë papers, private collection.

12 'The picnic at Dromineer', *Tipperary Vindicator*, 14 August 1844, p. 2.

13 Mr Crofts is named as the principal claimant against John Poe in contemporary reports of Solsboro as an encumbered estate. See, for example, 'Equity Exchequer', *Nenagh Guardian*, 11 March 1848, p. 3.

14 Francis Bowen, *The Principles of Political Economy* (Boston: Little Brown & Company), p. 520.

15 'Evictions in the half barony of Owney, Co. Tipperary', *Nenagh Guardian*, 2 September 1848, p. 2, cited by the *Limerick Reporter*.

16 'Nenagh Subscription Ball', *Tipperary Vindicator*, 26 September 1849, p. 3.

17. 'How say you, Charles Langley?'

1 'The Dublin markets', *Freeman's Journal*, 15 March 1850, p. 4; 'Sporting intelligence', *Freeman's Journal*, 15 March 1850, p. 2; 'Agricultural report', *King's County Chronicle*, 20 (March 1850), p. 4; *Advocate: or, Irish*

Industrial Journal, 20 March 1850, p. 15; 'Farming operations', *Freeman's Journal*, 22 March 1850, p. 3; *Farmer's Gazette*, 16 March 1850, p. 4; 'The weather – the crops', *Irish Farmers' Gazette*, 23 March 1850, p. 9.

2　*Irish Farmers' Gazette*, 23 March 1850, p. 9; *Limerick Reporter*, 26 March 1850, p. 2.

3　The purpose of the subterranean passage between Nenagh Gaol and the courthouse is described in the *Waterford Mail*, 13 September 1843, p. 3. The description of the passage is based on the author's personal observation.

4　The courtroom is largely intact today.

5　F. Elrington Ball, *The Judges in Ireland, 1221–1921* (London: John Murray, 1926), pp. 284–5; 351–2; Ciaran O'Neill, *Catholics of Consequence* (Oxford University Press, 2014), p. 115. Judge Ball resided at the palatial 85 St Stephen's Green, later sold to the Catholic university founded by Cardinal Newman; see *Irish Arts Review*, 10 (1994), 112.

6　*Nenagh Guardian*, 27 February 1850, p. 2; 6 March 1850, p. 3.

7　'Trial of Dr Langley for the murder of his wife', *Freeman's Journal*, 25 March 1850, p. 4.

8　'Trial of Dr Langley', *Nenagh Guardian*, 23 March 1850, p. 1.

9　'Trial of Dr Langley for the murder of his wife', *Freeman's Journal*, 25 March 1850, p. 4.

10　The opening of the trial is summarized in 'Trial of Dr Langley', *Nenagh Guardian*, 23 March 1850, p. 1. A more detailed account is given in 'Trial of Dr Langley for the murder of Mrs Langley', *Limerick Reporter and Tipperary Vindicator*, 22 March 1850, p. 1.

11　For this question, see 'The trial of Dr Langley for the murder of his wife', *Ballina Chronicle*, 27 March 1850.

12　*The Trial of Charles Langley, Esq., F.R.C.S.I.* (Dublin: J. M'Glashan, 1850), p. 33.

13　Scott was 'father of the Leinster Circuit', having been called to the bar as early as 1804; see *Thom's Directory of Ireland* (1850), p. 369.

14　'Murder of Gleeson', *Tipperary Vindicator*, 26 March 1845, pp. 1–2.

15　'Trial of Dr Langley', *Nenagh Guardian*, 23 March 1850, p. 1.

16　'Deaths', *Nenagh Guardian*, 23 May 1849, p. 3.

17　Leonard Shelford, *A Practical Treatise on the Law of Marriage and Divorce* (Philadelphia: John S. Little, 1841), p. 359.

18　*The Trial*, p. 47.

19　'Landed Estates Court Rentals' at www.findmypast.com; 'Notice to claimants and incumbrancers', *Nenagh Guardian*, 3 April 1850, p. 3;

'Encumbered Estates Commission – sale of estates', *Nenagh Guardian*, 7 August 1850, p. 2.

20 NLI, Genealogical Office, MS 512, Bewley notebooks (5), p. 117; Richard Bligh, *New Reports of Cases Heard in the House of Lords: On Appeals and Writs of Error*, vol. 4 (London: Henry Butterworth, 1833), p. 411.

21 Following the Tithe War of the early 1830s, the Tithe Commutation Bill of 1838 made landlords responsible for supporting the clergy by incorporating tithes through increased rental payments. In 1831, as the new incumbent of both the urban parish of Nenagh and the nearby rural parish of Knigh, the Rev. Mr Poe had encountered severe resistance to payment as the protest against tithes gripped the locality. For the first year of the conflict over £147 remained outstanding to him, but by the end of the following year, as more tenant farmers resisted, the sum had risen to £655. Nenagh's population held steadfast against the Established Church. By the end of the decade, the Rev. Mr Poe was so penniless that he was forced to suffer the indignity of appearing in the Court for the Relief of Insolvent Debtors; see *Tithe arrears, Ireland. Return of the arrears of tithe due in the several dioceses of Ireland*, from 1 May 1829, p. 17; see also 'In the matter of Rev. James Hill Poe, an insolvent', *Nenagh Guardian*, 22 February 1840, p. 3. The embarrassment spread to his relations. A Dublin satirical paper joked in 1834 that Ellen's brother William rode a horse named 'Tithepayer', over the lands of local tenant farmers in the £50 Nenagh steeplechase of August that year; see 'Nenagh personalities of a century ago', *Nenagh Guardian*, 23 February 1935, p. 4, extracted from the *Dublin Weekly Satirist*, 16 August 1834.

22 'Gaol appointments', *Nenagh Guardian*, 3 August 1842, p. 3; 'Nenagh Poor Law meeting', *Nenagh Guardian*, 19 June 1842, p. 3; 'Nenagh Union', *Nenagh Guardian*, 19 May 1849, p. 2.

23 A Late Professional Gentleman [R. Maunsell], *Recollections of Ireland* (Windsor Printing Works, 1865), p. 11.

24 E. H. Sheehan, *Nenagh and Its Neighbourhood* (Dublin and Bray: Record Press, 1948), p. 86.

25 'Equity Exchequer', *Nenagh Guardian*, 8 November 1848, p. 3; John Poe of Solsboro was in debt to everyone, but most notably to a relation of his brother's daughter-in-law, the Rev. Freeman Crofts from Cork, the principal claimant against his estate; and also his cousin, Lord Bloomfield, as well as his wife's brother, Thomas Bernard of Castle Bernard. He had spread his search for loans wide, tapping any family

connection to the rich and powerful. Among his creditors was the wealthy Earl of Donoughmore, to whom his wife was closely connected by her brother's marriage to Lady Catherine Hely-Hutchinson, the earl's daughter – see Poe of Woodville papers, National Archives of Ireland. There are several detailed indentures in this collection outlining the debts owed by John Poe. The estate's creditors soon forced him to sell Solsboro; James Jocelyn journeyed to Dublin to supervise the sale on behalf of his uncle. His diary of 18 November 1852 records that the 200-year-old estate – his inheritance – was *all sold in 20 minutes!!!* (Papers of Blanche Poë, private collection).

26 *The Trial*, p. 47.

27 'Coroner's inquest on Mrs Eleanor Langley', *Tipperary Vindicator*, 9 May 1849, p. 2.

28 For the Kingsley family, see NLI, Genealogical Office, MS 810, p. 22. A 'Dr Kean' is mentioned as one of several of the town's doctors in a satirical tract on Nenagh published in the *Weekly Dublin Satirist*, 23 August 1834; see 'Nenagh personalities of a century ago', *Nenagh Guardian*, 30 March 1935, p. 4.

29 *The Trial*, p. 53.

30 'Trial of Dr Langley', *Nenagh Guardian*, 23 March 1850, p. 1.

31 For the hissing in court, see 'Trial of Dr Langley for the murder of his wife', *King's County Chronicle*, 27 March 1850, p. 1.

18. 'The book of fate'

1 *The Trial of Charles Langley, Esq., F.R.C.S.I.* (Dublin: J. M'Glashan, 1850), p. 44.

2 Ibid., p. 43.

3 'Marriages', *Freeman's Journal*, 5 July 1849, from 'Nick Reddan's Newspaper Extracts', part 56, members.iinet.net.au; *Slater's National Commercial Directory of Ireland*, p. 295.

4 *The Trial*, pp. 37 and 43.

5 Ibid., p. 44.

6 Elizabeth Bowen, *The Shelbourne: A Centre in Dublin Life for More than a Century* (London: Harrap, 1951), p. 32.

7 William Thackeray, *The Irish Sketch Book* (New York: Charles Scribner's Sons, 1911), p. 28.

8 *Nenagh Guardian*, 30 April 1845, p. 4.

9 'Marriages', *Nenagh Guardian*, 2 March 1842, p. 3.

10 For their family background and association with Killiney Castle, see Sir Bernard Burke, *A Genealogical and Heraldic History of the Landed Gentry of Ireland* (London: Harrison & Sons, 1912), pp. 62–3.

11 *The Trial*, p. 40.

12 Ibid., p. 37.

13 Ibid., p. 38.

14 Ibid., pp. 38–9.

15 Ibid., p. 40.

16 Ibid. The 'undress circle' was an archaic term for one of the upper circles in a theatre occupied by 'decent men and women, who have hats and whole dresses . . . Why this place is called the Undress Circle no one knows, for it is only half a circle, and every one in it is fully dressed', *Zozimus*, 20 April 1872, p. 241. For the review of Lind's performance, see 'Theatre Royal', *Nenagh Guardian*, 28 October 1848, p. 1.

17 *The Trial*, pp. 40–41.

18 R. M. Levey and J. O'Rorke, *Annals of the Theatre Royal* (Dublin: Joseph Dollard, 1880), pp. 130, 137 and 141.

19 *The Trial*, p. 37.

20 Identified in the *Nenagh Guardian* simply as W. T. but by his full name in the *Limerick Chronicle*, 27 March 1850. He was married in 1835 to Frances, daughter of Major Taylor and Mary Anne Rolfe. William Tuthill appears to have had a house at 88 (38?) Fitzwilliam Place, Dublin; see *Nenagh Guardian*, 29 March 1845, p. 3. He also seems to have been a solicitor; see *Nenagh Guardian*, 24 February 1849, p. 4. He had a 1,307-acre estate in Tipperary; see http://landedestates.ie. His wife died on 31 December 1845; see *Freeman's Journal*, 4 January 1845.

21 'Coroner's inquest on Mrs Eleanor Langley', *Tipperary Vindicator*, 9 May 1849, p. 1.

22 *The Trial*, p. 37.

23 Ibid.

24 *Nenagh Guardian*, 22 February 1840, p. 3; 'The Nenagh Cricket Club', *Nenagh Guardian*, 9 June 1849, p. 2.

25 'The 52nd Depot', *Nenagh Guardian*, 15 May 1844, p. 3.

26 E. H. Sheehan, *Nenagh and Its Neighbourhood* (Dublin and Bray: Record Press, 1948), p. 4.

27 *The Trial*, p. 38.

28 Ibid., p. 37.

29 Thomas Lefroy, *Memoir of Chief Justice Lefroy* (Dublin: Hodges, 1871), p. 40. An absentee landlord in the area and a subscriber to the dispensary, Lefroy was always received there, he later recalled, in 'the most cordial and friendly manner'. He presided at several murder trials in the town and was an annual contributor to the Nenagh Dispensary, so would have been aware of the controversy surrounding Langley's appointment in the early 1840s. He was also an absentee landlord of a 1,000-acre estate in the Nenagh area, in the townland of Knigh just north of the town, in a parish administered by the Rev. Mr Poe; see Landed Estates Database, NUI Galway, http://landedestates.nuigalway.ie. In May 1849 he was listed among the defaulters of the local poor rate; but it was explained that '[he] ejected all the tenants out of the land, and, after they had been ejected, the collector had nothing to destrain, but the rates would be paid one of these days'; see 'The clearance system', *The Northern Star and National Trades Journal*, 26 May 1849, p. 6.

30 Jane Bennett, James Jocelyn Poe's wife, was the granddaughter of John Bennett, a Justice of the King's Bench, and niece to George Bennett, 'the unbending Tory lawyer', who was Father of the Munster Circuit. One of George's daughters was married to Joseph Sheridan Le Fanu, the writer of Gothic horror and chronicler of Irish Protestant angst, who came from Abington, eighteen miles south-west of Nenagh. Another of his daughters was the mother of Rhoda Broughton, who would go on to become one of the most popular writers of sensationalist fiction in the late Victorian period. The Bennetts were well known beyond this locality and connected by marriage to the much-respected Baron Pennefeather, a younger brother of the Lord Chancellor of Ireland, and to the earls of Glengall, and later the earls of Stanhope.

31 For John Bourchier, see *Slater's Directory* of 1846, p. 296. He is listed among the subscribers to the Nenagh Dispensary – see 'Dispensary meeting', *Nenagh Guardian*, 14 January 1842, p. 2. He was also from a well-known landowning family in Clare and Tipperary and had a Dublin residence at Killiney Castle; see Landed Estates Database, NUI Galway, http://landedestates.nuigalway.ie.

32 *The Trial*, p. 37.

33 Ibid., p. 41.

34 Ibid. Edward Tuthill and William Tuthill appear to have been brothers. They are mentioned together several times in Dublin newspaper sources and both entered the legal profession. Edward Tuthill is

described as the son of John Tuthill of Ballinalea, Co. Limerick – also referred to as Ballinlina or Ballinlinea or Ballylyna, part of the estate of Charles Langley's first cousin, John Tuthill; see 'Trinity Term', *Dublin Monitor*, 28 May 1840, p. 3; 'Trinity Term', *Dublin Evening Mail*, 29 May 1840, p. 3; Rev. Patrick FitzGerald and J. J. McGregor, *The History, Topography and Antiquities of the County and City of Limerick* (Dublin: Baldwin, Craddock & Joy), vol. 1, p. 346. Neither is mentioned in the family pedigree, suggesting they may have been illegitimate; see Burke, *A Genealogical and Heraldic History of the Landed Gentry of Ireland*, p. 708. The Catholic parish registers for St Mary's parish, Limerick, has a William Tuthill, son of John Tuthill and Margaret Ryan, baptized 27 November 1814; see Microfilm 02412/02, Catholic Parish Registers, National Library of Ireland, Dublin, Ireland.

35 *The Trial*, p. 44.
36 Ibid., p. 43.
37 Ibid., p. 42.
38 Ibid., p. 39.
39 Ibid., p. 46.
40 Ibid., pp. 38–9.
41 Ibid., p. 39.
42 Sir Bernard Burke, *A Genealogical and Heraldic Dictionary of the Landed Gentry of Great Britain and Ireland*, vol. 2 (London: Colburn & Co., 1863), p. 1205.
43 *The Trial*, p. 41.
44 Langley quotes her words in his own letter, *The Trial*, p. 40.
45 Ibid., p. 38.

19. 'Sweet dear Solsboro'

1 *The Trial of Charles Langley, Esq., F.R.C.S.I.* (Dublin: J. M'Glashan, 1850), p. 42.
2 Stephanie L. Barczewski, 'James, George Payne Rainsford (1801–1860)', *Oxford Dictionary of National Biography* (Oxford University Press, 2004; online edn, May 2011, www.oxforddnb.com). 'His plots are poor, his descriptions weak, his dialogue often below even a fair average, and he was deplorably prone to repeat himself': Adrian Joline, *George Payne Rainsford James* (privately printed, 1906), p. 75.
3 *The Trial*, p. 42.
4 Ibid., p. 45.

5 Ibid. John's illness is referred to in later family letters. In one letter from John to his brother Hill dated 24 September 1879, he refers to 'spitting of blood, from the throat this time, and not so serious, but still very distressing, & rendering me useless in the house, & only a trouble at such a time' (private collection).

6 *The Trial*, p. 41.

7 'Deaths', *Tipperary Vindicator*, 5 July 1845, p. 3, William Poe, second son of the Rev. Mr Poe, brought a new variety of potato back from Normandy in 1842, suggesting the family holidayed there, or that John and Barbara Poe had fled there to escape their creditors and live less expensively. 'Extraordinary produce', *Dublin Morning Register*, 3 November 1842, p. 1.

8 *The Trial*, p. 41.

9 Ibid., p. 42.

10 Ibid., p. 38.

11 Details on the planting of the beech trees along the road and around the fort can be found in a report on litigation over them between two branches of the Poes in 1859; see 'J. J. Poe vs H. H. Poe', *Nenagh Guardian*, 30 July 1859, p. 3.

12 The breed of cattle is mentioned in 'Auction', *Tipperary Vindicator*, 15 April 1848, p. 3.

13 He was dismissed from his post a few days after Christmas 1849. See 'Tipperary North Riding Assizes – Monday', *Tipperary Vindicator*, 30 July 1850, p. 3.

14 *Nenagh Guardian*, 3 February 1877, p. 4.

15 G. Jekyll, 'John T. Bennett Poe', *Gardening Illustrated* (1926), p. 312; Johnny would win the Victoria medal for gardening in 1902; see *Garden*, 25 October 1902, p. 278. His older brother, Hill, also a gardening enthusiast, discovered a new variety of snowdrop that bears his name – *Galanthus* 'Hill Poe'.

16 *The Trial*, p. 45.

17 Ibid., p. 43.

18 Ibid., p. 39.

19 Ibid., p. 43.

20 Ibid., p. 40.

21 Ibid., p. 44.

22 Ibid., p. 39.

23 Ibid., p. 43.

24 Ibid., p. 42.

25 Ibid., p. 43.

26 'Christmas', *Nenagh Guardian*, 23 December 1848, p. 2.

27 For Langley's comments on the weather, see *The Trial*, p. 45.

28 Lisa Surridge, *Bleak Houses: Marital Violence in Victorian Fiction* (Athens, Ohio: Ohio University Press, 2005), p. 53.

29 Charles Dickens, *Dombey and Son* (London: Bradbury & Evans, 1848), p. 471.

30 For a general discussion of this issue, see Claudia Nelson, *Family Ties in Victorian England* (Westport: Praeger, 2007), pp. 120–21.

31 Karen Chase and Michael Levenson, *The Spectacle of Intimacy: The Public Life of the Victorian Family* (Princeton University Press, 2000), p. 112; Adam Kuper, *Incest and Influence: The Private Life of Bourgeois England* (Cambridge, Mass.: Harvard University Press, 2010), pp. 66–8.

32 Ibid.

33 Ibid., p. 118; Rosemarie Bodenheimer, *Knowing Dickens* (New York: Cornell University Press, 2007), p. 151.

34 *The Trial*, p. 46.

35 'The proposed Marriages Bill', *Nenagh Guardian*, 30 March 1850, p. 3, cited by the *Evening Standard*.

20. 'God grant I may never again dream such a dream as I dreamed last night'

1 'Deaths', *Limerick Chronicle*, 28 June 1848, via www.limerickcity.ie.

2 'Deaths', *Limerick Chronicle*, 2 June and 24 August 1842, via www.limerickcity.ie.

3 *Limerick Chronicle*, 17 April 1844, via www.limerickcity.ie.

4 *Limerick Chronicle*, 17 September 1836, via www.limerickcity.ie.

5 *The Trial of Charles Langley, Esq., F.R.C.S.I.* (Dublin: J. M'Glashan, 1850), p. 42.

6 Ibid., p. 44.

7 'Dr Langley', *Freeman's Journal*, 4 April 1850, p. 4.

21. 'Mrs Langley's constitution'

1 'Dr Langley', *Standard*, 3 August 1849, p. 1; 'Doctor Langley', *Nenagh Guardian*, 1 August 1849, p. 3.

2 'Trial of Dr Langley for the murder of Mrs Langley', *Limerick Reporter*, 22 March 1850, p. 2.

3 *The Trial of Charles Langley, Esq., F.R.C.S.I.* (Dublin: J. M'Glashan, 1850), pp. 55–6; 'Trial of Dr Langley', *Nenagh Guardian*, 23 March 1850, p. 2.

4 Ibid. This part of Quin's testimony is mistakenly attributed in the *Nenagh Guardian* to Dr Frith.

5 *The Trial*, p. 56.

6 'Trial of Dr Langley', *Nenagh Guardian*, 23 March 1850, p. 2.

7 Ibid.

8 *The Trial*, p. 55.

9 Ibid.

10 Ibid., p. 53.

11 Ibid., p. 52; 'Trial of Dr Langley for the murder of Mrs Langley', *Limerick Reporter and Tipperary Vindicator*, 22 March 1850, p. 2.

12 *The Trial*, p. 56.

13 *Slater's Directory* of 1846, pp. 296–7.

14 Clare Graham, *Ordering Law: The Architectural and Social History of the English Law Court to 1914* (Aldershot: Ashgate, 2003), p. 240.

15 W. E. Vaughan, *Murder Trials in Ireland, 1836–1914* (Dublin: Four Courts Press, 2009), p. 123; see also Nancy Murphy, *Guilty or Innocent? The Cormack Brothers: Trial, Execution & Exhumation* (Nenagh: Relay Books, 1998), p. 39.

16 Vaughan, *Murder Trials*, p. 121.

17 Ibid., p. 123.

18 Ibid., p. 124. Between those qualified to sit on petty juries, the rank of 'esquire' rather than 'gent' was generally given to landowners and merchants of higher means, though this could be something of a grey area. On this point, see Andrew Tierney, 'Architectures of Gentility in Nineteenth-Century Ireland', in *Irish Elites in the Nineteenth Century*, ed. Ciaran O'Neill (Dublin: Four Courts Press, 2013), pp. 31–50 at 43–4.

19 'The long panel', *Tipperary Vindicator*, 3 April 1844, p. 3.

20 John George Hodges, *Report of the Trial of William Smith O'Brien for High Treason at the Special Commission for the County Tipperary* (Dublin: Alexander Thom, 1849), p. 60.

21 'Trial of Dr Langley', *Nenagh Guardian*, 23 March 1850, p. 1; *The Trial*, p. 33.

22 For a first-hand account of the first appearance of women in the Central Criminal Court, see 'The woman juror's new sphere', *Manchester Guardian*, 12 January 1921, p. 7. Mrs Eleanor Poë and her daughters, Molly and Blanche (grand-nieces of Anna Poe), were founder

members of the Nenagh branch of the suffragettes and were elected vice-president, honorary secretary and treasurer; see 'Local suffragettes', *Nenagh Guardian*, 26 October 1912, p. 2.

23 *Thom's Directory* of 1849, p. 540.

24 Sir Bernard Burke, *A Genealogical and Heraldic Dictionary of the Landed Gentry of Great Britain and Ireland*, vol. 2 (London: Colburn & Co., 1852), p. 1601; Barbara, wife of John Poe of Solsborough, was a daughter of Thomas Barnard and Mary Willington of Castle Willington; see Burke's *Genealogical and Heraldic History of the Landed Gentry of Ireland* (London: Harrison & Sons, 1912), p. 41.

25 See Landed Estates Database, NUI Galway, http://landedestates.nuigalway.ie; see also John Burke, *A Genealogical and Heraldic Dictionary of the Landed Gentry of Great Britain and Ireland*, vol. 1 (London: Henry Colburn, 1847), p. 231.

26 'Marriages', *Ballina Chronicle*, 25 July 1849.

27 'Short vs Bentley', *Freeman's Journal*, 26 January 1859, p. 4; 'Breach of promise of marriage', *Freeman's Journal*, 17 March 1859, p. 4.

28 'Nenagh Union', *Nenagh Guardian*, 16 February 1850, p. 1; 'Borrisokane Union', *Nenagh Guardian*, 28 September 1850, p. 1.

29 See Landed Estates Database, NUI Galway, http://landedestates.nuigalway.ie.

30 'Chancery', *Nenagh Guardian*, 23 December 1840, p. 3; 'Barony of Lower Ormond', *Nenagh Guardian*, 13 May 1846, p. 3; Griffith's Valuation – parish of Ballingarry, via www.askaboutireland.ie. See also the surviving census for 1821, LDS Film Number 992663; E. H. Sheehan, *Nenagh and Its Neighbourhood* (Dublin and Bray: Record Press, 1948), p. 21; Edmund Bewley, *The Origin and Early History of the Family of Poe* (Dublin: Ponsonby & Gibbs, 1906), Pedigree B. For Aquilla Smith, see Sheehan, *Nenagh and Its Neighbourhood*, p. 21.

31 'The trial of Dr Langley for the murder of his wife', *King's County Chronicle*, 27 March 1850.

32 The jurors' room is still in use today, though an artificial window now provides the impression of an external light source.

22. *'Who would not have done similarly?'*

1 There is some uncertainty concerning the time of day as the *Nenagh Guardian* gives nine o'clock, while most other newspapers give ten

o'clock. For the presence of the sheriff, see *Limerick Reporter*, 22 March 1850, p. 2.

2 *The Trial of Charles Langley, Esq., F.R.C.S.I.* (Dublin: J. M'Glashan, 1850), pp. 57–8.

3 'Court House, Nenagh – Friday', *Limerick Chronicle*, 3 April 1850, p. 3.

4 'Debates and proceedings in Parliament', *Spectator*, 7 (1834), 718.

5 See *The Trial*, p. 38.

6 'Reports of the Society for the Promotion of Amendment of the Law – Divorce', *The Law Review of British and Foreign Jurisprudence*, vol. 8 (May 1848–August 1848), p. 348.

7 Out of 325 Acts only four were at the wife's petition; see David Fitz-Patrick, 'Divorce and separation in Irish history', *Past and Present*, 114 (1987), 172–96 at 173; Diane Urquhart, 'Ireland and the Divorce and Matrimonial Causes Act of 1857', *Journal of Family History*, 38:3 (2013), 301–20 at 302.

8 Lady Morgan, *Woman and Her Master*, vol. 1 (London: Henry Colburn, 1840), pp. 15–16.

9 Mrs John Sandford, *Woman in Her Social and Domestic Character*, 6th edn (London: Longman, Orme, Brown, Green and Longmans, 1839), pp. 213–14.

10 'County Tipperary – North Riding', *Dublin Weekly Register*, 24 March 1850, p. 8.

11 Ibid.

12 *The Trial*, p. 55.

13 Ibid., p. 60.

14 'Trial of Dr Langley for the murder of his wife', *Dublin Weekly Register*, 23 March 1850, p. 8.

23. 'Suppressio veri'

1 'Dr Langley', *Freeman's Journal*, 4 April 1850, p. 3.

2 Burke's guide records the marriage of James Jocelyn Poe to John Bennett's sister Jane in 1843; for the social standing of John Bennett of Riverston, see his obituary in the *Nenagh Guardian*, 31 December 1862; for the legal career of his grandfather Judge John Bennett, see Francis Elrington Ball, *Judges in Ireland 1221–1921* (London: John Murray, 1928), vol. 2, pp. 175–7, 187 and 223. The physical description of John

Bennett is derived from a surviving photograph among the papers of Blanche Poë, private collection.

3 'Dr Langley', *Freeman's Journal*, 4 April 1850, p. 3.

4 'Dr Langley', *Nenagh Guardian,* 27 March 1850, p. 3.

5 'Dr Langley', *Freeman's Journal*, 4 April 1850, p. 3; 'Melancholy state of the country', *Limerick Reporter*, 2 April 1850, p. 2.

6 'Dr Langley', *Freeman's Journal*, 22 April 1850, p. 4; *Tipperary Free Press*, 24 April 1850, p. 3.

7 Parl. Deb. (series 3), vol. 111, cols. 1179–99 (13 June 1850). See also the article from the *Dublin Mail* reprinted in the *Nenagh Guardian*, 30 March 1850, p. 3.

8 Jennifer Phegley, *Courtship and Marriage in Victorian England* (Santa Barbara: ABC-Clio, 2012), pp. 161–2.

9 'Dr Langley', *Freeman's Journal*, 22 April 1850, p. 4, cited by the *Limerick Reporter and Vindicator*.

10 *Limerick and Clare Examiner*, 3 April 1850, p. 1; 'Thurles Quarter Sessions', *Limerick Reporter*, 23 April 1850, p. 2.

11 'Thurles Quarter Sessions', *Limerick Reporter*, 23 April 1850, p. 2.

12 'Nenagh Assizes – trial of Dr Langley for the murder of his wife', *Belfast Newsletter*, 26 March 1850, p. 4.

13 Ibid.

14 'Trial of Dr Langley', *Nenagh Guardian*, 4 May 1850, p. 3.

15 'Trial of Dr Langley for the murder of his wife', *Freeman's Journal*, 25 March 1850, p. 4.

16 'To the editor of the Limerick Chronicle', *Limerick Chronicle*, 3 April 1850, p. 3.

17 'Dr Langley – to the editor of the Nenagh Guardian', *Nenagh Guardian*, 6 April 1850, p. 3.

18 'Thurles Quarter Sessions: A scene – Dr Langley', *Nenagh Guardian*, 27 April 1850, p. 3.

19 'Dr Langley', an article from the *Cork Examiner* reproduced in the *Nenagh Guardian*, 10 April 1850, p. 4.

20 Thomas Carlyle, *The Works of Thomas Carlyle*, vol. 6 (Cambridge University Press, 2010), p. 39.

21 'Dr Langley', an article from the *Cork Examiner* reproduced in the *Nenagh Guardian*, 10 April 1850, p. 4.

22 'Is murder by torture a crime?' *The Times*, 26 March 1850, p. 5.

23 For Mill's use of the initials 'A. B.', see Nicholas Capaldi, *John Stuart Mill* (Cambridge University Press, 2004), p. 375, note 51.

24 *The Times*, 26 March 1850, p. 5.

25 'Is murder by torture a crime?', *The Times*, 26 March 1850, p. 5.

26 *Nottinghamshire Guardian and Midland Advertiser*, 4 April 1850, p. 2.

27 Donald G. Dutton, *Rethinking Domestic Violence* (Vancouver: University of British Columbia Press, 2006), p. 9; see also John Stuart Mill, *The Collected Works of John Stuart Mill, Volume XXV: Newspaper Writings December 1847–July 1873, Part IV* [1847], via oll.libertyfund.org,

24. *'Woman's frailty and sinful passion'*

1 Edmund Bewley, *The Origin and Early History of the Family of Poe* (Dublin: Ponsonby & Gibbs, 1906), Pedigree B.

2 Notebooks compiled by Sir Edmund Bewley in the course of genealogical and legal research, with index of wills: NLI, Genealogical Office, MS 512, 'Index & Wills'. The original Church of Ireland baptismal records for this period in the parish of Ballymackey were destroyed in 1922.

3 For headstones, see Nancy Murphy, *Gravestone Inscriptions, Co. Tipperary: Section B: Barony of Upper Ormond, Vol. 5: Parish of Nenagh, Kenyon Street Graveyard, St Mary's Church of Ireland* (Nenagh: Ormond Historical Society, 1992). There is also no record of her at Ballymackey; see Denise Foulkes, *Gravestone Inscriptions, Co. Tipperary: Section B, Barony of Upper Ormond, Vol. 8: Parish of Ballymackey* (Nenagh: Ormond Historical Society, 1984).

4 Jane Bennett of Riverston, Nenagh, wife to James Jocelyn Poe, was a first cousin of Susanna Bennett, wife of Joseph Sheridan Le Fanu.

5 'The Spirits Whisper', in Joseph Sheridan Le Fanu, Sir Charles Young, et al., *A Stable for Nightmares or Weird Tales* (New York: New Amsterdam Book Company, 1896), pp. 185–208.

6 'Strange proceedings – alleged trespass', *Limerick Reporter and Tipperary Vindicator*, 29 March 1853, p. 3; 'Nenagh new church', *Nenagh Guardian*, 7 January 1857, p. 2.

7 Two copies of this will survive in the papers of his daughter, Blanche Poë, private collection.

8 'Mr Parnell's plea: an investigation of the Maamtrasna case refused', *New York Times*, 18 July 1885, p. 1.

9 'An Irish marriage settlement', *Weekly Irish Times*, 29 November 1879, p. 2; 'Remarkable will case', *Irish Times*, 2 February 1883, p. 7.

10 Frank Callanan, *T. M. Healy* (Cork University Press, 1996), pp. 90–91.

11 Nathaniel Hawthorne, *The Scarlet Letter: A Romance* (Boston: Ticknor, Reed & Fields, 1850), p. 93.

12 Sir Bernard Burke, *A Genealogical and Heraldic Dictionary of the Landed Gentry of Great Britain and Ireland*, vol. 2 (London: Colburn & Co., 1863), p. 1205.

25. 'The interposition of a kind Providence'

1 Papers of Blanche Poë, private collection.

2 'Marriages', *Freeman's Journal*, 18 June 1850, p. 4; Cheshire marriage indexes for 1850, www.cheshirebmd.org.uk.

3 The witnesses were Edward Edwards and Sarah Colclough (who signed with a mark) – marriage certificate dated 4 June 1850, Chester Registration District. Edwards is listed as 'parish clerk' in Chester in the 1861 census. Both these witness names appear for the wedding of a local innkeeper ten years earlier in the same church; see Marriage Notes for Phoebe Bebbington and Thomas Griffiths, via http:// familytreemaker.genealogy.com.

4 For the address of Keith's Photographic Studio, see *Manchester Guardian*, 30 September 1854, p. 9.

5 *The Trial of Charles Langley, Esq., F.R.C.S.I.* (Dublin: J. M'Glashan, 1850), pp. 41–2.

6 Herman Melville, *Redburn: His First Voyage* (New York: Harper & Brothers, 1850), p. 209.

7 Online Parish Clerks for the County of Lancashire, Register: Baptisms 1850–1851, p. 368, entry 2937, www.lan-opc.org.uk.

8 For a photograph and foundation date, see www.lan-opc.org.uk. A short description of 44 Newlands Street is given in an advertisement of 1891, 'To be let – dwelling houses', *Liverpool Mercury*, 29 October 1891, p. 2.

9 See 1861 census for Newlands Street, www.ancestry.co.uk.

10 Alexander Brown, *Smith's Stranger's Guide to Liverpool and Environs* (Liverpool: Benjamin Smith, 1843), p. 220.

11 1861 census, www.ancestry.co.uk. Death certificate of Annetta Frances Langley, registered West Derby and Toxteth Park, 31 March 1862, General Register Office. Death certificate of Charles Henry Langley, registered 27 November 1860, West Derby and Toxteth Park, General Register Office.

12 Toxteth Park Cemetery: see www.toxtethparkcemeteryinscriptions.co.uk.

13 Quote from the *Liverpool Mail* of 6 November 1847, cited in Carmen Tunney and Pat Nugent, 'Liverpool and the Great Irish Famine', John Crowley et al. (eds), *Atlas of the Great Irish Famine* (Cork University Press, 2012), p. 508; James Matthew Gallman, *Receiving Erin's Children: Philadelphia, Liverpool, and the Irish Famine* (Chapel Hill: University of North Carolina Press, 2000), p. 28.

14 'Claim for breach of promise of marriage', *Liverpool Mercury*, 13 January 1876, p. 8. For the origin of the false name, see 'Harry Montague's Entertainments', *Staffordshire Sentinel and Commercial and General Advertiser*, 1 April 1876, p. 7.

15 'Claim for breach of promise of marriage', *Liverpool Mercury*, 13 January 1876, p. 8.

16 See 'Extraordinary action for breach of promise', *Sunderland Daily Echo and Shipping Gazette*, p. 3.

17 1881 census, www.ancestry.co.uk.

18 'Adjudications', *Birmingham Daily Post*, 27 March 1886, p. 8.

19 Death certificate, registered 24 August 1882, West Derby, General Register Office. Toxteth Park Cemetery: www.toxtethparkcemetery-inscriptions.co.uk. *England & Wales, National Probate Calendar (Index of Wills and Administrations)*, 1858–1966, p. 369.

20 Her parentage can be traced in the 1851 census, www.ancestry.co.uk. The marriage certificate, in the parish of St Chrysostom, is dated 12 August 1882. Elizabeth's age is listed here as thirty-five but this contradicts several census records for the Lake family which show she was forty-three in 1882.

21 *England & Wales, National Probate Calendar (Index of Wills and Administrations)*, 1858–1966, p. 73. For Barbara Burton's background, see the 1861 census, www.ancestry.co.uk.

22 Admiral Sir Edmund Samuel Poe, grandson of the Rev. James Hill Poe of Nenagh, became commander of the Mediterranean fleet in 1910; see 'Death of Admiral Sir E. Poë', *The Times*, 7 April 1921, p. 13.

23 See 1891 census, www.ancestry.co.uk.

24 'Adjudications', *Birmingham Daily Post*, 27 March 1886, p. 8.

25 'Cheshire Quarter Sessions', *Cheshire Observer*, 10 January 1891, p. 6.

26 See Brown, *Smith's Stranger's Guide to Liverpool* (1843), p. 228.

27 Julian Hawthorne, *Hawthorne and His Circle* (New York and London: Harper Brothers, 1903), Project Gutenburg ebook, unpaginated, via www.gutenberg.org.

28 She left her son £2,339. England & Wales, FreeBMD Death Index: 1837–1915, Record for Anna Martha Langley, General Register Office; *England and Wales Civil Registration Indexes*, General Register Office (see section 8a, p. 315, of death register for further details); *England & Wales, National Probate Calendar (Index of Wills and Administrations)*, 1858–1966, p. 63. Death certificate registered 12 January 1893, Wirral Registration District.

29 Jeremiah died in 1901 on Woodhey Road, Rock Ferry, in Cheshire, aged forty-nine, leaving the substantial sum of £4,606 to his second wife, Barbara Burton. *England & Wales, National Probate Calendar (Index of Wills and Administrations)*, 1858–1966, p. 73.

30 Nathaniel Hawthorne, *Passages from the English Note-books of Nathaniel Hawthorne* (London: Strahan & Co., 1870), vol. 1, p. 30.

He just wanted a decent book to read ...

Not too much to ask, is it? It was in 1935 when Allen Lane, Managing Director of Bodley Head Publishers, stood on a platform at Exeter railway station looking for something good to read on his journey back to London. His choice was limited to popular magazines and poor-quality paperbacks – the same choice faced every day by the vast majority of readers, few of whom could afford hardbacks. Lane's disappointment and subsequent anger at the range of books generally available led him to found a company – and change the world.

'We believed in the existence in this country of a vast reading public for intelligent books at a low price, and staked everything on it'
Sir Allen Lane, 1902–1970, founder of Penguin Books

The quality paperback had arrived – and not just in bookshops. Lane was adamant that his Penguins should appear in chain stores and tobacconists, and should cost no more than a packet of cigarettes.

Reading habits (and cigarette prices) have changed since 1935, but Penguin still believes in publishing the best books for everybody to enjoy. We still believe that good design costs no more than bad design, and we still believe that quality books published passionately and responsibly make the world a better place.

So wherever you see the little bird – whether it's on a piece of prize-winning literary fiction or a celebrity autobiography, political tour de force or historical masterpiece, a serial-killer thriller, reference book, world classic or a piece of pure escapism – you can bet that it represents the very best that the genre has to offer.

Whatever you like to read – trust Penguin.

read more
www.penguin.co.uk